Medieval Welsh Settlement and Territory

Archaeological evidence from a Teifi valley landscape

Jemma Bezant

BAR British Series 487
2009

Published in 2016 by
BAR Publishing, Oxford

BAR British Series 487

Medieval Welsh Settlement and Territory

ISBN 978 1 4073 0442 7

BAR Publishing is the trading name of British Archaeological Reports (Oxford) Ltd.
British Archaeological Reports was first incorporated in 1974 to publish the BAR
Series, International and British. In 1992 Hadrian Books Ltd became part of the BAR
group. This volume was originally published by Archaeopress in conjunction with
British Archaeological Reports (Oxford) Ltd / Hadrian Books Ltd, the Series principal
publisher, in 2009. This present volume is published by BAR Publishing, 2016.

Printed in England

BAR
PUBLISHING

BAR titles are available from:

BAR Publishing
122 Banbury Rd, Oxford, OX2 7BP, UK
EMAIL   info@barpublishing.com
PHONE   +44 (0)1865 310431
FAX   +44 (0)1865 316916
www.barpublishing.com

TABLE OF CONTENTS

TABLE OF FIGURES

ABSTRACT

Principally through the use of landscape archaeology, this thesis explores the medieval landscape of west Wales, particularly the cwmwd of Gwinionydd in the central Teifi valley, Ceredigion. With particular reference to the 'Age of the Princes' this thesis examines the reign of Rhys ap Gruffudd, the 'Lord Rhys' in order to locate territorial and settlement patterns. Despite the effects of Normanisation upon them it has been possible to demonstrate a degree of continuity of a complex and sophisticated landscape. The approach taken by Jones-Pierce, Glanville-Jones and Rhys Jones has been primarily document-based, concentrating on political change as a catalyst for changes in the settlement pattern, agrarian landscape and political geography. The focus of many previous studies has been the Marcher regions and the Englishries of north and south Wales, emphasising the fact that west Wales has not yet been subject to the same level of sustained academic study.

The main focus of this thesis aims to recreate the cwmwd-maenor-tref, territorial system administered by a pre-conquest Welsh aristocracy and will locate native tenures along with their specific agricultural regimes. A retroactive analysis of estate structures such as those at Llanfair and Llanllyr will establish their medieval antecedence and they will be considered alongside the monastic granges of Whitland, Strata Florida and Talley abbeys. 'Rules' concerning territory and settlement are known in an idealised form from the Laws of Hywel Dda.

This project has successfully drawn upon techniques including field survey, remote sensing, geophysics, mapping and terrain modelling using Geographic Information Systems and Lidar data. These methods have been complemented by excavation to target and clarify the interpretation of some of the survey results.

Thorough interrogation of the landscape is critical to a developing rural community that seeks sustainable uses for failing traditional agricultural regimes. My thesis can be seen as a trans-disciplinary landscape analysis that has implications for future approaches to the study of rural Wales. This successful study of an apparently inscrutable rural landscape will be relevant for the research and curatorial disciplines alike.

ACKNOWLEDGEMENTS

This thesis has been supported by a full doctoral award from the AHRC (no. 100007) without which this research would not have been possible.

Special thanks must go firstly to Professor David Austin, supervisor, mentor, inspiration and friend. Thank you.

Nigel Nayling, thanks for the patience and TLC.

Fortunate to live in the beautiful Teifi valley at Llanfair, special thanks must go to John and Wendy Kidd for their kind help, support and advice.

Thank you to Roderick Bale, Gordon Lumby, Daniel Jones and Susan Hurst who have taken time from their own research in order to help with fieldwork, research, dog-sitting, beer-drinking and all other aspects of this project. Invaluable help, good friends. Thanks.

The help and support of other members of staff at the Archaeology Department, University of Wales, Lampeter has been gratefully received especially Andrew Fleming, Martin Bates, Penny Dransart, Kathy Fewster and Quentin Drew. The support of Dee Williams, Ann Mackie and Maureen Hunwicks has been especially helpful.

Thank you to Toby Driver for the aerial survey during excavation at Llanfair plus all the other aerial photographs supplied here. Thank you to Dee Williams and Neil Ludlow for the ceramic identifications. Thanks to Dr Ros Coard for the bone identification. Thank you also to Neil Ludlow for his enviable knowledge of medieval Wales and for the advice and help of Richard Jones, Ken Murphy, Alice Pyper, Gwilym Hughes and all the staff at Cambria Archaeology. Thanks to John Davies for his useful information about the history and geology of Llandysul and all the members of Hanes Llandysul for their support.

Thank you to Gerald Morgan for his illuminating analysis of Ceredigion gentry. Jack Langton at Oxford was particularly kind in sharing his thoughts on the forest areas of the Bishop's of St David's. Rhys Jones was kind enough to reply to my awkward questions, thank you! David Longley has an enviable grasp of the medieval period in north Wales and has also been most kind and helpful.

Patience, kindness (and invaluable mechanical help with the back-filling of trenches!) was supplied by Tom and Eva Cowcher at Penrhiw. Thanks also to the other landowners, Vernon Griffiths at Fferm y Cwrt, diolch yn fawr i chi. Also thank you to Mr and Mrs Flower at Moelhedog, Mr and Mrs Philips at Llwynffynnon Uchaf and Dan and Pat Perks at Dancapel for access to estate maps.

For making the office a stimulating and entertaining place to work, many thanks also Stephen Jones, Trevor Jose, Jennie Cairns, William Whiteley, Pauline Bambrey, Lynn Morgan and Katy Smith.

Thank you to the library staff at Lampeter University who have patiently received some very strange and awkward requests from me over the course of this research. Thanks also to the staff of the Records Office and the National Library, Aberystwyth, very different but invaluable institutions. Thank you to the staff at Geoscan, one of whom rang me from the beach on holiday to help solve software problems! Thank you to Raluca Radelescu of the University of Wales, Bangor for hosting the Palaeography workshop at Gregynog, useful and unexpectedly enjoyable! Thank you to Professor Janet Burton and Andrew Abram of the History Department, University of Wales, Lampeter for occasional matters monastic.

Last but most important, thanks to the fieldwork team, to everyone above who helped with survey, excavation and fieldwalking plus the excavation team; Jennie Arnold, Stefanka Chadjas, David Sables, Julie Bezant, Camessa Wakeham, Anne Lawrence, Trevor Jose, Emile, Kim, Sue, Eliso and Geoff & Chris Snowden.

ONE: INTRODUCTION

Setting the Scene

This thesis proposes to identify traditional territorial and settlement structures and place them into a reconstructed 12th to 13th century Welsh landscape. This chapter will outline the aims of the thesis and introduce the study area. I will explain the history and character of Southern Ceredigion's physical landscape and then outline the turbulent political and military history of the Norman incursions, the subsequent lordship of Rhys ap Gruffudd, and the subsequent gradual fragmentation of his kingdom after his death and the final Norman victory in 1284.

This thesis is a landscape analysis at a variety of scales. Although the rural Welsh landscape suffers from a serious deficit of critically informed historical analyses it is not the intention of this thesis to develop the theoretical aspects of landscape analysis. I aim instead to develop the currently unsophisticated approaches to Welsh landscapes themselves. I aim to demonstrate that the dominant approaches are insufficient and historically-driven. I also aim to demonstrate that the curatorial, hands-off approach to a landscape that we do not understand will not generate further understanding but that modest archaeological intervention can greatly enhance the knowledge base.

I aim to challenge the prevailing hypotheses that pre-Norman Wales operated along simple tribal lines using unsophisticated social and political structures. Complex territorial institutions and efficient forms of revenue and fiscal management have traditionally been regarded as a 'new' development in direct response to the Norman threat between the 11th and 13th centuries, and it is generally accepted that only by installing the more successful elements of state-formation borrowed from the Normans did areas of north and west Wales survive the threat of occupation and defeat for over two centuries. Gwynedd in the north became one of the most powerful Welsh kingdoms of the Middle Ages under the reign of the likes of Owain Gwynedd, Llywelyn ab Iorwerth and Llywelyn Fawr. The historical prestige of these princes, supported by the surviving historical evidence of their new institutional processes; acta, surveys and rentals provides a resource unparalleled elsewhere in Wales. This factor has been largely instrumental in distracting attention away from the equally significant kingdom of Deheubarth in the south, especially the important 12th century reign of Rhys ap Gruffudd.

Norman invasion of parts of Deheubarth during the late 11th and early 12th centuries displaced what had gone before, disrupting existing tenurial patterns and lordship structures until Rhys was able to take power in 1165. His peaceful rule culminated in the creation for him of the unique office of Justiciar which essentially gave him the overlordship of both Welsh and Normans alike. He re-established a lineage so powerful that he became known as

Arglwydd Rhys, the 'Lord Rhys', and his lineage was the only one to retain any vestige of lordship after Edward's Statute was signed at Rhuddlan in 1284. Rhys was an accomplished politician, endowing both Cistercians and Premonstratensians with large estates as one of a suite of new strategies aimed at the consolidation of his kingdom. Earlier, traditional institutional practices are also illuminated though during Rhys's reign and those of his successors - practices that were based upon the administrative framework of the cantref and cwmwd. These structures had their origins in an early pre-conquest past and it is the constituent elements of this system that this thesis seeks to locate; the *maenor* or estate collecting the *gwestfa* payment based on the *tref* or township. These were populated by kin groups occupying the *tyddynod* or homesteads by *gwely* tenure and it is these institutions that are so poorly understood in landscape terms, and it is this period of Rhysian rule during the 12th century that will provide a useful historical axis around which I will place my analysis

Aims

Applying a multi-disciplinary approach familiar to landscape archaeologists to the existing historical narratives will prove to be particularly useful. The turbulent military and political events during the early Norman period and the subsequent Rhysian dynasty has provided a horizon of physical evidence in the form of new architectures - earthworks, castles and churches. A more limited but useful resource are contemporary accounts, like those of Giraldus Cambrensis (Brewer, 1873; Colt-Hoare, 1976 and Forester, 1887) for example and chronicles such as the Brut y Tywysogion (Jones, 1955a). This period also witnesses the adoption of new forms of administration and governance that generates certain documentary cohorts such as charters to Cistercian and other religious houses (Evans, 1878 and Pryce, 2005), later Edwardian surveys (Dodgshon, 1994) and, later still, Dissolution surveys (Dugdale, 1817-1830). This historical evidence has hitherto been only partially helpful in landscape reconstruction. I will combine it (fig. 1) with a retroactive analysis of some of the estate holdings that proliferate along the central Teifi valley. This will involve the use of maps and other documents, place name evidence, topographical survey, geophysics, remote sensing and excavation in order to interrogate the antecedents of these estates and their relationship to medieval institutions. This will enable me to address the following:

- The reconstruction of settlement and territorial structures during the 12th - 13th centuries.
- An assessment of the degree of survival and continuity or otherwise of such structures.

I will demonstrate that, using these techniques, it will be possible to reconstruct landholdings and territory for the 12th to 13th century period in the central Teifi valley. Normanisation had a considerable fragmentary effect in the early 12th century but the reign of Rhys and his descendants will be demonstrated to have had traditional and conservative as well as modernising elements. This will be revealed within certain territorial structures. For much of rural Wales the only detailed evidence for the structure of the medieval landscape is the monastic grange. The granges created by the emerging European monastic houses preserved the vestige of the early medieval clas-church estates. I will demonstrate that the geography of these religious estates also preserved within them other pre-conquest territorial elements based upon the cwmwd-maenor-tref system. I will also assess how far 'native' agricultural practice is preserved within the grange structure which will be a useful way of analysing the preservation or otherwise of ancient territories. This should be possible because such practices are at odds with the adoption of new Norman management regimes such as the enclosure (sometimes into strips) of *rhandir*, 'shareland',

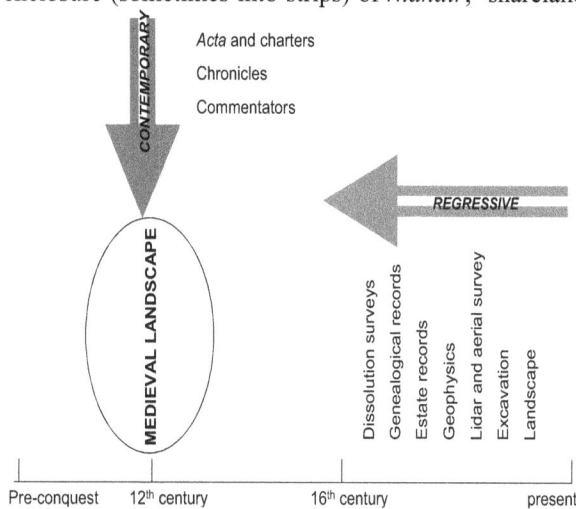

Figure 1. Approach and method. Contemporary evidence will be combined with a retrogressive analysis of a range of later data.

or former common grazing land and the adoption of 'forest' in areas patronized by the powerful Norman Bishops of St David's. Survey, excavation and geophysics targeted at specific areas will demonstrate the medieval antecedence of these gentry and monastic estates.

The effects of Normanisation evident in the scant documentary resource will be analysed alongside both landscape archaeology and the historical techniques available to the field archaeologist and will demonstrate that the basic structure of today's landscape is in fact rooted in a sophisticated medieval framework. This thesis does not propose new methodologies but, by compiling a suite of familiar techniques, seeks to challenge existing approaches to rural landscapes and will change the way that the reconstruction of rural landscapes in this area is approached. By using traditional desk-based and landscape research techniques I will be able to locate previously undiscovered medieval archaeology. Excavation at Llanfair for example has contributed enormously to the understanding of this project but it has to date been the only church site excavated in Ceredigion and, outside castles,

has been only one of a very small handful of medieval sites investigated in this region. I challenge the principle of 'preservation in situ' for rural archaeologies and my approach will inform the landscape and heritage management process, train new archaeologists and reveal a new horizon of medieval archaeology which will become visible for the first time.

Outline of Approach

In a discussion on the history and development of the Welsh nation and its identity, Gwyn Williams (1985: 5) wrote that "landscape does not make history; men and women do". Although this thesis is not about identity and Welshness per se issues like this have heavily influenced both the established historical narratives and the research that I have conducted. Specifically political aspects of what became Welsh Nationalism did not emerge until the 19th century with influence from European nationalism but always took a gentler path than, say, Irish politics. The reasons for this are outside the scope of this paper but the result meant a more scholarly debate punctuated only by sporadic low level protest action in the community. At the time that Ireland was creating new narratives about its past in order to define its separateness from England, Wales was looking at its own history with a more measured, parochial stance. The longevity of bardic tradition outlasting Roman, Christian and Edwardian was promulgated by Iolo Morgannwg. Specifically militant groups like the Free Wales Army emerged around members drawn from the Lampeter area in the early 1960s and they began to assert their independence from England. These groups provenanced their actions by the use of historical narratives referring to the Age of the Welsh Princes from the 10th century Hywel Dda through the 12th century Lord Rhys of Deheubarth, Llywelyn Fawr in the 13th century and Owain Glyndwr in the early 15th which lent to the eponymous Meibion Glyndwr campaign appropriation of him as a kind of folk hero - members also attained social support. This created a specific narrative, one of the Age of the Princes; a landscape deeply imbued with a great literary and scholarly past, the Laws of Hywel Dda, rewritten perhaps by Rhys, demonstrated a civilized society capable of complex levels of governance and with a deep, deep antiquity. Even so historical narratives have insisted that this was an essentially a tribal landscape albeit a noble one with a proud Druidic ancestry. This folkloric anecdotal history was deeply embedded within the academic. The landscape that represents the 'land of castles', that is the Wales that we recognize today with roughly its county borders, administrative centres, cultural and political geography therefore was entirely as a consequence of Norman conquest. In other words, the Normans created Wales. Therefore it has been difficult for Wales to re-create itself, to create its own narratives, agenda and policies, to create new opportunities for culture and business. We know all there is to know about Wales; we know where all the castles and churches are, the rest was an 'empty', 'tribal' landscape, an attitude that is perhaps supported by a lackof fresh approaches to existing data. This thesis seeks to challenge these notions, to reject the limiting 'celto-nostalgic' narratives that have driven Wales for so long and to introduce a sophisticated medieval landscape that paralleled the trajectory of the rest of medieval Europe.

Archaeological theory is almost exclusively played out on the field of prehistory and the medieval period fares especially poorly in this respect. The way humans create, interact with and experience their surroundings is discussed in phenomenological terms for the Neolithic by Tilley (1994), Bradley (1998) and Thomas (1999) for example. These and other types of cognitive approaches have not been used for the medieval period with any great success as yet and this has had a detrimental effect on the way medieval landscape narratives have been constructed in the past. The study of historical periods has traditionally been a combination of empiricist, inductivist approaches which stress history merely as a sequence of political and cultural events. Various systems and models have been devised in order to explain the processes that cause these events. These functionalist approaches declare that all institutions, beliefs and morals are interlinked like a living organism.

The subsequent rejection of these types of systems thinking as too rigid has advocated a more theorized, cognitive approach that has made the use of models and systems as explanation unfashionable. As Johnson (1999: 71) points out, however, most people actually are "systems thinkers" and that it is natural for us to perceive landscape and culture for example as distinct units. Whilst we deny using model as explanation it is actually something we do all the time: Tom Williamson's (2000: 58) study of post-medieval enclosure seeks to challenge those who see it as a unified, structured process but nevertheless he attempts to "identify some general rules which help to explain what happened". Since a model is predicated on a set of rules (as was the act of enclosure), he is actually just creating a model by way of explanation that is not necessarily unsuccessful. Since he sought (ibid: 71) to "explain the social and ideological causes and implications" of enclosure, we could even name Williamson's model for example, 'The Socio-ideological System of Enclosure Model' and use to test its validity in other areas. Williamson's sensitive and compelling study demonstrates that we can still use system and model as an approach if we apply them in a theorized and sensitive way. We can then select certain elements from functionalist and systemic approaches in order to explain how we think society and landscape works, but only if we also consider conflict, agency and other cognitive factors. Traditional systems analysis will be looking from the top-down for elites as catalysts but many historical archaeologists are no longer content to place emphasis upon power relations (Hicks, 2005: 386). Therefore I shall use fracture, difference, change and conflict in order to construct new models and systems from the inside-out.

The medieval world was deeply imbued with rules, boundaries and structures. The correct order of things was reinforced through the organization of the landscape and structure of society. Social behaviour is closely related to the organization of space in the medieval world for Duby (1988). The development of feudalism to capitalism is reflected in changing notions of space, from public to private. Allegory and romance is chief in the late medieval period where the chivalric knight was the mirror of Christian morality (Austin, 1984: 71). The symbolic landscape depicted in the Tres Riches Heures of the Duc de Berry, depicts a visual moral map (ibid.) with the castle as a symbol of power and authority at the top, endorsed by heaven.

For Taylor (2000: 51), the ornamentation of certain medieval landscapes acted as a symbolic reflection of societal values. Gilchrist (1999: 244) relates the heavily formalized use of space during the medieval period directly to social agency. She proposes that changes in belief, liturgy and moral values can be read in the changing internal layouts of church buildings for example. Humans structure their lives, their relationships with each other and with space. Giddens' (1993) structuration approach, recognises the input of human agency and has become a particularly popular way of explaining behaviours of the later historical period (eg. Dobres & Robb, 2000). The overwhelming amount of detail about the individual from historical periods has lent itself well to this approach. More recently, the behaviour of individuals within these processes has looked at the underlying structures within society and the way that people either subvert or reinforce these rules. Johnson's (2000) more recent work has used some of these agentic approaches in the study of late medieval buildings and he has also studied the development of an enclosed landscape in the post medieval period (1996).

We have seen that agency is presently the most popular theoretical 'tool' for historical archaeologists. There is a problem however. This does not lend itself well to landscape analysis and change over time, and medieval landscapes in particular remain behind current new theoretical approaches. Although we should not see humans within these wider schemes of change as merely pawns, human beings are inherently predictable and we cannot reduce the understanding of long-term social processes to what we do as individuals. We should avoid being too attached to a Westernised 'cult' of the individual. Instead I will emphasise community and family as an agent for landscape change and start to move the emphasis away from the power inherent within individuals, an approach that I feel will prove especially useful for the study of rural archaeologies.

Johnson (2005: 112) critiques the traditional approach that most historical archaeologists use when he says it is about amassing data for its own sake. For him, the 'archaeology of record' remains insular in scope and particular in content. Orser (1999: 273) proposes that one way of reinvigorating and retheorising historical archaeology is to "think globally, dig locally" with the aim of creating a modern, world archaeology. This approach is popular, especially in the revisionist construction of post-colonial narratives. But others have criticized this global, metanarrative approach. Dan Hicks (2005: 375) advocates a more contextual or 'situational' interpretation that recognizes contradiction and diversity. He explores alternatives to the excessive emphasis upon 'interpretation' and 'meaning' in archaeological practice which he contends has distance archaeologists from their material, "away from messiness, complexity and partiality".

It is important that I address the messiness, complexity and partiality of this medieval landscape. For many, the study of late and post medieval archaeology is about the development of new processes such as capitalism, commodification and enclosure. We can contest these on a local scale for example, we can see that in the middle Teifi valley, enclosure happened at a much later date than other areas. A mid-18th century estate map for the Castell Hywel estate shows enclosure limited to the very narrow strip along the valley floor and apparently unfinished hedge lines imply that enclosure was still an ongoing process at this time. I suggest that there are regional, local and community-scale influences here that mask global narratives such as capitalism and enclosure and these processes cannot any longer be used as an explanation of change in the Welsh landscape. Other factors are at play. The development of the 'gentry estate' in this area in the late medieval period cannot simply be attributed to the failure of the feudal medieval order and the advancement of a capitalist mentality. Archaeological elements within the landscape will demonstrate the importance of memory, identity and kin. Within this rural landscape, a landscape devoid of grand architectures, and whilst great change is taking place during the 12th and 13th centuries, deliberate and repeated reference to tradition and custom allowed the retention of community histories of a deep antiquity that had specific and unique effects on this landscape.

I have demonstrated that certain elements and practice inherent within models and other systemic ways of thinking are still relevant as a way of studying and explaining landscape. I have also demonstrated that the study of agency at the scale of the individual merely creates a reversal of the top-down analysis, that is, a bottom-up approach that becomes meaningless as a way of landscape explanation. We are moving away from the importance of attaching specific meaning to object and space and away from trying to find global explanations such as capitalism in order to explain them. Against the modern sub-text of a devolving Wales I aim to re-locate the medieval Teifi valley within a new landscape model. This will enable a locational narrative at a variety of scales using a variety of techniques. I will re-cognify the landscape at a regional scale testing the most relevant of the elements from models such as continuity and sophistication from Glanville Jones' multiple estate and kinship ties from Jones Pierce's work. I will demonstrate the effect that the habits and practices of

particular communities had on local landscapes and I will embrace the mess and noise of archaeological material in order to populate that landscape from the inside-out.

The rest of this chapter introduces southern Ceredigion and describes the physical and cultural character of the region. The historical framework leading up to the Norman impact on the area in the 11th-12th centuries is reviewed and the subsequent impact of Rhys ap Gruffudd's lordship is outlined. Our understanding of the landscape in this period is almost entirely understood in terms of this military narrative and the castle-building projects of Normans and Welsh alike are summarised in order to introduce the various political structures and institutions. Chapter two provides the background to historical and archaeological study in this region. It particularly considers the work of Jones-Pierce (1939, 1940, 1941a, 1941b, 1942-3, 1947, 1951, 1959a, 1959b and 1967) and his ground-breaking analysis of the documentary history of north Wales and studies the socio-political atmosphere that influenced other scholars. Although key studies of early estates in Carmarthenshire by Glanville Jones (1972b and 1984) demonstrated the validity of an approach that embraced both document and landscape together the traditional approach has generally been one of political geography driven by historical process. My approach allows the integration of landscape archaeology and history and a detailed methodological outline and approach is presented following a critique of the current research status of medieval Wales.

Chapter three is designed to introduce the specific landscape components that characterised Wales at the moment of conquest. Early Welsh texts supply an invaluable written account of an ideal administrative landscape including the cwmwd, maenor and tref (Owen, 1841). In order to absorb the complex and contradictory versions, I have modelled the various redactions and looked at the way other scholars have used the various redactions to analyse some Welsh landscapes. These introductory chapters serve to highlight the qualitative and quantitative challenge to this thesis.

There exists a lack of a critically informed landscape analysis within Wales but also challenging is the very poorly understood archaeological potential. Seeking to address this poor understanding, Chapter four aims to create on a regional scale a broad pattern of lordship for southern Ceredigion under Lord Rhys at the close of the 12th century. This demonstrates that the landscape units highlighted in the law texts were still in use at this time and that the uniquely 'modern' lordship of Rhys fossilised much of this pre-Norman landscape in grants to monastic houses. Chapter five pursues these units in and around the cwmwd of Gwinionydd and is able to demonstrate a complex and ancient landscape drawing on the methods introduced in chapter two. The maenor and the tref of medieval Gwinionydd are sought and certain forms of complex render and tenure are also reconstructed. The gwestfa and the gwely are investigated as key aspects of settlement and territory and the status of the central Teifi valley and the potential of the archaeological record in low-lying agricultural areas emerges. Chapter six examines more closely the evidence for the gwely and the occupants of the tyddyn or homestead. The retrogressive analysis of estate structures has supplied evidence for the specifically Welsh settlement practice of rhandir at Bettws Bledrus and Llandysul. The medieval antecedence of the dispersed farmscape is highlighted at Moelhedog farm and Llanfair and this evidence has allowed the recreation of a 12th century farmscape and the development of new models for secular organization in pre-Norman Wales. The concluding discussion in chapter seven reiterates the main conclusions from the landscape analysis, contextualises the methodological approach and touches briefly upon potential future concepts to be investigated.

The information generated has emerged in a very visual way at a variety of scales and because of the nature of this analysis and the complexities of map and place name evidence, tables, maps and figures will be placed within the text as relevant and not within a separate appendix thus removing the need for excessive cross-referencing throughout the document.

The Study Area

The study area will focus on the northern flanks of the central Teifi valley in southern Ceredigion. Because this study aims to illuminate some of the complex settlement and territorial systems in place during the 12th to 13th centuries. The defining cultural and political unit is the *cwmwd* or commote, and the focus in this case will be on

the cwmwd of Gwinionydd (fig. 2). Cymydau were often paired within the larger cantref and it was these that formed the framework for the modern hundredal system not formalised in Wales until 1546. Gwinionydd comprises some 39,000 acres and presently contains nine parishes. The central parish of Llandysul is one of the largest in the county at 17,640 acres and forms the focus of some of the closer-grained fieldwork and survey. The small town of Llandysul is situated on the northern banks of the Teifi and is some 19 miles upstream of the county seat at Cardigan on the coast to the west, and 13 miles downstream of the small market town of Lampeter. Essentially reflecting groups of parishes and tithe districts, the cwmwd and cantref units were mapped for the first time in the early 20th century by William Rees (1932 and 1951). They were reconstructed using a range of often scarce administrative and other documentary sources, and although they have since provided an invaluable resource some of the boundary detail will benefit from closer scrutiny. The complex way that cwmwd Gwinionydd, its parishes and their sub-units fit into the administrative framework of medieval Ceredigion will also be explored.

Landscape Character

Contextualisation of Gwinionydd within its physical and cultural landscapes requires a more distant or regional perspective than may be employed later in addressing issues of, for instance, specific boundaries. The cwmwd sits within the region of the central Teifi valley, parts of which have previously been the subject of landscape characterisation under Cadw funded initiatives in collaboration with CCW and ICOMOS (Cadw, 1998 and Cadw, 2001). Indeed Wales has been a fertile area for the development of such approaches to characterisation and designation of historic landscapes (Rippon, 1996 and 2004: 70-74). This valley region is considered in this introductory section through examination of the underlying, solid and drift, geology, followed by sections on topography with subsequent increasingly cultural sections on landscape and land use.

Geology

The underlying geological sequence for this region is relatively well studied. The submerged offshore plain is Lower Palaeozoic in origin, whilst the narrow, shallow coastal strip overlying this is of the Silurian period (fig. 3). The lower Teifi valley around

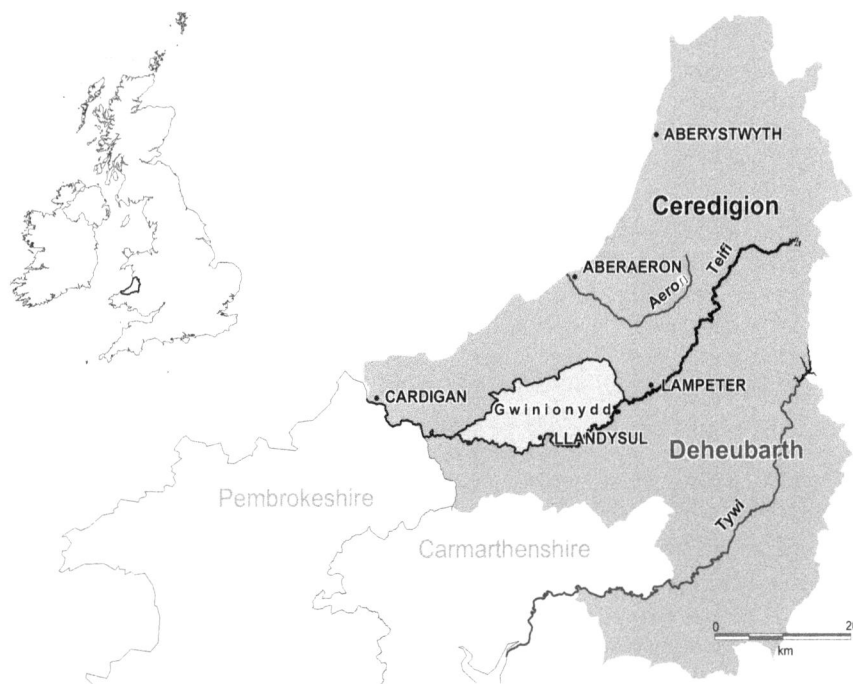

Figure 2. Location map. Deheubarth with Cwmwd Gwinionydd in southern Ceredigion.

Cardigan is comprised of Ordovician silt and mudstones and as the land rises inland we see a series of Pleistocene clays, gravels and sands with marine deposits plus valley and hillslope accumulations which provide the parent materials for soils (Bowen, 1994: 6).

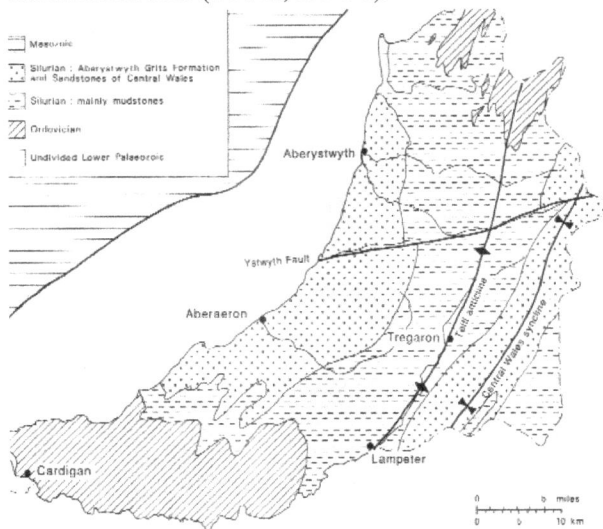

Figure 3. The solid geology of Ceredigion (Bowen 1994: 8)

It is the precise nature of these later glacial deposits that remains a complex and sometimes controversial topic (McCaroll, 2001). This region is the point where glaciers based in the Irish sea 'overlap' with the United Kingdom ice sheets based in the mid-Wales upland, thus the precise origins of glacial deposits in west Wales remains ambiguous. Areas south of Llanrhystud in the central coastal area of the county demonstrate a blue-grey clay rich in marine foraminifera and calcareous fragments which demonstrates its Irish Sea origins, whilst a number of sarnau or end moraines running out into Cardigan Bay emphasise the south-westerly orientation of the terrestrial ice lobes. These sarnau or causeways are visible at low tide along with prehistoric land surfaces and submerged forests and offer evidence for the origins of the mythical Cantref Gwaelod or 'drowned country'. Whilst the British Geological Survey (BGS) has mapped both the underlying and drift geology of the coastal zone around Cardigan, precise glacial information for the complex sequences of the Teifi valley remain incomplete and the BGS is currently in the process of mapping the middle Teifi valley area in more detail (M. Hambrey pers comm.).

Topography

West Wales is characterised by a series of dissected plateau forming a stepped landform that rises from the coastal plain inland to the central uplands of mid Wales. The Cambrian mountains create a central spine to Wales with their highest point in Ceredigion in the north with Pumlumon at 2,468 ft. This massif forms the main watershed for the whole of Wales with the rivers Severn, Wye, Elan, Irfon, Tywi, Cothi, Teifi, Ystwyth, Rheidol, and Twymyn rising here.

Narrow, deeply incised river valleys drain these upland areas, emptying from the north-east to south-west into Cardigan Bay. The Teifi reflects this trend rising in the southern Cambrians issuing into Cardigan Bay after travelling some 75 miles. The lakes forming the Teifi headwaters were exploited as fisheries by the Cistercians situated at Strata Florida Abbey (Toulmin Smith, 1906). The Teifi drains into Cors Caron below the abbey and pollen analysis has provided a record that spans later prehistory into the medieval period when clearance and agricultural change attributed to the Cistercians is evident (Hughes et al., 2001: 91). By the time the Teifi reaches Lampeter it is wide enough to form a more significant physical barrier and it is here that it forms the county boundary where Roman river crossings once accessed the nearby fort at Llanio. The central stretch of the Teifi valley between Lampeter and Newcastle Emlyn affords a modest but fertile ystrad or valley floor. A series of spectacular narrow gorges below Llandysul and at Cenarth, Llechryd and Cilgerran give way finally to the wide, shallow estuarine meadows around Cardigan.

Soils and Vegetation

This complex glacial history means we presently have a rather coarse understanding of Ceredigion's soil origins and composition and this perhaps contributes to our lack of understanding of pre-industrial agriculture. Enough evidence does exist to show that much of southern Ceredigion consists of well-drained loamy soils, becoming wetter and more peaty in the upland zone between the middle Teifi and Aeron valleys (Rudeforth 1994: 22). These soils are thin and acidic and, especially from the 18th century onwards, lime was imported to a number of kilns constructed along the coast.

Thicker peats on upland areas are characterised by open heather and Molina-dominated stagnopodzols. These usually remain uncultivated but in the Dyfi estuary in northern Ceredigion, earthy peats have been formed through repeated cultivation and provide excellent arable and grazing land (ibid.). The modern ploughing and improvement of peat uplands around Gors Goch demonstrates the threat posed by agriculture to this resource. Shallower, drought-prone Ranker soils are commoner in parts of the fertile south west where cereals, especially barley for stock feed, are occasionally grown today. Coastal brown sands in the Cardigan area are prized as a source of sand and gravels.

Despite the thick fertile, silty Brown alluvial soils along the lower and middle Teifi valley they are seldom cropped, mainly being laid to grass meadow. This is traditionally explained in terms of flood risk and Rudeforth (1994: 24) for example highlights the apparent evidence of early settlement sites away from flooding on hilltops and well-drained lower slopes. There are, however, very few gley soils along the valley bottoms which are mostly well drained and flooding is largely predictable and seasonal in nature. It will also become apparent that settlement patterns represent a much more complex picture than that explained by soil composition and flood risk alone and some of the sites investigated below lie on this 'uninhabitable' flood plain at Llanfair and Llandysul for example.

The transition from the Ordovician of the lower Teifi valley to the Silurian mudstones of the upper occurs right inside the study area, around the middle Teifi valley somewhere between Lampeter and Llandysul. It is this zone that begins to mark the transition from the mild and fertile lower Teifi to the wetter, shallower uplands and whether this transitional zone has had a conspicuous impact on land use in the historic period will be investigated below.

Pollen analysis from central Ceredigion demonstrates that woodland clearance from about the Neolithic period onwards led to the development of upland peats that are now dominated by molinia or purple moor grass (Walker et al., 2001: 25). Currently, unenclosed upland grazing occurs mainly in the north of the county but within the study area, wetlands have been drained and improved to form pasture. At Cwrt farm near Cwrtnewydd the scars of drainage channels cut by the present owners' father during the early post-war period can still be seen. The traditional upland grazing zone is lower than in the north at around 200 metres and there is no unenclosed common or rhos within the study area although the now-enclosed upland is still occasionally dominated by gorse and molinia.

The Cultural Landscape

The central Teifi valley area as politically defined by Gwinionydd is also a topographically distinct area defined by the shallow river valley and its gentle south facing slopes and catchment areas. The region is rural but not remote and heavily influenced by agricultural stock production; smaller dairy farms diversifying to beef, and sheep in recent years. Ieuan ap Sulien writing at Llanbadarn Fawr around 1090 describes the 'fertile region' of Ceredigion bounded by Pumlumon to the east, the sea to the west and to the north and south by the Rivers Dyfi and Teifi (Kirby, 1994a: 318).

Essentially this is a landscape of dispersed farmsteads with few small hamlets and the small towns of Adpar, Llandysul (fig. 4) and Lampeter are situated along the banks of the Teifi. Field boundaries on early OS and tithe maps show small, irregular field enclosures along valley floors and sides and the evidence is that very little of the higher ground remained unenclosed.

Large fields hedged with single thorn species generally represent late enclosure and are confined only to the highest areas above 200 metres. Land was drained and improved and grass was cultivated in order to provide grazing. This has not always been the case and as I intend to demonstrate below, even the highest upland areas were often utilised for arable production, both in the medieval period and well into

the 19th century. Small pockets of species-rich wetland areas also remain in this higher zone and there are some smaller wetlands just to the north of the study area at Rhos

Figure 4. The small market town of Llandysul developed around St Tysul's church on the banks of the Teifi.

Garn Whilgarn, Rhos Ymryson, Rhos Garn Wen and Rhos Lawr Cwrt all in the upland zone between the Teifi and Aeron valleys. The boggy areas around Blaencathal and Gors Goch in the north east are designated as SSSIs as are the Grannell, Clettwr, Ythan and Teifi rivers. As Special Areas of Conservation, these rivers are also afforded the highest level of protection under the law. The more heavily settled and farmed lower zones have fewer of these designated areas and these are characterised by a patchwork

Figure 5. Crug y Whil mound (a deposit of glacial sands) on the floor of the Teifi Valley near Rhuddlan Teifi surrounded by a typical patchwork of small, hedged fields.

13

of smaller fields (fig. 5).

The Teifi forms a modest physical barrier and the bridges at Newcastle Emlyn, Henllan, Llandysul, Maesycrugiau and Lampeter are late in date but are positioned at narrow points, replacing earlier fordings. The only confirmed medieval bridge is attested at Llanfihangel-Ar-Arth (Lloyd, 1935: 316-7). The modest stream systems that drain the middle Teifi region are the Grannell in the east, the Cledlyn, Clettwr, Gwenffrwd, Cerdin, Nythan, Merwydd, Hoffnant, Bachnog, Iago, Cynllo and the Afon Cwm-wern at the westernmost edge. The Teifi meanders back and forth across a shallow plain no more than half a mile wide at any point and settlement on the valley floor is sparse, generally confined to low knolls and plateaux just above the floodplain. Occupation that does brave the floodplain comprises isolated larger dwellings and minor gentry houses at Dolhaidd, Dancoed, Gilfachwen, Dol Llan, and Llanfair. Although fertile, the valley floor is rarely cultivated and is reserved for pasture and meadow. Fields are medium sized and irregular, often hedged with mixed-deciduous species and here there are few banks, walls or fences.

The dominant theme of this landscape is the farm. The valley sides are generally gently sloping and it is here that, dotted along the spring line, the dispersed farmsteads typical of the area lie. Along the steep sides of the narrow Nant Ythan that feeds the Cerdin just north of Llandysul for example, we can see the chief farms of Blaenythan, Pantscythan, Pant-y-Rhedynen, Cwm-ul and Troedrhiwffenyd. These are situated on narrow platforms cut into the steep valley side and are mentioned in a rental dated to 1564 (Richards, 1964a). Smaller, later cottages and byres are situated on the upper slopes above c.200 m.

Considered to be of little merit architecturally, the earliest of these Georgian-style farm complexes date to the late 18th century with a main phase of rebuilding in the middle 19th century (fig. 6). Generally double-fronted, stone under slate and arranged at one end of a three-sided courtyard of outbuildings these are described by Lloyd et al (2006),

Smith (1988 and 1998) and Peate (1944).

These buildings replaced earlier stone and clom (clay) thatched cottages that seldom survive although the former dwelling at Shadog, Llangeler with its gorse under-thatch now serves as a barn. Constructed of earth and clay in layers these early structures are built on low stone footings which support a scarfed-cruck, thatched roof. A small concentration of these buildings survive particularly in the central Teifi and Aeron valleys where the National Trust estate at Llanerchaeron includes former estate cottages at Pontbrenmydr and Wigwen Fach where the distinctive wicker and daub fire-hoods are still visible. These are tentatively stylistically dated to the late 16th century (Evans pers. comm.) but preserve the clom and cruck tradition known from excavation at Llanerchaeron of a 14th century domestic structure (Evans, 2003). Other examples of traditional clom and cruck buildings can be seen at Ty Glyn, near Aberaeron, Gelli near Trefilan, at Aberarth, Llan-non and spectacularly restored examples can be seen at Rhiwsion, Llanwenog and at Cribyn to the north in the Aeron valley. If many of these surviving structures do date to the 16th and 17th centuries it is likely that some of the larger gentry houses may also conceal an earlier core. But none of these have been securely dated and the recently dendro-dated structure at Gwastad in the Aeron valley (fig. 6) is the earliest in the county at between 1530 and 1575 (Nigel Nayling pers. comm.). The biography of the typical farmstead in this region is thus poorly understood but their morphologies and distinctive characteristics will be studied below in order to develop a methodology to indicate early antecedence.

These early farms are generally surrounded by small, irregular fields, enclosed by steep earthen banks which are sometimes stone-faced with herringbone-style patterns (fig. 7). These walls often line relict trackways and paths that formerly linked neighbouring farms. The hedges topping the early banks are generally multi-species including oak, hazel, rowan, gorse, thorn and holly which is often left to grow on as a standard. Later hedges tend to contain fewer species and quick-growing ash can suggest an earlier hedge

Figure 6. 18th century former farmhouse at Moelhedog.

Figure 7. Steep hedge banks above the Teifi valley.

than is actually the case and along with quickthorn is associated with the enclosures of the 18th to 20th centuries. Beech hedging was common during the 19th century and has often has grown out leaving quite large avenues of mature trees but remnants of hedge laying can sometimes be seen in low, lateral branches. Beech was also used in later, more genteel contexts in order to improve the approach to a gentry farm and avenues of large beech trees line many farm entrances and trackways. An 18th century estate map shows the former avenue of trees approaching the abbey farmhouse at Strata Florida and an impressive avenue of 18th century limes approaches the now levelled former plas at Peterwell, Lampeter. For agricultural purposes, blackthorn and quickthorn were used as a quick-growing, economical species with good impenetrability and are common on the upland enclosures, often without the ubiquitous hedge bank. Enclosure occurred late and was a contentious process in many areas. During the 18th century, the Castell Hywel estate at Pontsian, north of Llandysul saw small irregular fields clustered around the main farms along the lower slopes with large areas of open, unenclosed uplands (James, 2001: 141). But the encroachment onto the uplands was not confined to gentry landowners and many 'squatter' settlements emerged from the late 18th century and reflect the desperate exploitation of land traditionally held by common right, but formerly only for grazing.

Where the valleys are too steep for settlement, for example around Henllan gorge and the narrower tributaries they are wooded with mixed oak seldom over 100 years old and often heavily coppiced or cleared between the wars. Tir coed or woodland was a vital resource in medieval Wales and in the pre-conquest period was subject to intricate valuations, definitions and apportionments. 12th and 13th century sources with earlier origins illustrate the correct coppicing and pollarding procedure and preserved woodland, coed cadw, specifically for pannaging and underwood was particularly prized (Linnard, 2000: 21).

Woodland within the study area is confined to steep-sided wooded slopes (fig. 8), many of which have been recently re-wooded as the 1st edition Ordnance Survey maps indicate. At Dancapel in Llangeler for example, steep valley sides to the east were criss-crossed by trackways and field boundaries accessing springs and quarries but are now densely wooded. The scarcity of large timber trees is reflected in the local building traditions where the scarfed-cruck made by jointing two smaller timbers replaces the cruck blade more familiar in the Welsh borders (Smith, 1988). Only two buildings with full cruck blades are known from Ceredigion, Gwastad Gwrda has combination of both scarfed and full crucks, apparently contemporary with each other. Even major dwellings exhibit this feature with a large scarfed-cruck roof supporting the earliest phase at Llanfair, Llandysul dating probably to the 17th century.

The larger medieval churches at Llandysul and Llanwenog are focal points within this dispersed landscape and the earliest fabric here dates to the 14th century (Hughes &

Jenkins, 1967). Figure 9 shows the distribution of castles and churches showing their dedications. Churches are not prominently sited; rarely breaking the sky line they are situated below ridges on middle slopes. Llanwenog church for example is set below a knoll and retains the vestige of its outer circular 'llan' enclosure. Also occasionally exploited is a valley floor siting as at Llandysul church which is very close to the Teifi and which regularly suffers from flooding. These are the earliest extant buildings within this rural landscape, although there is evidence for earlier religious activity in the form of early medieval inscribed stones. The Deccabar stone at Capel Mair in Llangeler is

Figure 8. The wooded south-facing slopes of the Clettwr valley, viewed from Moelhedog Farm.

inscribed in Latin and ogham and will be considered alongside other evidence as the site of an early church. The Velvor stone at Llandysul unusually commemorates a woman, where there is also a cross-marked slab and the large Latin and ogham Trenactus stone at Llanwenog that stood on the purported site of a lost chapel mound by the Teifi near Crug Y Whil farm. The dedication to popular medieval saints is also evident in Mary at Llanfair and Llanfair Treflygen and Michael at Llanfihangel and the earlier 'Celtic' saints for example, David, or Dewi, at Capel Dewi, Geynog at Llanwenog, Gwynen at Llanwnnen, Gwenffrwd at Fardre, Cynon at Capel Cynon, Celer at Llangeler, Bridget at Llansantffraid, Cynllo at Llangynllo, Tyfriog at Llandyfriog and Tysul at Llandysul. There is a paucity of evidence for medieval secular settlement in this area and Giraldus Cambrensis (Forester, 1887: 505-506) famously described the habits of late 12th century rural Wales: "They neither inhabit towns nor villages, nor castles, but lead a solitary life in the woods, on the borders of which they do.vvnot erect sumptuous palaces, nor lofty stone buildings, but content themselves with small huts made of the boughs of trees twisted together, constructed with little labour and expense, and sufficient to endure throughout the year". Limited urban settlement began to occur around newly built castles from the 12th century. Newcastle Emlyn castle to the west of the study area is overlooked by a motte to the north but is also the location of one of the important early Welsh-built stone castles built in c. 1240 by Maredudd ap Rhys, grandson of the famous Lord Rhys (Evans, 1922: 70-72). There are numerous

Figure 9. Medieval castles, ringworks and mottes; castles (marked with a cross) are shown with their dedications.

mottes strung along the Teifi valley, and whether of Welsh or Norman provenance is often unknown. Contemporary Welsh annals written at Strata Florida Abbey known as the Brut y Tywysogion, or Chronicle of the Princes record the building of the large motte at Trefilan in the Aeron valley by Rhys's son, Maelgwyn who died at the nearby hamlet of Llanerchaeron in 1231. The castle was subsequently finished by his son, Maelgwyn Fychan (Jones, 1955a: 230). Other defensive earthwork sites exist at Castell Gwinionydd, just east of Llandysul and Castell Ddu at Llanwnnen. These ring-work sites are poorly understood but assumed to be Welsh-built and of pre-conquest date. Castell Gwinionydd is named for cwmwd Gwinionydd that it sits centrally and evidence presented below suggests that it was connected to the early administration of the cwmwd.

Political and Military History

Little is understood of the Post-Roman period in rural Wales. The political geography of Demetarum from which 'Dyfed' derives, had been centred on the Roman Moridinum at Carmarthen and the recently discovered fort and civitas at Llandeilo Fawr may have formed the antecedent of the medieval Royal seat of Deheubarth at Dinefwr. Irish settlement in the southwest from the 5th to 6th century onwards is also poorly understood but is attested by the rath in parts of Pembrokeshire and the ogham inscriptions that stretch further north up the coast as far as the central coast of Ceredigion. *Gwthefyr* or *Gwrtheryn*, the British king, *Vortepor* can be placed in this period and is reputed to have built a stronghold on the banks of the Teifi (Davies & Hogg, 1994: 249). His memorial stone inscribed, *memoria Voteporigis Protectoris* in both Latin and ogham stood at Castell Dwyran near Narberth; according to the Mabinogion, this was the caput of the early princes of Dyfed, a set of tales that linked many Teifi valley locations: Cwm Cych and Rhuddlan Teifi for example (Kirby, 1994b: 322).

The 9th century Historia Brittonum relates the expulsion of the Irish from Britain by Cunedda and the sons of Cunedda became the eponymous founders of many of the kingdoms of Wales, Ceredig providing us with Ceredigion. These foundation myths are linked to identity and memory and were to do with institutional power and legitimisation where we can see hints of the early importance attributed to pedigree and lineage with many medieval princes claiming descent from Cunedda (Harvey & Jones, 1999). The Cunedda lineage also provided the ancestry for a number of saints, Dewi, Carranog and Teilo. In the later 8th century, Seisyll became an early founder of the Deheubarth core when he added the three cantrefi of Ystrad Tywi to Ceredigion to create the kingdom of Seisyllwg. This is also alluded to in the Mabinogion, the main source for which, the *Llyfr Gwyn Rhydderch* (Peniarth MS 4) the White Book of Rhydderch is the earliest redaction of the four branches of the Mabinogi and was written at Strata Florida Abbey, probably for the influential steward, deputy justiciar and dosbarthwyr (lawyer, officer), Rhydderch ab Ieuan Llwyd

(c. 325-1400) from Parcrhydderch in the parish of Llangeitho in Ceredigion (Griffiths, 1994: 56).

In 909, Hywel Dda united the fractured Kingdom of Dyfed with Seisyllwg to become the early kingdom of Deheubarth and came to rule much of Wales. Through the descent of Rhodri Mawr and his son Cadell, Hywel's father, he became a member of the Dinefwr branch of the dynasty. His reign was a peaceful one and it was his parliament at Whitland in 945 that ratified the law codes, copies of which survive from the late 12th century onwards. Sulien of Llanbadarn became Bishop of St David's in 1073 and his son, Rhigyfarch wrote the Life of St David's. The kingdom passed via Hywel's lineage eventually in 1078 to Rhys ap Tewdwr.

Norman military activity in the area began at the close of the 11th century with the death of Rhys ap Tewdwr and the invasion of south west Wales by Marcher lords. Castles were established at Carmarthen, Cardigan and Pembroke. Quickly erected mottes were built, sometimes on new sites when the conquest began in earnest in Wales at the turn of the 12th century. Pushing northwards from Pembrokeshire and Carmarthenshire they reached the banks of the Teifi where Cantref Cemais was recreated as a Barony whilst neighbouring Cantref Emlyn was brought under partial control when the commote of Emlyn-Is-Cych was created as the Lordship of Cilgerran. Ceredigion was seriously threatened when Roger de Montgomery built the new castle at Cardigan in 1110. Ceredigion remained administered via the Norman caput at Cardigan until Rhys ap Tewdwr's grandson, Rhys ap Gruffudd was able to retake much of the former kingdom in 1165 where the relative peace of his reign terminated in the gradual fragmentation through his sons' in-fighting.

The Lordship of Rhys ap Gruffudd

The process of 'Normanisation' occurred much later in Wales than elsewhere in Britain and necessitated the creation of Marcher lordships along the Welsh borders and the south east. New administrative techniques illuminated traditional practices and how much they represent the former status or a totally new way of doing things is perhaps reflected in the outcome of studies into Domesday Book, for example, that demonstrates the incorporation of native English practice into new administrative terminologies and systems. It was not until the signing of the Statute of Rhuddlan in 1284, however, that the whole of Wales was brought totally under the control of the English Crown, over 200 years since 1066. In this time, Gwynedd in the north and Deheubarth in the southwest remained largely under native rule. We know of the extensive estates granted to religious during this period by Welsh rulers but precisely how they relate to existing territorial structures has been obscured by conquest and change. In order to unpack the complexities of ownership and landholding at this time it is necessary to look at the intricate military action during this period, often the only source of historical evidence available.

Whilst the first Normans appeared in Ceredigion as early as 1073 and 1074 they faced and were defeated by Rhys ap Tewdwr in 1081, Prince of Deheubarth at the Battle of Mynydd Carn somewhere south of Cardigan (Lloyd, 1911: 384 and n. 88). These events were chronicled by a contemporary writer based at the clas monastery of Saint Padarn at Llanbadarn near Aberystwyth. This text, that was later moved to the Cistercian abbey of Strata Florida, came to be known as the Brut y Tywysogion or the Chronicle of the Princes (Jones, 1955a) and demonstrated the status of the newly founded monastery. On Rhys ap Tewdwr's death in 1093, Roger de Montgomery, the first Earl of Shrewsbury, marched through Ceredigion from the north unto Cardigan where he built a timber motte, possibly on the early site of Din Geraint. Even though he was forced to retreat the following year destroying other castles in his wake, Cardigan had established itself as the Norman caput which developed as the administrative centre of the county. In 1099 Ceredigion along with much of Powys was claimed by Cadwgan ap Bleddyn ap Cynfyn of Powys. Enraged by the elopement of Cadwgan's' son, Owain and the beautiful Nest from Cilgerran castle, Henry I granted Ceredigion to Gilbert Fitz Richard de Clare in c. 1110. Here began a campaign of motte building in earnest with a peak around the 1130s but continuing into the early 13th century.

The Norman hold on Ceredigion during the early 12th century continued under Gilbert Fitz Richard, despite an unsuccessful rout by one of Rhys ap Tewdwr's sons, Gruffudd ap Rhys. On Gilbert's death in 1117 his son Richard Fitz Gilbert succeeded. On the death of Henry I in 1135 Richard returned to Cardigan but was ambushed and killed at Crickhowell and the lordship of Ceredigion was thrown into disorder. The Royal princes of Gwynedd took advantage and, with the help of Gruffudd ap Rhys and other Welsh leaders, Owain and Cadwaladr, the sons of Gruffudd ap Cynan of Gwynedd, they crossed the Dyfi southwards into Ceredigion with several thousand soldiers and within three years every Norman castle had fallen except Cardigan (Jones, 1955a: 115). With the Norman stronghold based here, administration of the local Welsh campaign seems to have been focussed upstream around the middle Teifi valley where, in Gwinionydd alone, there are nine fortified sites. Rhydowen is believed to be 'Owain's ford' and close to where Owain's son Hywel, rebuilt the Norman motte at Castell Hywel around 1150 (Morgan, 2005: 73).

The following years saw the defence of Deheubarth and its dynastic rights by the sons of Gruffudd ap Rhys. Anarawd tried unsuccessfully to take Cardigan castle but his brother Cadell took Carmarthen and Llanstephan from the Normans in 1143 where Anarawd was killed. Maredudd succeeded Cadell in 1153 but due to ill health his younger brother Rhys ap Gruffudd succeeded to the turbulent kingdom of Deheubarth in 1155. Following immense pressure from Gwynedd to the north and the Normans to the south he built a motte at Tomen Las on the banks of the

Dyfi in order to deter Owain Gwynedd (Jones, 1955a: 43). This act characterised his subsequent reign which was one of consolidation and great political maturity. In 1158, however, Rhys was forced to surrender to Henry II and Ceredigion was granted to a nervous Roger de Clare, the Earl of Hertford, who set about reprovisioning Rhys's other strongholds at Castell Hywel, Ystrad Meurig, Dineirth and Llanrhystud (Turvey, 1988: 42).

Despite two royal campaigns against him in 1159 and 1163 Rhys regained control of Ceredigion in 1164 and finally took Cardigan Castle in 1165. Following Owain Gwynedd's death in 1170, Rhys became the most powerful Welsh ruler and in 1171, Henry II acknowledged Rhys's recent re-acquisitions of Ceredigion, Ystrad Tywi, Emlyn, Ystlwyf, and Efelffre, appointing him Justiciar (Pryce, 2005: 8). Rhys rebuilt the castle at Cardigan and in a highly symbolic act held what has been recognised as the first Welsh Eisteddfod there in 1176. Rhys was an accomplished diplomat and politician and realised that the best method for consolidating his new Kingdom was to give it away; that is to monastic and religious houses thus essentially diffusing the military potential of vast swathes of Ceredigion, a fashion continued in lesser form by his successors. That he was a considered politician and prolific castle builder is evident but the exploitation of resources necessary to maintain this trajectory have never been explored and indicate the management of a sophisticated landscape.

Rhys's reign was relatively stable but in its closing years his successors warred amongst themselves. Rhys's son Maelgwyn proved particularly troublesome and he was imprisoned by Rhys, escaping in 1192 and destroying Ystrad Meurig castle the following year. In 1194 he and his brother Hywel imprisoned their father at Nevern though he was later released by Hywel. Rhys died on the 28th April 1197 and the "greatest Welsh prince to have graced the political stage during the golden age of Welsh independence" (Turvey, 1988: 109) was interred at St David's cathedral church ending over 30 years of relatively peaceful rule. In a modern move Rhys had named his eldest son Gruffudd as his sole heir according to Anglo-Norman law. Under the Welsh law of cyfran, Maelgwyn would have been entitled to claim an equal share of his father's dynasty. Enraged, Maelgwyn defeated Gruffudd at Aberystwyth and took possession of much of Deheubarth and plotted with King John, to whom he traitorously sold Cardigan Castle (Jones, 1955a: 183). Gruffudd later retook lands apart from Cardigan and Ystrad Meurig but died in 1201 allowing Maelgwyn to take Cilgerran which he lost to William Marshall in 1204. Maelgwyn was expelled from Ystrad Tywi by another brother Rhys Gryg who took Cantref Mawr and Dinefwr thus consolidating the Ystrad Tywi branch of the lineage, whilst the sons of Gruffudd, Rhys and Owain, took Cantref Bychan.

Llywelyn the Great of Gwynedd annexed Uwch Aeron in 1208 but by 1216 after a council at Aberdyfi, Llywelyn restored most of Deheubarth. To Maelgwyn was apportioned Cantref Gwarthaf, Carmarthen, Cemais and Emlyn, Mallaen in Cantref Mawr and Hirfryn with Llandovery in Cantref Bychan, along with the cymydau of Gwinionydd and Mabwynion. Rhys Ieuanc and Owain were restored to all of Ceredigion except that land belonging to Maelgwyn. Rhys Gryg was given Cantref Mawr and Cantref Bychan, again, save the land that Maelgwyn held, plus Cydweli and Carnwyllion in Dyfed. After Rhys Ieuanc's death in 1222, his land was divided between Maelgwyn and Owain. William Marshall II's successful campaign returned Carmarthen and Cardigan to the Crown in 1223 and Maelgwyn died in 1231 at Llanerchaeron and was buried at Strata Florida; his son Maelgwyn Fychan inheriting what by now comprised Ceredigion Is (below the) Aeron.

Maelgwyn Fychan led skirmishes into northern Ceredigion where he gained cymydau there with a view to relieving the monks of Strata Florida of Ystrad Meurig (Pryce, 2005: 11) but was dispossessed of them by Maredudd, son of Rhys Gryg and Maredudd son of Owain, he only retained Perfedd in the far north and Is Coed in the south. The overlordship established by Llywelyn did not continue long after his death with his son Dafydd (proclaimed at Strata Florida in 1238) dying in 1246. Authority in Ceredigion became fragmented between minor Welsh lords and the Crown. Northern Ceredigion became subject to crown rule via Henry III and all the tithes of the vast parish of Llanbadarn for example went to the crown, although administered at a local level by a Welshman, Gwilym ap Gwrwared, grandfather of the famous bard, Dafydd ap Gwilym (Morgan, 2005: 78). By 1256, however, Llywelyn's grandson Llywelyn ap Gruffudd swept the Normans away from Gwynedd and northern Ceredigion which he gave to Maredudd ap Owain who ruled peacefully here for twenty years. Henry III finally confirmed Llywelyn with the title of Prince of Wales in 1267 though he came into conflict with the new king, Edward I in 1273.

With the death of Rhys in 1197, the rule of the dynasty of Deheubarth had begun to disintegrate. Petty squabbles and feuding rivalry allowed Llywelyn and the house of Gwynedd to assume overlordship. Although the last great Welsh ruling dynasty was that of Gwynedd, it was the Rhysian lineage that was the last to retain any native lordship in Wales; in Gwinionydd. Following Maredudd's rule his son Owain retained the cwmwd of Anhuniog whilst his other son Gruffudd kept Gwinionydd. The failure of Gruffudd's line meant that Owain's young son, Llewelyn ab Owain inherited the estates and, as a minor during the Edwardian conquest, was created a ward of court and was allowed to retain lordship of the now diminished lands. Nevertheless he became known as the Lord of South Wales and his estate was centred at Llandysul. Llywelyn's son Thomas married Eleanor of the descent of Llywelyn the Last of Gwynedd. One of their daughters married Gruffudd Fychan, Lord of Glyndyfwrdwy and their son, Owain became known as Owain Glyndwr who could claim descent from both the line of Gwynedd and the line of Deheubarth. His rebellion caused Henry IV to confiscate his land; however, a pardon issued by Henry V was accepted on his behalf by his son, Maredudd. As a vital territory central to the Deheubarth estate Gwinionydd had survived the conquest and in-fighting until the conquest of the whole of Wales in 1284. Despite this turbulence it is here that many ancient territories and institutions survive and these served to distinguish this region into the post-medieval period with the fossilisation of small lordships and gentry estates.

Centres of Authority

McNeill and Pringle (1997) have highlighted the massive concentration of mottes along the Welsh borders demonstrating the brutal and overpowering process whereby the Norman Marcher lords launched their assaults. There is a smaller but still significant concentration clustered around the central Teifi valley (see fig. 9 above). Studies to establish the contemporaneity of such structures have been lacking but, as McNeill and Pringle point out, areas with fewer mottes such as the northern March may be due to the relatively stable lordships of Gwynedd and Chester but this pattern cannot be assumed for Gwinionydd with the prolific castle-building policies of Rhys in evidence.

The deliberate establishment of castles on formerly significant secular sites remains untested and the distribution of fortified sites as a general clue to earlier settlement and territory must be considered cautiously. Longley (1997: 43) noted a correlation between 11th century mottes in Gwynedd and politically important Welsh secular royal centres centred on the llys or court and their attendant demesne settlement known as the maerdref. But out of the 31 maerdrefi he identified, only five castles (plus another possible three) could demonstrate a definite correlation, indicating the complexity of the situation. Longley (ibid. 53) still insists that Norman mottes may be useful in identifying former llys and maerdref structures but he does point out that Norman fortification is purely a stage in the "continuous evolution of centres of power and authority" and goes on to suggest that Iron Age hillforts maybe the early forerunners of high status sites. Johnstone (1997) developed this approach in the study of 13th century Gwynedd as a context for the excavated llys site at Rhosyr. He linked 11 mottes with proposed adjacent llys sites, evidence for which was particularly strong in Meirionnydd where (with the exception of the llys at Ystumgwern) all of the mottes could demonstrate some sort of link to a former Welsh site and he went on to speculate that a phase of llys fortification immediately preceded the building of mottes.

In an attempt to identify former Welsh centres of secular power within Ceredigion, ten of the most 'important' castles have been linked to the county's ten cymydau:

Castle	Cwmwd
Din Geraint and	
Blaenporth	both in Is Coed
Castell Hywel	Gwinionydd
Stephen's Castle	Mabwynion
Aberystwyth	Creuddyn
Caerwedros	Caerwedros
Castell Flemish	Penardd
Dineirth	Anhuniog
Ystrad Meurig	Mefenydd
Razo's Castle	Perfedd
Walter's Castle	Genau'r Glyn

(cf. Rowley, 1983: 225-226)

Figure 9 (above) however illustrates the immense and complex campaign of castle building by both Welsh and Norman over a long period of time. With little evidence of the structure of the early Welsh secular court, to emphasise the link between llys and motte would be to oversimplify. Mottes were often hastily erected military structures differing entirely in function from an administrative llys site, which may have been only lightly defended. Castell Flemish, proposed as the caput of Penardd is actually an Iron Age hillfort that shows no evidence of use during the medieval period. The castle referred to at Llwyn Gwiniau stands only a mile distant from Castell Flemish but is only a low mound and doubt is cast on its identification as a motte (Davis, 2000: 43). Alternatively, a compelling case can be made for the centre of pre-conquest political authority in Mefenydd at Ystrad Meurig to the north-west which was the focus of intense activity during the 12th and 13th centuries. The location, morphology and unusual nature of the earthworks there hint at early origins that may represent an early secular high-status site, perhaps a llys site.

Roger de Montgomery's timber castle at Cardigan on the coast briefly became the centre of Norman lordship in 12th century Ceredigion, and it was Cardigan that came to symbolise for the Welsh the caput of Norman oppression in the county. Not surprising then that Cardigan became the prize for Welsh rulers, only to be taken successfully by Lord Rhys who held his highly symbolic Eisteddfod there as an expression of statesmanship. It was at Cardigan that Rhys received Archbishop Baldwin and Giraldus Cambrensis here during their tour of Wales to raise support for the Third Crusade (Colt-Hoare, 1976). A town developed around the castle and Cardigan was eventually to become the county seat. Although the defended site of Din Geraint predates Roger de Montgomery's arrival in 1093, there is no evidence that medieval secular occupation of any significance existed here prior to this and the importance of Cardigan grew directly as a result of Rhys's victory.

Is it possible then to correlate castle sites of importance with formerly significant Welsh structures in Ceredigion and if so, what can they tell us about settlement, ownership and lordship in this rural area? Although we know that both

the Welsh and the Normans constructed mottes, different types of fortification should also be considered in reconstructing the military picture. We do not have the level of documentary evidence available elsewhere and it has been difficult to date activity at most sites. Ring-works in Wales remain poorly understood as a defensive ditch and bank surrounding an area of varying size. Positive identification therefore remains a problem and many may have Iron Age or even Norman provenance. Some of these were subsequently developed with a motte, and sometimes a major stone castle as at Kidwelly, Carmarthen and Dinefwr.

It is this progression that has perhaps led to the general assumption that ring-works were essentially undeveloped, primitive and thus Welsh in construction. Within a five mile radius of the ring-work and suggested site of the former llys at Castell Gwinionydd there are 19 other fortified medieval sites, including the motte at Castell Hywel and the ring-works at Llanwnnen and Dol Wlff. It is difficult to suggest the contemporaneity of these sites based on location and typology alone but the complex evidence suggests intricate patterns of lordship and patronage of different estates that emerges into the post-medieval period as proliferate but modest gentry holdings. Indeed the supposition that Castell Gwinionydd represents the site of the former royal llys for Gwinionydd will be challenged in light of emerging evidence from nearby Rhuddlan Teifi.

The Emergence of the Gentry Estate

The development and consolidation of the medieval estates of the uchelwyr or gentry class is most evident in the emergence of the 18th and 19th century gentry landscapes of the 'Tivyside' area. Lloyd (1989: 50) locates this loosely between Lampeter and Cardigan but centred on the Llandysul region and considers it the hub of social activity for the three counties (of Pembrokeshire, Carmarthenshire and Ceredigion). Traditional inheritance structures such as cyfran or partible inheritance may partly explain the proliferation of gentry homes and estates in this area and, as will be demonstrated, many of the habits of the later gentry have their genesis in the medieval period. Indeed, it is the particular political and cultural upheavals of the 12th to 13th centuries that may have fossilised native structures and behaviours in such a distinct manner in Gwinionydd.

Griffiths (1994) proposed that the dramatic emergence of the 'gentlemanly' class in the Teifi valley at this time may be due to the late and rather headless and anonymous administrative government of the post-conquest period. Incentives to attract incomers to the new boroughs of Cardigan and Aberystwyth had been only partially successful. In 1280 the lordship of Aberaeron was awarded to John de Knovill and the top strata of political control that was exclusively Norman. By 1287 the southern portion of the county had been brought under complete control (Jones Pierce, 1959b: 268). The administrative focus was again at Cardigan but a new castle and borough were also created at Aberystwyth in 1277 and on the 24th May 1282, Gilbert de Clare was to "receive burgesses and others willing to come to the king's town of Llanbadarn to dwell therein" (Griffiths, 1978: 32). Aberystwyth was somewhat isolated from other centres of Norman control and whilst it was made clear initially that Welshmen were not welcome within the town walls of Cardigan, a high proportion of welsh names appear as burgesses at Aberystwyth during the early 14th century (ibid.)

Acting as absentee landlords the Norman governmental officers had little in common with life at local level and, coupled with the removal of the top strata of Welsh royal lineages, a vacuum developed in society. Local entrepreneurs and lesser aristocracy were quick to exploit this lacuna and co-operation with local government officials encouraged the consolidation of social and political power into the hands of numerous families and emerged as a new gentry class. An arms-length approach to administration was practised in Ceredigion as a result and this meant the unique retention of early forms of tenure and institution. The local uchelwyr flourished and began to take up important local posts.

Notable local entrepreneurs included (a different) Rhys ap Gruffudd who was born in 1283 and became lord of Llangybi (Rees, 1924: 37). By 1308 he had become steward of Cardigan, later gaining the leases of the royal estates at Lampeter, Trefilan and Silian and by 1334 he had received a knighthood. Although undoubtedly one of the most powerful Welshmen in the area he was by no means unique. Ednyfed Fychan had been granted an estate at Llanrhystud by Llywelyn Fawr in the 13th century and by lineage some of his estate had passed to Rhys ap Gruffudd who was his cousin. Other estates in Cellan, Mabwynion, Llechweddlwyfan in Creuddyn and Rhydonnen in Perfedd passed to descendants of Ednyfed (Griffiths, 1994: 56).

The middle-class gentry had begun to consolidate their estates by the start of the 15th century as at Castell Hywel where families had enjoyed success and established new halls on former caputs at Cilgwyn and Alltyrodyn for example. A new fiscal economy paralleled new governmental duties and local power structures were developed. The family of Owain Glyndwr were still resident at the newly created 'manor' of Gwinionydd Is Cerdin, and this created a degree of political pressure that was probably behind the decision by some local gentry to support the Glyndwr uprising although for example, Philip ap Rhydderch had his estates in Mabwynion, Silian, Talsarn and Trefilan confiscated in 1401 for his part in the uprising. Ceredigion represented an important family heartland for Glyndwr and five local men were amongst his top officers. The effect on the county was tremendous and by 1409, returns from the borough of Cardigan were only just beginning to recover where no fairs were being held and rents were respited. Governmental control over the cymydau of Gwinionydd, Iscoed, Caerwedros, Mabwynion and most of Anhuniog was not re-established until the end of 1409 (Rees, 1924: 273, n. 4). In 1402 the government outlawed those poets and bards who might inflame passion and rebellion but many local families were just as keen to protect and consolidate their growing estates and sympathy for Glyndwr's cause waned after the first decade of conflict.

But these families recorded their status in lineage not acreage. The Lloyds of Gwastad Gwrda had their pedigree recorded by Dwnn in the late 16th century as descendants of Gruffudd Foel of Ty Glyn (Jones, 2004: 141). David Lloid ap Hugh o'r Clwyd Jack also signed for Dwnn at Lloyd Jack becoming high Sheriff of Cardiganshire in 1597 (ibid. 179).

Thus, this region of west Wales had been conquered late and administered by a succession of disinterested absentee landlords. The top layer of rule was Norman but the local uchelwyr, who were keen to demonstrate their descent from Welsh aristocratic lineages, began to emerge within local politics, consolidating their hereditary estates through marriage, purchase and customary tenure. Many of these gentry estates emerged into the post medieval period essentially intact and represent the yeoman status farmsteads still characterising today's landscape. The potential of these for the reconstruction of a medieval landscape has hitherto not been considered.

TWO: BACKGROUND

Introduction

This chapter proposes that the dominant approach to medieval Wales has been one of generalising, historically-driven narratives. It accepts that the subject matter is difficult and the landscape inscrutable but argues that combining approaches derived from historical geography and archaeology can be applied with successful results. It stresses, however, that the development of models and their use as a mode of explanation can be useful in examining a medieval administrative landscape that was itself predicated on complex rules and systems. But it also stresses that the current trend to generate the type of Euro-history popular today can obscure local 'noise', that the agency perceived in the community and individual needs to be addressed.

Antiquarians, Poets and Scholars

A strong tradition of literature had long existed within the Teifi valley and during the 14th century a cultural renaissance can be attributed to the area with the heads of numerous minor gentry houses supporting the services offered by bards, poets, linguists, genealogists and translators (Griffiths, 1994). Local families were increasingly gaining important administrative posts locally and in 1304, Ieuan ap Moilwyn of Mabwynion cwmwd was appointed as seneschal of Ceredigion by Sir John Haveryng and Thomas de Canterbrug (Rhys, 1936: 323). The poet Llywelyn Brydydd Hodnant composed awdlau or odes to him and his son Ieuan Llwyd, and his son's wife, Angharad, was feted by Dafydd ap Gwilym as "dispenser of bounty at banquets, of the wine-board's abundance, the patron of poets in their pride" (Griffiths, 1994: 56).

Dafydd also added a variety of poems to blank pages in the *Hendregadredd* manuscript, a document produced at Strata Florida for Ieuan and representing an important source of 'poetry of the princes' (Huws, 2000: 193). Ieuan's son also reached an important level in local government. From 1386 to 1389, Rhydderch ap Ieuan Llwyd served in administration at his home in Mabwynion, becoming steward of Cardigan in 1386 and deputy-justiciar in 1388-9 (Griffiths, 1994: 56). As an expert in Welsh legal matters he was called upon to settle local disputes as a dosbarthwyr, according to the Welsh laws. Contributing enormously to local cultural activities, texts were commissioned and influenced by him - his son went by royal request to a congress of poets at Pembroke castle to validate the lineage of William Herbert of Raglan (ibid.). Like his father, Rhydderch also valued literature and the *Llyfr Gwyn Rhydderch* containing the earliest copy of the Middle Welsh tales now collectively known as the Mabinogion was compiled for him, also probably at Strata Florida by one of the same scribes attributed to the *Brut Y Tywysogion* (Huws, 2000: 227). Other noteworthy poets surfaced in the Teifi area and during the 1330s, Einion Offeriaid, also of

Mabwynion rewrote important grammatical mandates, reasserting the social position of the bard in a new post-conquest culture. Many of the later Tivyside gentry were keen to ally themselves to the medieval gentry. Despite this, Crompton Fitzwilliams of Cilgwyn in Newcastle Emlyn bemoaned the parochial self-interests of the local intellect in a personal journal written in the late 19th century. His contempt for the local "petty princelings" expresses the unrelenting gentry pursuit of their ancient pedigrees (Aberystwyth, Ceredigion Record Office, uncatalogued material relating to Newcastle Emlyn and Llandysul parish).

The obsession with lineage and pedigree characterised the studies of George Owen of Henllys who died in 1613. His father William was heir to the Barony of Cemais in northern Pembrokeshire and, as a wealthy lawyer, his son was also educated at the Inns of London. Owen became an eminent antiquarian, naturalist and geologist and many of his contemporaries owned documentary records of their descendants' which Owen copied into genealogical records, also creating flamboyant heraldic rolls for family records (Charles, 1973: 109). His insistence on his ancient feudal rights as lord generated constant lawsuits but compelled him to conduct extensive surveys of the Barony making detailed lists of the fees, dues and rentals of his principal freeholders (ibid: 73). His compilation of the *Hundreds, Castells, Parish Churches and ffayres...in all the Shiers of Wales* in 1602 preceded his important Description of Penbrockshire (Owen, 1892; 1897; 1906 and 1936) which pxaralleled the thorough and successful approach taken by Richard Carew's *Survey of Cornwall* (Halliday, 1953). Born a generation later in Shropshire, Edward Lhuyd had family connections to the south Wales gentry and also became an eminent historian and geographer. He traveled widely in Wales and copied from manuscripts and documents publishing his replies by questionnaire to his *Parochial Queries in Order to a Geographical Dictionary, a Natural History, etc., of Wales* (Lhuyd, 1909-11) in 1696 detailing the extent and character of parishes across Wales, their ancient monuments and customs providing a valuable insight into Tudor Wales. This was followed in 1707 by the *Archaeologia Britannica: giving some account...of the languages, histories and customs of the original inhabitants of Great Britain* (O' Sullivan & O' Sullivan, 1971). Other historians also assiduously collected 'histories' and 'antiquities' and Samuel Rush Meyrick published his *History of Cardiganshire in 1810* (Meyrick, 1810).

This antiquarian legacy flourished, especially suiting the gentleman scholar many of whom were, or were influenced by, land-owning families. The minor gentry families of the Tivyside cultured a fascination with antiquities, history and genealogy. Thomas Johnes' library at Hafod in northern Ceredigion was renowned and well-visited but the more modest collection at Llwynderw at Pentrecwrt near Llandysul housed the important Golden Grove books and was described as a most valuable collection of books and manuscripts (Baker-Jones, 1999: 165). The collection came to be housed at Alltyrodyn, Rhydowen was rivalled only by the Brigstocke library at Blaenpant near Cardigan whilst the important deeds, charters and pedigrees housed at Bronwydd north of Newcastle Emlyn also formed an invaluable resource for the interested gentleman antiquarian or genealogist.

An increasing interest in Welsh history and culture was strengthened in Owen Morgan Edwards who, as a young boy in school at Bala, was punished via the *'Welsh Not'* for speaking his native tongue and joined the influential Dafydd ap Gwilym Society at Oxford (Edwards, 1906). Some of his most important contributions included *Cartrefi Cymru, Famous Welsh Homes* (Edwards, 1896), several histories of Wales (eg Edwards, 1901) and the journal *Cymru* from 1892. One of the last and greatest of what can be described as the 'antiquarian tradition' was Sir John Edward Lloyd who became Wales's most eminent historian around the turn of the century. Educated in, and lecturer at Aberystwyth he served as the chair of the Board of Celtic Studies until 1940. His authoritative *History of Wales* (Lloyd, 1911) was the first really authoritative treatment of all the main historical sources and it remains a key text today. It was followed by a *History of Carmarthenshire* in two volumes and *The Story of Ceredigion* (Lloyd, 1935; 1937 and 1939). This work reflected a monumental task in terms of research and reflected the fashionable 'collecting' mentality of the time. Subject-oriented critique and analysis of the medieval world was yet to follow.

The study of medieval territory and its structure was central to the works of Jolliffe (1926 and 1962) and Vinogradoff (1905) who sought to illuminate the social and economic conditions of early England. Jolliffe proposed that the villein of Norman times was a descendant of the Anglo-Saxon freeman, and that the typical Anglo-Saxon settlement would have been a free community. The status of the freeman diminished as a direct result of the Norman Conquest; a premise subsequently assumed for medieval Welsh society. Studies of Welsh manuscripts dating to the 12th and 13th centuries and collectively known as the Laws of Hywel Dda allowed Seebohm (1904 and 1933) and Ellis (1926) to illuminate social and legal customs in pre-conquest Wales. Reference to a handful of medieval documents, mostly with a north Wales bias, especially the Anglesey rentals and surveys of 1294, the 14th century Court Rolls of Aberffraw and the Denbigh Extent of 1335, allowed them and others such as Lloyd (1937) to explore the social and legal institutions and customs of what they termed the 'Celtic tribal' system.

The notion of an early society that was tribal in nature was developed by Seebohm (1904: 87) who noted a "passage from nomad life to settled occupation". He was amongst the first to advocate the study of socio-political behaviours as a way of explaining territorial systems such as the cantref, cwmwd and maenor. For Jolliffe (1954: 57), the emergence of these territorial structures around the 10th and 11th centuries paralleled the emergence of new forms

of over-kingship. The increase in use of written documents records courtly codes, charters and rulings and was interpreted as evidence for the development from kingship to governance. But evidence for the complex institution of the maenor can be pushed back to the pre-9th century period (and will be examined below) and it is clear that what the documents were describing were complex systems with early origins.

Early 20th century studies of medieval Wales attracted a more academic approach and have produced several eminent scholars. For the archaeologist and historian researching medieval Wales the work of Thomas Jones Pierce in particular has provided an invaluable resource for over 70 years. His great contribution and influence means his work is worth considering here in more detail. Accepting a lectureship at the University College of North Wales, Bangor, Jones Pierce quickly realised that a proper analysis of Wales's medieval history would entail a careful study of the primary source documents. At his own expense he took a year's study leave in order to study Chancery and Exchequer records and lawbooks dating to the post-conquest period in Gwynedd. He systematically amassed material for a series of seminal papers concerning the development of tribal societies and the emergence of new systems of proprietorship at the close of the medieval period (1939; 1940; 1941a; 1941b and 1942-3).

The task was a complex one coming during a period when the translation and editing of contemporary texts had scarcely begun. His attitude towards the social and agrarian institutions of medieval Wales exemplified a novel approach that differed from that of many of his contemporaries. Though relying heavily on the kinds of tribal customs depicted by Ellis (1926) and Seebohm (1933) for example, Jones Pierce used the minutiae of local records in order to define in detail specifically Welsh institutions visible for the first time during the 12th and 13th centuries. His first article (1939) in this series sets the tone for the following four articles, reflecting a certain reticence to acknowledge total Welsh subjugation under Anglo-Norman control.

Jones Pierce instead suggested that the 13th century administrative system was an essentially pre-conquest survival. He investigated the ten cymydau of Caernarvonshire which were subdivided into rural districts, roughly coeval with the modern parish, known as the township or tref but he also noted the survival of kinship and other social structures within these divisions (Jones Pierce, 1939). He proposed that the commutation of traditional labour dues to a money rent was not as the result of new Anglo-Norman administration but that forms of fiscal complexity were already "far advanced in some districts", had their origins in a pre-conquest context and occurred even in "mountain cymydau far removed from the main currents of change" (1939: 18). Whilst still accepting tribal influences, it was not enough to merely be ancient and 'noble', Jones Pierce had demonstrated the sophistication and complexity of a pre-conquest society for the first time.

The gradual demise of native systems such as the bond community was generally accepted to be the result of a combination of post-conquest 'progress', Anglo-Norman administrative changes and plagues during 1349-50. Jones Pierce also proposed that the consolidation of landholdings in the later middle ages formed the nuclei of gentry estates whereby following the example set by English burgesses, native uchelwyr or gentry began to "participate in the race for property" (ibid: 34).

These early gentry families formed the focus of his next paper (Jones Pierce, 1940). The later 16th century land disputes relating to the township of Dinorwig indicate that decayed and escheat bond land along with encroachment provided a substantial holding for Thomas William of Faenol, and in 1589 Sir John Wynn of Gwydir was summoned for encroachment on crown lands at Gwydir (ibid: 6-7). Despite the interesting focus on the emergence of gentrified families in the early modern period, Jones Pierce's real interest lay in identifying and following the demise of the bond vill. The relationship between the bond and freemen of Wales was a recurrent theme in much of his subsequent work especially in his complex studies of Anglesey (1951) and Ceredigion (1959b).

The latter years of the 19th and early 20th century began to see new forms of Welsh cultural nationalism begin to influence everyday Welsh life and this generated new interest in the 'Celtic arts'. Through diverse initiatives a Welsh language heritage was being assembled and defined and in 1933 a Welsh Language Board was established. Despite the longevity of the language the lack of a Welsh literary academia provided the incentive to create new standards and a National Library for Wales was established at Aberystwyth, receiving its Royal Charter in 1907. In 1922 the Urdd Gobaith Cymru, the Welsh League of Youth was established and held their first National Eisteddfod in 1929 at Corwen. The establishment of a Welsh Parliament was seen as a means of entrenching the nationalist inheritance and the radical language campaigner Saunders Lewis founded Plaid Cymru in 1925 and in 1937 the BBC established a distinct service for Wales. In 1949 the Labour government established an advisory body known as the Council for Wales and Monmouthshire and in 1951 the subsequent Conservative government established the Ministry of Welsh Affairs by granting responsibility for Welsh affairs to an existing Cabinet minister.

By 1955 Cardiff was acknowledged as the capital of Wales and in 1957 the Council for Wales and Monmouthshire launched a campaign for the establishment of a Welsh Office. Welsh historical culture was undergoing a new revival and needed to develop a gravitas of its own - to move beyond the Druidic histories espoused by the *Myvyrian Archaiologies* and the conservative romantic nationalism espoused by Iolo Morgannwg in the 19th

century. Jones Pierce's interest in pre-conquest institutions and indigenous tenurial systems quietly paralleled these contemporary issues without being overtly patriotic or nationalist.

This period of unsettling nationalist themes had resonances for the academic world. A lecturer in Welsh at University College Swansea, Saunders Lewis lost his post in 1936 after being imprisoned following an arson attack at Penrhos airforce base. Despite widespread nationalist protest the village of Capel Celyn and the Tryweryn valley near Bala were drowned in 1965 in order to supply water for the City of Liverpool. Eight hundred acres of land were drowned, as well as the school, the post office, the chapel and the cemetery, in order to create the Llyn Celyn reservoir. Writing at a time of pioneering Welsh cultural movement Jones Pierce cannot fail to have been influenced by the swift moving politics perhaps prompting his move away from interest in bond and 'peasant' tenures to write the Nobility and Gentry in 1967 (Jones Pierce, 1967). The irony of research themes involving Welsh history during English conquest writing at a time of positive (and often militant) moves towards a Welsh language movement and devolved government cannot have evaded him.

Despite his close involvement with the Cambrian Archaeological Association, Jones Pierce found little inspiration for his studies outside of documentary sources and there are few references to archaeological studies within his articles. Influence probably occurred in the other direction, his historical findings informing the very scarce rural Welsh archaeology. Archaeology was not an academic pursuit in the early 20th century but the pursuit of the informed gentleman; the history, classics and geography scholar. However, by the time of Jones Pierce's appointment, jointly at the College and at the National Library at Aberystwyth, a new style is evident in his investigation of the Clennenau estate (1947). The physical evidence of the landscape is considered alongside the documentary sources, describing farm buildings and speculating on the origins and antiquity of some of the structures. Map-regressive techniques familiar to the landscape archaeologist are briefly in evidence and Jones Pierce combined place-name and topographical evidence in order to form a physical premise to his conclusions. He also examined the possibility of Dark Age origins for the clan and tribal-based social system of the gwely before going on to describe detailed land rentals. Here he wrestled with the extent and nature of the gwely or clan-based holding of the native Welsh, concluding that the traditional practice of cyfran was at odds with the gwely as a native institution of hereditary freeholding. In order to avoid the fragmentation of newly emerging consolidated estates he suggested that there must have been a natural inclination towards primogeniture, citing the evidence of the Clennenau MSS whereby the majority of the estate was entailed on the younger, and favourite son of John ap Maredudd. The Morris family eventually consolidated seven distinct interests in the Clennenau hamlet into a single estate. It is clear that Jones Pierce saw the origins of these large estates as firmly in the later medieval period, an institution that effectively removed and replaced older tenurial traditions. He became increasingly interested in the broader issues concerning the origins and mechanics of Welsh tenurial systems.

Whilst by now very familiar with the historical fabric of north Wales his studies of medieval Ceredigion (1959b) must have been exasperating in terms of the contrasting and divergent practices apparently in operation. Jones Pierce posed three questions;

1   Was it possible to identify any continuity   in native practice after Norman rule?
2   What novel effects did Lord Rhys's rule have during the 12th century?
3   Precisely what influence did the Edwardian conquests have on the social organisation of Ceredigion?

Ceredigion was one of the last Welsh territories to fall to the Normans and the influence of new administrations was felt only lightly in this rural area. Jones Pierce's 13th and 14th century sources also indicated that outside Cardigan and Llanbadarn, most traces of Anglo-Norman settlement had been obscured by Welsh occupation and that at this time Welsh names outnumbered English by a ratio of 15 to 1 (1959b: 270). Social and economic patterns appeared to stay predominantly Welsh with the new administration exerting little influence. However, ancient renders and institutions uniquely still in use in Ceredigion such as the gwestfa and the gwely had an 'artificial' appearance that Jones Pierce (ibid: 319) attributed to a comprehensive rearrangement during the relatively stable rule of Lord Rhys.

An effect of this was to truncate systems based upon taeog or bond services operated around the ancient llys and maerdref system. Distinctions between bond and free tenures were essentially now invisible in Ceredigion, so had the upheavals of the 12th century resulted in permanent disturbance "involving some extinction and flight" asked Jones Pierce? In many ways this is one of his most frustrating papers. The paper formed the substance of an address presented to the Cardiganshire Antiquarian Society and on its publication two interesting appendices concerning the nature of the maenor and maenol and the Manor of Anhuniog (immediately north of the Aeron) appeared, reflecting Jones Pierce's struggle to clarify and understand these systems. Some of his most interesting allusions to the cymydau of Anhuniog and Mabwynion are referenced to an article published a year earlier by T.I. Davies (1959) who frustratingly neglected to reference his sources. The documentary sources are much poorer than those for North Wales though it stands out as an almost unique attempt to recreate the medieval Ceredigion landscape. Essentially, Pierce sees four major factors in play at the end of the medieval period in Ceredigion;

- a long-established settlement pattern
- a widespread peasant proprietorship
- a network of rights anchored to ancient clanlands
- a body of innate tenurial law and custom

Although Jones Pierce acknowledged medieval Wales as turbulent and rapidly changing during this period he did not preclude the possibility of complex indigenous involvement and change even before the conquest period. Although he remained apparently objective and moderate his often difficult writing style makes a complex and poorly understood subject opaque and even more difficult to unravel. But he recognised that in order to identify the precise structure of tenurial patterns and the considerable impact of ecclesiastical tenures the landscape deserved closer scrutiny. It is, however, testament to his seminal work that medieval archaeological projects in North Wales (Johnstone, 1997; Longley, 1997 and 2001 for example) have a historical framework with which to work.

The Study of the Welsh Landscape

Welsh culture was studied in closer detail by other scholars and when the Welsh Folk museum (now Amgueddfa Werin Cymru or the Museum of Welsh Life) opened in 1948 it did so with Iorwerth Cyfeiliog Peate as its first curator. Peate's seminal work, *The Welsh House* (1940, 1944 and reprinted in 2004) was tellingly subtitled, *A Study in Folk Culture*, and was more than simply a study of rural vernacular architecture, focusing instead on cultural anthropologies as a mode of explanation for material form.

The late 19th century survey of a traditionally-constructed farmhouse near Strata Florida by Stephen Williams (1899) had been interpreted as 'obviously medieval' and consequently placed at the lowest end of the social scale. Peate's approach was more forgiving and referred to the medieval Law codes when examining the medieval house. His *House of the Welsh Laws* (Peate, 2004: 109-131) for example gave a detailed account of the different redactions of the Laws relating to building custom and tradition. The codes also stipulated the nine buildings of the king's llys, a hall, chamber, kitchen, barn, kiln, privy, dog kennel, stable and chapel or dormitory. The codes are extremely detailed and the lists of building components and their values allowed Peate to link the use of traditional materials and techniques to the sociological aspects of the gwerin or folk and their homes. Peate also drew parallels with the 9th century Irish Crith Gablach which describes eight sizes of house corresponding to the eight ranks of chiefdom. He also describes a Neolithic 'house' from Ireland that, divided into a long central space with side aisles evidently the sleeping compartments, parallels Dutch and west German examples, all having parallels with the long house (ibid: 52-53). He was trying to establish a continuity of great antiquity for building traditions of Western Europe of an essentially 'Celtic' character.

Archaeologists were also attracted to the tracing of wider evidence for the ancient and noble customs described in medieval texts. Excavations of upland house platforms at Gelligaer Common, Glamorgan during the 1930s revealed that the three houses excavated each contained a large central post-hole with another at one end behind the hearth (Fox, 1939). Dated to the early 14th century, the absence of any evidence for cruck construction led Fox to infer a simpler, native Welsh construction but also linked it to the kinds of construction mentioned in the Law codes. Detailed analysis of the documentary record by historians such as Lloyd, Seebohm and Ellis had provided Fox with a convenient cultural context for her findings and she placed the buildings in the context of an upland Welshry in clear contrast to the sophisticated lowland Englishry nearby.

These upland remote strongholds seemed to represent a survival of territories based upon kinship and custom which were essentially determined by a remote upland terrain ideal for native, small-scale pastoral agricultures. In 1962 Lawrence Butler (Butler, 1963) excavated the interior of a hut platform at Bwlch yr Hendre an area under threat due to a new hydro-electric scheme in the upper Rheidol valley. Bwlch yr Hendre predated the 18th century permanent settlements along the Camddwr valley floor and Butler considered the anthropogenic effects on the landscape of peat cutting, mining and droving. For Butler, however, the lack of material culture seemed be entirely consistent with its use as a simple *hafoty* or 'summer house', of the type described by Sayce (1956 and 1957) for example as a seasonally-occupied dwelling as part of a transhumant economy.

The excavation and dating of 'native' structures and their relevance and association to the wider landscape has barely moved on since Butler's fieldwork but surveys on the Black Mountains in Carmarthenshire by Ward (1997) have demonstrated the potential for future archaeological excavation. A poorly documented excavation of an upland long-hut near Llanddewibrefi in Ceredigion produced limited evidence of medieval occupation (Lewis, 1927) but a group of rectilinear buildings at nearby Bryn Cysegrfan produced dating and occupation evidence linked to over thirty pillow mounds dating to the 14th century that were indicative of sophisticated seigniorial management of this upland zone (Austin, 1988). More recently, excavations at Llanerchaeron have revealed significant medieval settlement dating to the 14th century associated with later gentry mansion and early church of St Non's (Evans, 2003). But despite a new report (Roberts, 2006) that has recorded over 7000 deserted settlement sites in south west Wales, the above sites (apart from castles) remain the only excavations of medieval sites in the county.

Successful excavations outside Ceredigion, however, have yielded rich deposits at the upland site of Hafod y Nant Criafolen in Clwyd for example where the unexpectedly rich remains have challenged the primitive and ephemeral nature of these upland sites (Allen, 1979). The extensive nature of the excavations focused beyond the internal floor plan of buildings and this helped to identify the location of the midden, contributing to the rich haul of information from this important site. Stone-built structures, outhouses and middens also revealed pottery, spindle whorls, whetstones, decorated bake stones and scourers, worked bone scoops, horse shoes and nails and an iron sword dated occupation to the 15th and 16th centuries.

Again from north Wales, the excavation of four building platforms at Cefn Graeanog have been tentatively dated to the middle 13th century (Kelly, 1982: 869). Environmental sampling revealed the processing of barley and oats and possible construction materials such as hazel, bedstraw, bracken, juncus and elder. Kelly makes close reference to the use of such materials in the north Wales redactions of the Law codes but makes the observation that climatic downturn and plague during the late 13th and 14th centuries explained a change from the more expensive cruck timber and turf construction to readily available stone (ibid: 884) but it is likely, however, that a range of customs and practice were in use.

This limited archaeological investigation has resulted in a poor understanding of the landscape in the southwest and has led to approaches expressed in terms of evolutionary development. In Cornwall for example, Harvey (1997) described a series of progressively more sophisticated steps resulting in increasingly complex organisational systems. He proposed that the earliest attempts to define territorial boundaries could be seen as a result of the introduction of the tithe and other forms of Anglo-Saxon administrative control; ancient and relatively stable origins for some of the larger, simpler territories is conceded however. Nevertheless, some of the tithing districts for West Cornwall were linked to former township regions based on early tribute and food renders and vestiges of the three-acre unit were also noted, perhaps as a part of a hierarchical territorial framework designed for the control and exploitation of resources at an early date (ibid: 19).

Gresham (1987) described a similar pattern emerging from 12th century Gwynedd, again alongside the emergence of tithe organization. He, like Harvey, considered the relationship between parochial and township or tref systems. Although the township or tref systems were by now heavily obscured Gresham attributed their creation to the result of deliberate policy by Owain Gwynedd (d.1170) in direct response to the pressures of Norman aggression (ibid: 138). Paralleling the regularisation of parish and tithe areas under Diocesan reorganization, the 13th century charters of Llywelyn ap Iorwerth and later royal extents dated 1352 reveal that by the end of the 12th century the whole of Gwynedd was laid out in an apparently 'deliberate' and 'regular' system of administrative territories. This supposition was proposed by Gresham despite the fact that he conceded that there was no record of this happening or of the method under which it was carried out (ibid: 141). Physical and topographical rules were nevertheless outlined by Gresham that would have allowed the systematic laying-out of territories, this new order "provided the semi-feudal basis required by Owain Gwynedd to maintain the military strength of his land" (ibid: 143). Some of Gresham's territorial 'types' include the parish coextensive with a single township, or, more commonly the larger parish containing several townships or portions of them. No mention at all remains of Gresham's surveyors who "were responsible for directing the lines to be taken by the parish boundaries" and it seems remarkable that such an ambitious act of land survey and reorganisation left no historical record despite the otherwise rich documentation available for this period in north Wales. Rhys Jones proposes the creation of a foundation myth for Gwynedd in the early 9th century by Merfyn Frych in order to create the time depth and continuity necessary to legitimise his control (Harvey & Jones, 1999). If we accept Gresham's attribution of the reorganisation of boundaries to Owain Gwynedd is it just as likely that he would have utilised existing institutions' boundaries as a way reinforcing and legitimising his rule.

This process whereby a leader's ambition to consolidate towards the creation of a nation state is defined by Jones as a territorialisation of power; a change in situation whereby "territory was identified and ordered through society to one in which society was ordered through territory", notions heavily based upon social structures proposed by Sahlins in the 1960s (R. A. Jones, 1998c: 135 and Sahlins, 1968). For Jones then the emergence of systems based upon the cantref, cwmwd, maenor/maenol is entirely due to a conscious state-formation process. An archaeological approach to these themes would be familiar with the landscape at differing levels of resolutions over differing time scales. The complex arrangements of societies over millennia are evident through physical materiality, a consideration apparently absent from the above debates.

The ascribed superiority of Gwynedd is examined elsewhere by Rhys Jones (1998a and 2000b) where he proposes a deliberate increase in resource exploitation as part of a Europe-wide ideology of state formation during the medieval period. Although many of his hypotheses are similar to Gresham's, Jones (2000b: 510) takes a more close-grained approach, discussing specifically Welsh institutions and custom at a sub-parochial level, for example the commutation of gwestfa dues to the twnc pound. He perceives this change as a way of increasing the level of income and control over that income. But his observation that "smaller and smaller communities were being told their exact fiscal and judicial duties" directly led to the increased definition of these smaller units is to over-simplify. People would have understood at a deep level whose land was whose, who owed what to whom and why; and at a period much earlier than the 12th century when it was recorded in written form for the first time.

The notion of increasing fission and complexity developing over time underpins much of Jones's work. For example,

the cantref in Gwynedd was divided into two cymydau in such a regular manner as to suggest that the cwmwd was planned entirely as a subdivision of the cantref at a later period (R. A. Jones, 1998b). These approaches stand in direct contrast to the fundamental principles of nested hierarchical territories with an Iron Age antecedence proposed by Glanville Jones (Jones, 1976). Central to the approach taken by modern historical geographers like Rhys Jones, Gresham and Harvey is a reluctance to address the landscape at the smallest scale, that of the individual and community. Early schemes are described as native, simple, fluid and disorganised. The increased complexity of later medieval systems apparently comes as a contrast to what went before and prescribes an increasingly complex society and landscape. We can sense the influence of early scholars when we read about the inexorable progression of a tribal society to a settled, complex, feudal one; Seebohm, Ellis, Vinogradoff, but their early valuable contributions have not yet been advanced by modern scholars.

Medieval Ceredigion is therefore very poorly understood and almost entirely defined in terms of comparison and analogy to other regions of Wales and England. Determinist attitudes towards economy, production, settlement and climate are proposed as catalysts for societal organisation. Evolutionist notions of state formation and nationalism see simple primitive tribal societies reacting to purely external pressures. In considering the early state formation processes in Wales, Rhys Jones also uses the extensive survival of contemporary documentation from north Wales to suggest Gwynedd as a core from where new state formation processes were adopted under the catalyst of external influence and pressure. He goes as far as to suggest that Norman attacks "probably offered the best opportunity for the creation of a unified Welsh state" (Jones, 1998a: 668). Pryce, however, proposed that the shift of Welsh writers towards the use of Anglo-Norman terms Wallia and Walenses around the 12th century provided the Welsh with a new opportunity to express their national identity, "it is highly unlikely that they did so reluctantly or saw themselves as thereby surrendering cherished notions of identity in the face of pressure from outside" (Pryce, 2001: 796).

Current Landscape Models and the Multiple Estate

The origins of 'modern' approaches to the analyses of territorial development in Wales can be attributed to the seminal work of Glanville Jones (e.g. 1972b and 1976). The multiple estate model conceived by Jones involved series of hierarchical territorial units, grouped together to form a discrete estate to better exploit a series of resources and, in effect, be self-sufficient. The multiple estate has been debated, primarily because it relied on the schematic, idealised and difficult laws outlined in the Law codes. Various redactions of the codes describe the division of large standard areas of land, composed of 50 farmsteads or trefi, belonging to the king, his reeve, and his tenants.

The multiple estate model has been challenged although without much vigour (Davies, 1982; Jones, 1998c and Jones, 1999). Gregson (1985: 346) offered a direct challenge to the model when she outlined her problems with definition, method and application but in so doing she (unwittingly) provided the most succinct definition of an ideal multiple estate that would include the following attributes:

1. A group or group of associated upland and lowland townships containing vills, hamlets and other settlement groupings occurring within the bounds of medieval or earlier estates…we would expect to find: a royal vill; an important estate centre, the focus of a rural deanery, the centre of a great monastic manor, the centre of a hundred or a medieval market. In addition this group should show a continuity of association as far back as the immediate pre-Norman period.
2. A social hierarchy comprising a lord or morphological surrogate such as a hall-court complex.
3. Ministerial group whose responsibilities included the administration of the lord's demands.
4. Freemen owing cash rents and light labour services.
5. Bondmen owing heavier labour services.
6. A developed service network perhaps with the specialisation by different groups, construction, food production, military service etc.
7. Evidence of early settlement place names.
8. Archaeological evidence indicating perhaps Romano-British settlement, Iron Age fortification or pre-historic routeways.

Gregson went on to demonstrate that, with the exception of Aberffraw, Glanville Jones' 23 multiple estate examples did not actually contain all of the criteria mentioned. Jones's (1985) rebuttal used Gregson's check list in order to update the evidence for the places listed. For Yeavering, where few of the diagnostic criteria were present, Jones emphasised the deficiencies in the documentary record and used the archaeological evidence to supplement the record. He went on to demonstrate that the places did in fact satisfy most, if not all, of the criteria contending that pre-Norman Britain was far from being an empty wasteland populated by an unsophisticated nomadic tribal society. Jones (ibid: 361) maintained that these estates reflected arrangements of "great antiquity" although only recorded in detail from the 11th century onwards indicating the need for careful landscape analysis beyond simple historical investigation.

Some of Wales's apparently early territorial and administrative units do survive into the early modern period. The cantref, literally meaning 'one hundred tref', was composed of two or more cymydau or 'neighbourhoods'. The similarity with English Hundreds, the basic area of medieval local government and policing below the level of the shire, and indeed with similar groups of settlements on the Continent, is striking. Many English Hundreds in the west Midlands, it is worth noting, were

composed at Domesday not of 100 hides, but of 50, and it is possible to see pairs of such Hundreds which considered together seem to echo the Welsh cymydau and cantrefi.

This administrative geography is also partially visible in England as the creation of shires, hundreds, rapes and lathes and in Denmark for example as syssels and herreds (R. A. Jones, 1998b: 169). Essentially the cantref is regarded as a subdivision and regularisation of kingdoms based upon the gwledydd or 'countries/regions'. The origins of these were assessed by Rhys Jones (1998b) who described the cantref as the formalisation of boundaries between neighbouring princes and lords resulting in the consolidation of territories through developing overlordship. He places this development at around the 9th to 10th centuries for north Wales based on the models for organisation in the north Wales redaction of the Law codes. The names of certain cantrefi; Dunoding, Rhufoniog and Edeirnion for example contain personal name elements which indicate small or petty kingdoms (ibid: 171).

These forms of early state administration may be compared to 8th century Ireland where increasing hierarchies of lordship became centred on dynastic overlords, the ri ruirech, at Tara and Cashel. The formation of these administrative kingdoms was part of a state formation process concerned with renders and obligations rather than later legal jurisdiction in order to maximise economic resource (R. A. Jones, 1998b: 173). It is generally accepted that the cwmwd represents a later division that postdates that of the cantref although it does appear in pre-1100 sources (Davies, 1982: 235, n. 68). Glanville Jones (1992: 100) also proposed the origins of the cantref as the administrative subdivision of a larger kingdom, possibly adopted during the 9th century and whilst these cantref would have been further subdivided into cymydau they did not crystallise into administrative units until later.

Rees's (1924 and 1932) study of medieval rentals (apparently) combined with tithe and parish information allowed him to produce a series of maps attempting to recreate the 14th century geography of Wales. Essentially though the historical evidence was insufficient to enable Rees to map the boundaries of many of the smaller territorial units with any accuracy but the influential later studies by Melville Richards (1961 and 1969) somewhat augmented this work and the detail supplied by place name studies allowed Richards to produce greater geographical detail. Rees' maps and territories were used by linguists in attempts to geographically provenance medieval texts and law Codes by studying their dialectical features and continue to be used today (Wmffre, 2003).

Glanville Jones had asserted that the maenor or multiple estate formed a basic, discrete unit and its constituent trefi were not divisible by partition, inheritance or gift. The issue of property and heritable land is complex. Cyfran is discussed by Jones-Pierce (1959b: 267) who suggests that the successive sharing of estates with every generation led to fragmentation, a situation that became so unwieldy that post-conquest reorganisation and, for example, Lord Rhys's attempts to adopt single succession or primogeniture was an attempt to regularise and consolidate territorial organisation. For this reason, Davies (1982: 77) also envisaged problems with the identification of pre-conquest landholdings to any degree of accuracy, citing many examples of division and fragmentation. For instance during the 8th century Lifris recorded how Gwynllyw took the principal holding of his father's kingdom with his brothers dividing the rest amongst them, whilst rivalry led to Gwyddnerth murdering his brother Meirchion and Caradog killing his brother Cynan in the 11th century (ibid: 78).

A memorandum in the margins of the *Lichfield Gospels* (kept at Llandeilo church until the late 10th century) records the outcome of a dispute between two parties over the ownership of Tir Telych, the 'land of Telych'. Glanville Jones (1994) proposed that the location of Tir Telych corresponded to landholdings within the former cwmwd of Caeo centred on a group of farmsteads at present-day Bryn Telych. The marginalia describes a lengthy dispute with Elgu the son of Gelli in the tribe of Idwared who retained possession of Tir Telych but had to pay compensation to the claimant, Tudfwlch, of a horse, three cows and three newly calved cows. Jones asserts that the motivation behind, and the subsequent recording of the dispute over this modest landholding is related to its proximity to the gold mines at Dolaucothi.

The dispute seems to have been focused on a change in course of the river Cothi, downstream of the mine workings. Jones suggests that a significant amount of gold particles, tailings, satellite ores and fine sand produced by hushing and washing processes during the Roman period could have provided valuable resources for later landowners downstream and on lower floodplains. The marginalia does not give us direct clues to territorial organisation although the remarkable survival of Tir Telych from the 9th century allowed Jones to reconstruct the holding using 19th century records for the group of farms at Bryn Telych, Cefn Telych and Ynysau Ganol.

Using information primarily supplied by Rees's 14th century maps, Jones was able to place Tir Telych within the wider cwmwd of Caeo which was subdivided into maenorau or multiple estates (fig. 10). Maenor Rhwng Twrch a Chothi to the north east was mirrored in the south west by Maenor Llansawel. In between them, Y Faenor Isaf containing Tir Telych and Dolaucothi gold mines. These multiple estates were further subdivided into gwestfa districts. These are irregular in size and Jones (1994: 89) points out that this is at odds with Jones-Pierces' observation that the regularity of gwestfau in Ceredigion for example represented a reorganisation by the Lord Rhys in the late 12th century.

Maenor Rhwng Twrch a Chothi and Y Faenor Isaf combine together to form the present parish of Cynwyl Gaeo. The former maenor contained four gwestfa districts, Blaentwrch, Maesllangelynen, Cwmtrwch and Cwm-Cothi while Y Faenor Isaf contained five gwestfa; Maestroddyn, Penarth, Cwm Blewog, Tre Cynwyl Gaeo and the largest, Gwestfa Y Faenor Isaf.

Melville Richards (1964b: 18) has discussed the significance of is, and uwch within cantref and cwmwd names and suggests that the isaf or lower may be better translated as nearer, 'this side of', or 'the most important', possibly because it would refer to low lying fertile arable lands acting as an early focus for the administration of the wider community. Thus Jones (1994:88) observes that the king's llys or court is likely to have been located within Gwestfa y Faenor Isaf, probably near the mine workings at Dolaucothi and possibly on an oval-shaped mound near the river. He illustrates this point suggesting the presence of a motte as a signifier of later medieval authority. In the post-Norman period he suggests that the llys may have been at the village of Cynwyl Gaeo which, during the 14th century was a principal bond settlement of the cwmwd with the principal church just one mile away and housing the Reginus memorial stone and in 1633 Cynwyl Gaeo village was also the venue of the king's court (Rees 1924: 222).Jones has been able to provide a physical and tenurial context for a 9th century landscape using 19th century farm and parish boundaries. He suggested that the gold mine became part of the estate of a sub-Roman leader and their successors and went on to make a spatial link between the extent of mine workings and shape of Gwestfa Y Faenor Isaf. The importance of this piece of work lies in the different strands of evidence that Jones had brought together. Using the etymologies of tribal and family names recorded in the 9th century memorandum Jones was able to ascribe lineage, status and territorial organisation to cwmwd Caeo. The physical study of the terrain using 19th century tithe maps and evidence suggested by medieval Law codes all combine to provide a compelling methodology. Jones had demonstrated that it is possible to posit reconstructions based on place and personal name and much later cartographic evidence. These methods form the basis of a model that will be improved and enhanced by this project.

Sources and Methodology

A variety of techniques will enable me to locate and interpret the maenor, tref and tyddyn within the middle Teifi valley and specifically Gwinionydd. I aim to investigate these sites archaeologically and to place these within a reconstructed medieval cultural landscape. I have two primary sources of information:

The Documentary Record

The appearance of a dense and complex civil and governmental administrative documentation during the medieval period saw a new horizon of documentary record.

It will be demonstrated that although Ceredigion had social and cultural trajectories distinct from the rest of Wales, historical documentation can be used to investigate the survival of pre-conquest systems. Ceredigion is, however, poorly served by medieval rentals and surveys of the types known from elsewhere, but what does exist can be roughly distinguished by its secular and ecclesiastical subjects.

Secular rentals, surveys and law codes

The enormous wealth of detailed but often contradictory information supplied by the forty MSS that comprise the Laws of Hywel Dda were transcribed in 1841 and form an enormous body of research in their own right (Owen, 1841). The schematic models for an idealised Wales have formed the basis for many of the landscape reconstructions and these will be considered in some detail.

A survey of gwestfa payments dated to the early reign of Edward I gives us the names of the gwestfa districts for Ceredigion (eg Dodgshon, 1994 and Wmffre, 2004) but many of these remain unidentified, unlocated and the extent of all of them remains unknown. Those for Gwinionydd will be recreated and mapped in Chapter five.

Late 13th century Minister's accounts (Rhys, 1936) have also supplied detailed but incomplete information about the types of rentals as do the later rentals supplied by the Black Book of St David's which details the tenancies for the Bishop's of St David's holdings in 1326 (Willis-Bund, 1902).

The evidence supplied by 16th century rentals (Richards, 1964a) for half of the cwmwd of Gwinionydd that are still paying the gwestfa or chief rent has also been mapped onto GIS and has been vital in helping to reconstruct earlier settlement patterns. Exchequer proceedings have provided information about the post-Dissolution process and the way in which monastic granges were carved up in this process (eg James, 1955 and Jones, 1939). A collection of documents relating to Llandysul parish has furthered the links between Llandysul and The Bishops of St David's, charting the progress of holdings in Nantcwnlle for example. The tithe surveys have also proved an invaluable source for a pre-industrial landscape, often preserving strip field remnants for example. Tantalisingly, the tithe schedules for this area do not preserve field names, a great loss and one that would profit from further research. Due to the general appetite for family history, the census records are available online from *http://www.ancestry.com* for example and, in the case of Llandysul provided information about the names and extent of the parish's constituent hamlets. I am grateful to Mr and Mrs Flower for copies of a 19th century schedule and map of Moelhedog farm, Mr and Mrs Perks for a copy of an 18th century estate map for Dancapel and Seton Philips of Llwynffynnon Uchaf for the same.

Religious grants and records

The *Taxatio* (Record Commission, 1802) demanded by Pope Nicholas IV records the wealth of individual churches in 1291 and has demonstrated the significant status of Llandysul church for example.

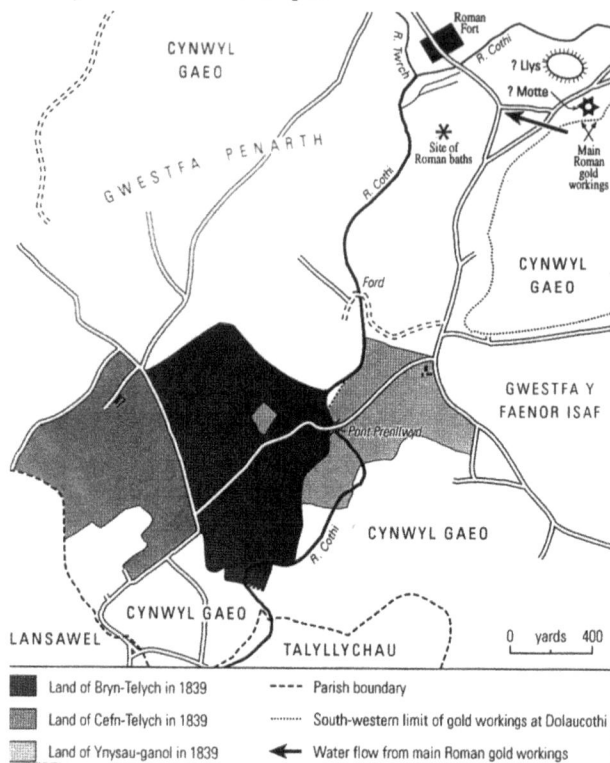

Figure 10. Bryn Telych in relation to the Dolaucaothi gold mines (Jones 1994:83).

Lord Rhys was instrumental in granting vast swathes of his kingdom to both Cistercian and Premonstratensian houses, some of which he founded himself. Where the text of these grants survive they form an invaluable record, especially the early charters to Strata Florida that have been helpful in proposing the former Llanllyr estates (eg Pryce, 2005 and Williams, 1889), and specifically an Inspeximus dated to 1331 that contains detailed boundary clauses relating to grants of land near Llandysul to Talley Abbey (Evans, 1878). Although written in Latin, some of these preserve some of the earliest Welsh place name forms that we have including topographical descriptors.

The *Episcopal Registers of the Diocese of St David's* (Isaacson, 1917) have also provided useful information about the nature and extent of the Diocese between the 14th and 18th century and this has been useful in the reconstruction of the extent of the 12th century Diocese that was substantially smaller than that which emerged in the post-medieval period. Dissolution surveys (Dugdale, 1817-1830) have produced scant but useful information regarding the fortunes of former monastic holdings in Llandysul.

These sources have all been studied as published except for the later estate documents and papers relating to Llandysul and Manorforion and the 1331 Inspeximus where the primary document was analysed in order to check the accuracy of the translation of place names. Most of this published material dates to the late 19th or early 20th century and is accompanied by interpretation and translation that has occasionally proved challenging in itself. For example, the precise nature of free and bond tenancy has never been satisfactorily addressed due to the complex and contradictory nature of the record but the debate has crystallised into either bond or free when it is obvious that a range of different terms are in use; taog, aillt, bileyn. Likewise uchelwyr, gwas and breyr have been translated as 'free notable' and the subtle difference between them has been somewhat lost. It is important to address this level of complexity so original forms have been used wherever appropriate and supplied with a translation wherever possible.

Most of the information derived has been linked to the identification of place names which has led to the identification, for example, of early grants to Strata Florida and gwestfa districts that have not been hitherto identified. The study of place names has been greatly facilitated by the monumental place name volumes compiled for Ceredigion by Wmffre (2004). This has been greatly useful in tracing the history and development of the place name but occasionally less helpful with the origins and meanings. Troedrhiwffenyd farm near Llandysul is said to have partly derived from *penyd* meaning penance, but its position located below the upland *mynydd* is more accurately named by the 1st edition Ordnance Survey map that gives the name as Troedrhiwfynydd containing the mynydd element. This is just one example and demonstrates the pitfalls for the unwary in using place name evidence.

The Physical Landscape

My second source is the physical landscape; topography and etymology affording an approach familiar to landscape archaeologists. For Wales (and indeed much of England) a horizon of built elements begins to emerge from the 12th century onwards with new ecclesiastical, military and secular architectures such as mottes and the new stone churches, bridges and castles. Identified and mapped by Cathcart-King (1959) for example, precise dating and their relationship to territory and settlement remains problematic and the relationship between fortifications at the neighbouring areas of Maerdref and Rhuddlan Teifi has proved more complex than has generally been assumed. The main tool to enable the manipulation and analysis of the landscape at a variety of scales has been facilitated by Geographic Information Systems (GIS) and the spatial analysis of the landscape through mapping has been one of the main approaches taken by this project. *MapInfo* version 7 and *ArcGis* v9.2 have proved powerful tools for landscape visualisation, analysis and presentation and have been used where appropriate in conjunction with digitised historical maps. For almost the entire survey area, the earliest surviving mapping is the tithe surveys of early 19th

century. These, alongside the 1st edition Ordnance Survey maps generally dating to the 1890s have proved valuable in charting the trajectory of the agricultural aspects of landscape change for example but it will be demonstrated that the field systems, settlement and development has actually had limited impact and the landscape has remained remarkably stable over the last 150 to 200 years. In most cases therefore this has allowed the use of accurate and detailed modern maps in order to present much of the data within this thesis. The scope of this project ranges from the regional county level to that of individual fields and a variety of map bases have been sourced digitally from the Ordnance Survey under licence via Digimap and, apart form the tithe maps, all the maps produced throughout have been supplied by *Digimap*. The 1:50,000 and the 1:25,000 base maps have proved especially useful at a regional level. At closer range, the 1:10,000 raster base map has been used in conjunction with the vector digital Landline at the same scale. This has allowed the import of other forms of digital data such as profile and contour. This has been useful for example in the analysis of potentially early farmsteads that all lie at or below the 200 metre contour for example. These digital map bases have greatly facilitated the addition and manipulation of supplementary information in layers such as rectified aerial photography, topographical survey, geophysical survey and its interpretation and the location of excavation trenches. All photographs are by the author unless otherwise stated.

The primary source for the existing archaeological resource has been the *Historic Environment Record* (HER). Formerly known as the sites and monuments record, the responsibility for this resource in Wales falls on several bodies committed to the production of the *Extended National Database in Wales* (ENDEX). As such, this is at present a scattered record with much overlap. Where I have cited the HER it will include the consultation of the following databases: the former sites and monuments record at Dyfed Archaeological Trust, Llandeilo, including paper and computer-based records; the CARN database operated by the Royal Commission on the Ancient and Historic Monuments of Wales (RCAHMW) at *http://www.rcahmw.org.uk/data/* and the map-based record also hosted by the RCAHMW and based on the same information but as yet, incomplete, called Coflein at *http://www.coflein.gov.uk/*. The provision of reliable, complete and academically rigorous online databases has dramatically improved in recent years and the seminal works of Melville Richard in a pan-Wales place name study is hosted by Bangor University and now available at *http://www.e-gymraeg.co.uk/enwaulleoedd/amr/*. Likewise the Historic Landscape Characterisation process undertaken for Ceredigion for Cambria Archaeology is published online at *http://www.acadat.com/HLC/*, the Celtic Inscribed Stones project hosted by University College London at *http://www.ucl.ac.uk/archaeology/cisp/* has also proved a useful resource.

A sophisticated form of topographical survey is being

increasingly used by archaeologists in order to analyse landscapes at high-resolution. Light Detection and Ranging (LiDAR) is an airborne mapping technique that uses a laser to repeatedly measure the distance between the aircraft and the ground and data for the survey areas at Llanfair and Moelhedog has been provided by the Environment Agency at a resolution of two metres. Input to GIS operating *ArcGIS* 9.2 has allowed the analysis of the data in 3 dimensional form allowing the identification of a new earthwork enclosure at Rhydowen and aspect analysis at Moelhedog for example has indicated the 'cherry picking' of the south-facing farmsteads of the Castell Hywel estate that formed part of Rhys' grant to Talley Abbey. The above techniques, historical and physical, have also allowed the potential of Llanfair to become apparent and geophysical survey and archaeological excavation during 2004 allowed the identification of substantial medieval deposits, the results of which have been discussed in chapter six. It is envisaged that a final excavation report will be deposited with the Dyfed Archaeological Trust as the local archaeological curator and the material recovered is to be retained by the landowner that it may be displayed by the local history society, Hanes Llandysul.

This has allowed the construction of a set of historical and physical information that has been analysed and presented via GIS. The efficacy of such an empirical approach used for the reconstruction of a medieval landscape occupied by a largely non-literate society devoid of documentary material needs unpacking has characterised my approach throughout.

THREE: TERRITORY DEFINED

Introduction

The previous chapter outlined the ways in which the integration of historical analysis and landscape will be successful in pursuing landscape reconstruction. This chapter aims to introduce the specific landscape units of medieval Wales as outlined in medieval texts. It recognises the schematic and idealised nature of the models but allows for the possibility that there was a consistent and demonstrable relationship between them and the physical landscape. It also flags up the dangers inherent in placing too much emphasis on administrative precision but establishes the premise that the complex settlement and territory did not start with the advent of documentary record around the 12th century but that it may be possible to establish earlier antecedents.

In order to reconstruct the medieval settlement and territorial patterns for Gwinionydd it is necessary to outline the framework that existed in some form prior to the turbulence of the 12th and 13th centuries. This paper will not be concerned with the origins of the cwmwd-maenor system that early medieval Wales is predicated on suffice to say that many of the institutions survive in name from at least the 9th century. Jones Pierce (1959b: 272) was puzzled by the lack of evidence in Ceredigion for *taeog* or 'bond' communities that would have indicated the presence of the llys-maerdref-demesne, a system much more visible in North Wales (eg. Johnstone, 2000). This lack of evidence for the llys-maerdref-demesne system may be linked to the absence in Ceredigion of the maenor, the 'umbrella' institution described by Glanville Jones as the 'multiple estate' that bound all these elements together. Beyond scant place name evidence we have no concrete evidence for definite llys-maerdref units or maenorial estates in the southern Ceredigion area and the status and tenure of the occupying individuals is even more poorly understood.

This chapter will introduce the evidence outlined in the medieval Law texts, evidence that describes the idealised territorial structure and tenure dating to the 13th century but with earlier origins. This will enable me to define the territorial units that should form the basis for territory and settlement in Ceredigion that have hitherto remained largely unidentified. Elsewhere, the law texts formed the basis for models of explanation which will be explored here. Glanville Jones's multiple estate model will be explored with reference to Carmarthenshire and will be compared to a recent critique of this approach and suggestions for north Wales offered by Rhys Jones.

The Evidence of the Laws

The fullest historical evidence for territorial organisation is presented in a number of medieval redactions of customary law collectively known as the *Laws of Hywel Dda*. The Laws comprise some forty manuscripts held in a variety of different collections and different redactions contain clues as to their place of production. Aneurin Owen organised the manuscripts into three groups named the '*Venedotian Code*' or the Book of Iorwerth relating to Gwynedd and north Wales, the '*Gwentian Code*' or Book of Cyfnerth relating to southeast Wales in particular and the '*Demetian Code*' or Book of Blegywryd relating to southwest Wales and Deheubarth in particular (Owen, 1841). Most of the manuscripts describe the reform of law attributed to the reign of Hywel Dda (d.950) which probably formed the source codex for these later revisions although some of the rules contained within may be even earlier.

The earliest manuscript dates to the early or mid 13th century and, although written in Latin, appears to be a copy of a Welsh original. Although the redactions differ in detail, they are strikingly similar in content. The Book of Iorwerth contains the most complete and schematic statements of territorial organisations but the Book of Cyfnerth and Book of Blegywryd preserve archaic forms thought to date to the late 12th century reign of Rhys ap Gruffudd (Turvey, 1988: 95), remarkable when, as Pryce notes, Ceredigion and Carmarthenshire operated along non-literate lines, land for example changing hands without documents well into the Tudor period (Pryce, 2000: 36).

The complete model outlined by Iorwerth is presented in diagrammatic form (fig. 11) and serves to demonstrate the schematic and idealised nature of the territorial model. What is evident is that the named elements are nested within each other in a regular and fixed way that is often difficult to reconcile with the complex appearance on the ground. The tref represents the basic element from which everything else was calculated. The largest administrative territory was comprised of 100 trefi and the cantref survived, although not wholly unchanged, in the 16th century hundredal system. The tref was the basic unit of administration and was the unit that was assessed for payment of the gwestfa. The food rent mentioned as early as the 9th century in the verse, Canu Llywarch Hen was later commuted into a cash payment known as the *twnc* pound worth 240d (Owen, 1841).

Groups of trefi collectively formed the maenol. In the Iorwerth model, two of the trefi that were not assigned to any maenol were reserved for the King. One as the demesne land servicing the court or llys was known as maerdref and was administered by the *maer y biswail* or 'land reeve', the other was reserved for summer pasture, the hafod. The laws further state that one maenol was assigned to the *cynghellor* or chancellor and another to the reeve or maer (blue). Four further maenolau (red) were to be assigned to the King's bondsmen to provide support or *dofraeth* for the *cylch* or circuit of the two royal officers and other members of the ruling households. The rent was known as the kylchmaer in 1355 when it was worth £12 in Elfael and a similar rent called the kylch march was payable at Emlyn (Rees, 1924: 98 and 226). The dofraeth became known as a commorth literally, 'aid'. In the Tywi valley where the commutation of this payment was later, an 'oat rent' was rendered on the bond communities. The 'oat money' was required of the free holders of the Manor of Gwynioneth Iskardin in 1651, the parishes of Llandyssel Iskarden, Llangynlo, Llanvayre Orllwin, Llandevryog and Llanvayre Trefflygon at 14d each to a total of £3. The lordship also collected oat rent from the detached parishes of Dehewid, Killie, Llanigcharron and Trevigod at 14d each to a total of 26s (Richards, 1960a).

The remaining six maenolau (green) were to be occupied by free notables; *uchelwyr* or *breyr* that were supported by their own bond under-tenants. These latter eight maenolau collected the gwestfa, assessed on the trefi. The uchelwyr were also to provide military service when required and light labour on the king's buildings. The bondsmen of the royal maerdref were to provide more onerous labour

services such as harrowing, reaping, sowing and carrying under the supervision of the maer y biswail. Jones points out that the bond tenants of the eight free maenolau plus the servile population of the remaining four maenolau plus the two bond royal townships meant that the idealised Iorwerth model meant that the majority of inhabitants within the cwmwd were bond (Jones, 1972b: 299).

The evidence in the Laws for areas outside those covered in the Iorwerth model is poor and often contradictory but they do describe differences between a bond maenor and a free maenor. Table 1 below summarises this information:

A Bond Maenor:

1 rhandir = 312 *erwau* or 47 statue acres
4 rhandir = 1 tref at 1248 erwau or 188 statute acres
     7 trefi = 1 bond maenor at 8736 erwau or 1316 statute acres

A Free Maenor:

1 rhandir (shareland)= 312 erwau or 47 statue acres
3 rhandir = 1 tref at 1248 erwau or141statute acres
13 trefi   = 1 free maenor at 16224 erwau or 1833 statute acres

Table 1. The South Wales Laws (cf. Owen 1841)

Jones Pierce (1959b: 281, app. 1) also noted, however, that in the northern Iorwerth redaction, the position of the gafael and the rhandir is reversed giving a rhandir of 64 erwau equating more to the 47 or 60 of the south. In any case the gafael is not recorded in south Wales by this time and the north Wales' maenol had all but disappeared except the cantref of Arfon which was said to have contained nine maenolau for example completely at odds with the schematic law texts. In the south at Ystrad Tywi, however, the large Maenor Meibion Seisyll covered roughly one third of its cwmwd, comprising three gwestfa districts (ibid.) and for the cwmwd of Caeo, Jones (1994) identifies the subdivision into nine gwestfa each paying a uniform rent of 53s 4d per annum. Thus we can see a confusing variability in size and name of various units which nevertheless underpins the 'multiple estate' framework - a complex hierarchy of nested territories.

The documents only record the forms of tenancy that the units were held by and the

The Llyfr Iorwerth Model
(Owen 1841: 91)

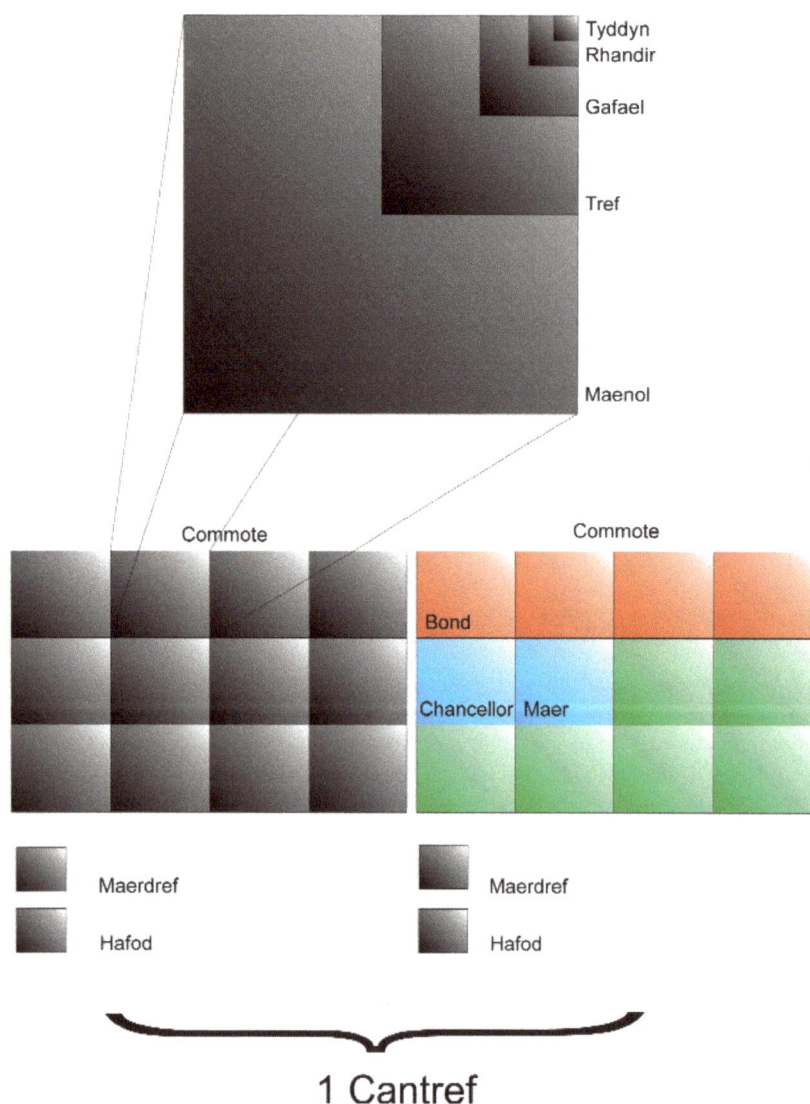

Figure 11. The Iorwerth model of territorial organisation represented diagrammatically.

geographies that they related to are difficult to identify. The maenor had all but disappeared from Ceredigion by the 12th century, to be replaced by the gwestfa as a uniformly applied tax based on the gwestfa district. If it was possible to identify and locate these gwestfa units, it may be possible to identify the tref upon which it was rendered in southwest Wales. To elaborate upon this it is necessary to unpack the relationships between the maenor, tref and the rhandir and to attempt to identify their physical manifestation on the ground in the late 12th century which should be possible because, as Longley (2004) speculates, the tref was firmly located in geographical space. Rhys Jones (1998c: 139) stated that there was no direct relationship between the maenor and the cwmwd/cantref in the south Wales texts but they were both in use as territorial units at the same time as in both north and south Wales where the boundaries of the cwmwd were said to 'belong to the king' (Jones, 1976: 11).

The land divisions present a mathematic exactness that is related purely to administrative ideals that have proved difficult to identify on the ground however. In the south Wales redactions, the maenol is referred to as the maenor, and the Book of Blegywryd distinguishes between the seven trefi of the maenor fro 'lowland bond maenor', and the thirteen trefi within the maenor urthtir 'upland free maenor' (Owen, 1841: 262). The Book of Cyfnerth notes the subdivision of the bond tref into three sharelands or rhandir and four within each free tref (Jones, 1989: 179). Three of the four bond rhandir were for occupancy with one reserved for pasture whilst on a free tref, two were for occupancy with one reserved for pasture (ibid: 180). Each rhandir ideally contained 312 erwau (Welsh acres) "between clear and brake, wood and field, wet and dry' with 12 (Welsh) acres reserved for buildings" (Owen, 1841: 374 my parenthesis). The unit of measurement is explained as an eighteen foot rod and Jones (1989: 180) has calculated that a rhandir of 312 erwau would equate to only 47 statute acres; divided into 32 acres for occupancy with only 1¼ acres for the buildings. Confusion occurs when the same passage in a Latin redaction gives a larger rod for the measurement of the erw resulting in 60 statute acres for occupancy with 2½ acres for buildings.

Liber Landavensis, the Llandaff Charters, written during the 1120s records 158 land grants made over the preceding five centuries (Davies, 1982: 6). Most (three-quarters) of the land grants were for three modii of land with only 14 percent for grants of four modii. The groups of modii in the charters were associated with a single named settlement or villa but Davies (ibid:12) is careful to indicate that these were not nucleations but units of land, the boundaries of which have been demonstrated to match features on the ground today allowing the identification of surviving ancient landholdings. A modius was of the order of 35-40 statute acres which equates well with the rhandir of some of the redactions (Jones, 1985: 355). With groups of either three modii (occasionally four) mentioned, most of the grants appear to have been of bond vills, that is, a bond tref

containing three rhandiroedd (Jones, 1984). Longley (2004) notes that the gwestfa (in the southern Law redactions) was assessed on a maenor of seven rhandir so calculates the maenor at seven times 312 erwau giving 2,184 acres. Jones (89: 180), however, explains that 'rhandir' should have read 'tref' as it does in all other texts and that the terms rhandir and tref are interchangeable and probably represent one of the sources of confusion.

Clearly the tref as a unit comprising three or four sharelands predates the law texts considerably, as does the different composition and nature of the free and bond trefi. Caution should be applied before translating literally to geographical space however. The units were recorded in relation to renders and were primarily concerned with assessment. The same unit could represent a variety of spatial extents perhaps demonstrating regional differences or the different quality and nature of the land in question. Nevertheless the texts are careful to describe the unit of measurements used in each area for each unit and the implication has to be that the relationships between the units at least existed as a series of nested elements within an estate, reminiscent of Glanville Jones' multiple estate.

The Cantref

If the complexities of the maenor and tref units are to be reconstructed, the cantref upon which the building blocks of the kingdom were predicated must be identified. To consult Rees (1951) or Richards (1969) one would get a false impression that we know exactly what the cantrefi were and what their extent was. This is not the case. The only unequivocal pre-conquest cantref name for Ceredigion to survive in the historical literature is Penweddig which, it is presumed, became the later hundred of Genau'r Glyn (Kirby, 1994b: 318). It has therefore been assumed that the creation of the hundred system during the Acts of Union in 1536 has preserved the other cantrefi names. This is also problematic as the example of Dyfed below shows.

Some of the best evidence for early cantrefi are given in the 13th century Mabinogion texts where the seven cantrefi of Dyfed are named (Jones & Jones, 2003: 3). George Owen (Owen, 1892) identified these in during the late 16th century and he added their constituent cymydau, in this instance three cwmwd per cantref. His list is reproduced below but contains several mistakes apparently traceable to mistranslation and interpretation of the manuscripts.

Cantref	Cwmwd
EMLYN CANTRED	ywch kych
	Yf kych
	Leuethir
DOYGLETHE	Amgoed
	Penant
	Evelfrey
ARBERTH	Penrin ar lais
	Esker o lef

		Talagharn
ROSE (ROOSE)		Hwlfordd
		Castell gwalch-may
		y garn
KEMES		ywch nyfer
		Yfnyver
		Trefdraeth
PENFRO	Coed yr haf (Coed Rhaf, now Amroth)
		Penfro
PEBIDIOK		Mynyw
		Pencaer
		Pebidiog

Whilst Owen was an accomplished historian, antiquarian and genealogist this list is greatly suspect. Information was gleaned from the lists contained in the Description of Wales by Sir John Price and Humphrey Lloyd completed in 1559 and published in Powel's Historie of Cambria (Powel, 1811). The place names and their territories had been formulated from obscure and often tentative references contained within the manuscripts that collectively make up the Mabinogion. For example, the cymydau said to be included in Arberth and Doygelddy all in fact formed part of Cantref Gwarthaf, except Efelfre (Velfrey), in Carmarthenshire (Owen, 1892: 45). Henry Owen (ibid.) also pointed out that there was no ancient cantref of Arberth or Narberth and that the commote of Leuethir or 'Elfed' was also in Cantref Gwarthaf not Emlyn. He considered Penant to be a corruption of Peuliniog which is a region of uncertain status also within Gwarthaf, pointing out that the commotes of Doyglethe 'Dungleddy' are actually Wiston (Castell Gwis) and Llawhaden (Llanhuadain). Henry Owen was also uncertain whether there was a cwmwd of Pebidiog within the Cantref of Pebidiog and explained it as a mistake due to repetition. The misinterpretation of lists presented in the *Red Book of Hergest* and the *Cwtta Cyfarwydd* are also reinforced by *Leland's Itinerary*, much admired by George Owen (although these texts also mention an apparently fictitious Cantref Y Coed which had been omitted by George Owen). It is frustrating that, writing so soon after the Act of Union in 1536 that the precise constitution of pre-Conquest cantrefi and commotes is so confused.

It appears therefore that the new hundreds may not be entirely based upon the original cantrefi. The new hundreds actually subdivide both Gwinionydd and Caerwedros cymydau (fig. 12). The two halves of Gwinionydd are split between two hundreds: Gwinionydd Is Cerdin lies in Troedyraur Hundred and Gwinionydd Uwch Cych in Moyddin Hundred. Other sources hint at the situation prior to the Union. Writing in 1756, Lewis Morris stated that the names of the Ceredigion cantrefi were Penweddig which contained Genau'r Glyn, Perveth and Creuthyn; Canawl (or canol meaning central) which contained Mevenyth, Anhunoe and Pennarth; Castell which contained Mabwynion and Caerwedros and Lywren (Hirwen) which contained Gwinionydd and Iscoed (Porter, 1993). Castell probably refers to Castell Moeddyn which gives us Moyddin Hundred, this is the name of a large Iron Age hill top enclosure located just outside the north-west boundary of Gwinionydd and as Meuddin Fawr, it was a former grange of Llanllyr, then Strata Florida.

The neighbouring cymydau of Gwinionydd and Mabwynion contain the same personal name elements and this has allowed the suggestion that the two cymydau comprised a pair that were established in order to provide military strength along the southern Ceredigion border (Griffiths, 1994). The reconstruction of the original cantrefi above, however, indicates that in fact the cymydau belonged to separate cantrefi; Gwinionydd in Hirwen and Mabwynion in Castell Moeddin and it is evident that the four original cantrefi respect the cymydau territories. The fracturing of these units must have occurred later with the establishment of the hundredal system and probably owes much to complex later medieval administration and ownership patterns for example at the Dyffryn Teifi estate that formed the basis for the modest lordships of the Lloyd family of the Newcastle Emlyn area during the post-medieval period.

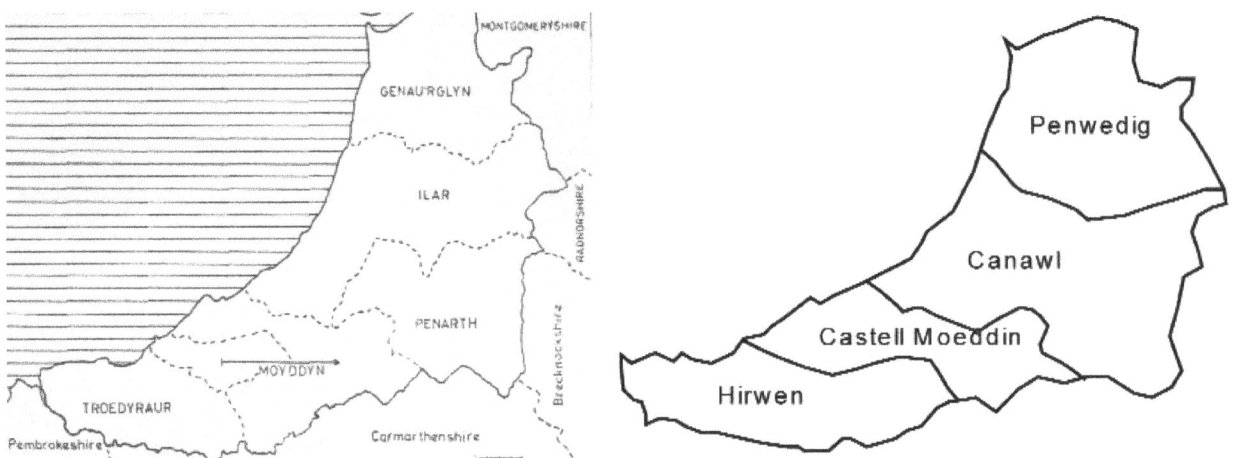

Figure 12. Left, the hundreds after 1536, splitting Caerwedros and Gwinionydd in half (Richards 1969: 252). Right, the proposed original cantrefs, respecting cwmwd boundaries.

The Maenor

Glanville Jones (1976) established associations between his seminal multiple estate and the ancient maenor of southern Wales. But in his examination of the maenor, Rhys Jones (R. A. Jones, 1998c) maintained that the relative silence of the south Wales texts meant that the maenor had ceased to be relevant to later medieval territorial organisation. Offering a substantial challenge to the nested hierarchies of Glanville Jones' multiple estate, Rhys Jones suggested that the maenor and the maenol were in fact different institutions. In his model (fig. 13) the maenol was discrete to North Wales while the maenor appeared purely in the

holdings in a politically motivated reorganisation. In state formation terms, Rhys Jones saw the maenor as institutionally immature reaching its zenith during the 9th century.

Regarded as a 'first step' towards the territorialisation of power this approach is firmly based on a 'tribal model' of social and spatial organisation whose institutional boundaries would only encompass areas settled lowland agricultural land. This meant that areas like woodland and moorland would remain "relatively free from either settlement or administrative divisions" (R. A. Jones, 1998c: 138) rather contrasting with the descriptions of the reserved

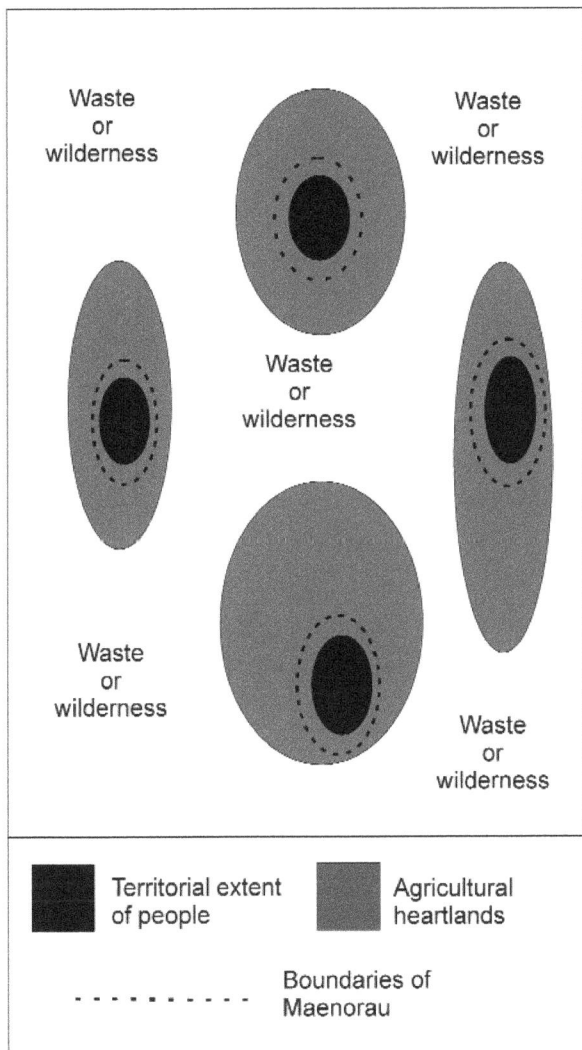

The South Wales Maenor   The North Wales Maenol

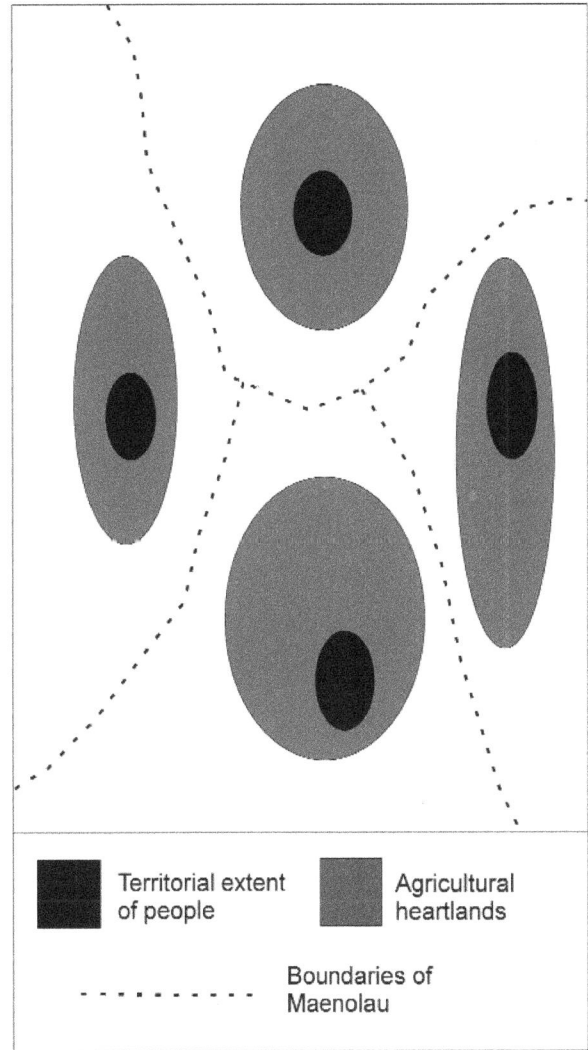

Figure 13. Rhys Jones's maenor model (R. A. Jones 1998c: 141).

south, although in greater numbers. Rhys Jones described Gwynedd as one of the most institutionally mature organisations in Europe at this time and he attributed the creation of the north Wales maenol to state formation policies put in place by Owain Gwynedd during the 12th century as a deliberate attempt to consolidate territorial

grazing of the rhandir between "clear and brake, wood and field, wet and dry".

Rhys Jones' model states that large consolidated territories would have been rare and substantial areas of Wales would have existed outside the control of tribal leaders. Owain's new maenol brought all land into administration for the first time and for the first time, 'wilderness or waste' became more than 'no man's land'. Rhys's landscape reconstruction is hard to reconcile with the archaeological evidence of thousands of years of complex settlement, even at remote and high altitudes and his model has more to do with the abstract mechanics of state formation rather than reality on the ground and, as such is well suited to the formulaic codes stated in the Laws which is the product of medieval lawyers

struggling with a complex and ancient set of realities.

Despite the assertion by Rhys Jones that the maenor in south Wales was dispersed and had been in decline since the 9th century, enough evidence survives to suggest that the cwmwd had been subdivided into maenorau in a systematic way and that occasionally these units survived into post-medieval administration. The attempt to describe the maenor unit, however, still leads to confusion. For example, the Demetian Code does not, as Dodgshon (1994: 345) claims, make clear that a cwmwd is subdivided into described by Iorwerth. He constructed a rather clumsy and improbable model to explain this (fig. 14, top) having to add 4 extra trefi at the end to meet a 50 trefi target. In fact the south Wales texts remain completely mute on the relationship between the maenor and cwmwd. Using early post-medieval surveys for southern Carmarthenshire, however, Rees had noted the division of cwmwd Kidwelly into quarters and Perfedd and Iscennen plus Mabelfyw and Mabudrud on the southern banks of the Teifi also containing four maenorau each (Rees, 1924: 203). four maenorau in contrast to the twelve Glanville Jones (1976: 12 and 1992: 97) used this evidence to propose his own model (fig. 14, bottom) for a south Wales cwmwd, different to Dodgshon's but also with the adherence to the ideal content of 50 trefi. Jones noted, however, that the maenor fro, or lowland bond maenor should contain seven trefi according to the Book of Blegywryd which (as Dodgshon's model had demonstrated) caused mathematical problems. Jones simply doubled this figure, proposing that the maenor of the King should be larger than others so that the bond maenor would contain 14 trefi split into 7 lowland and 7 upland. Whilst this model still owes as much to mathematical precision, Domesday does,

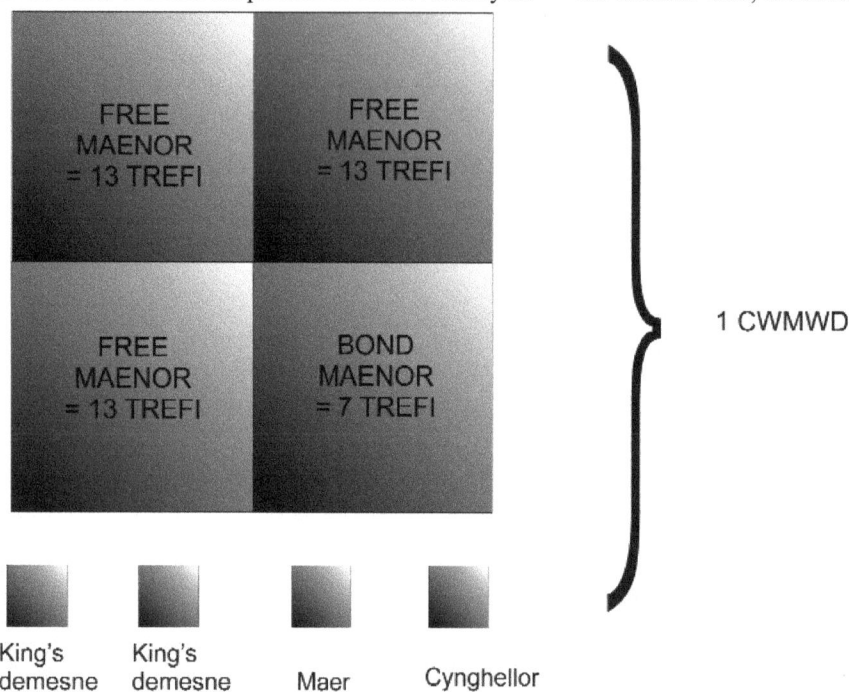

The Glanville Jones Model
(1976:12 & 1992:97)

1 CWMWD

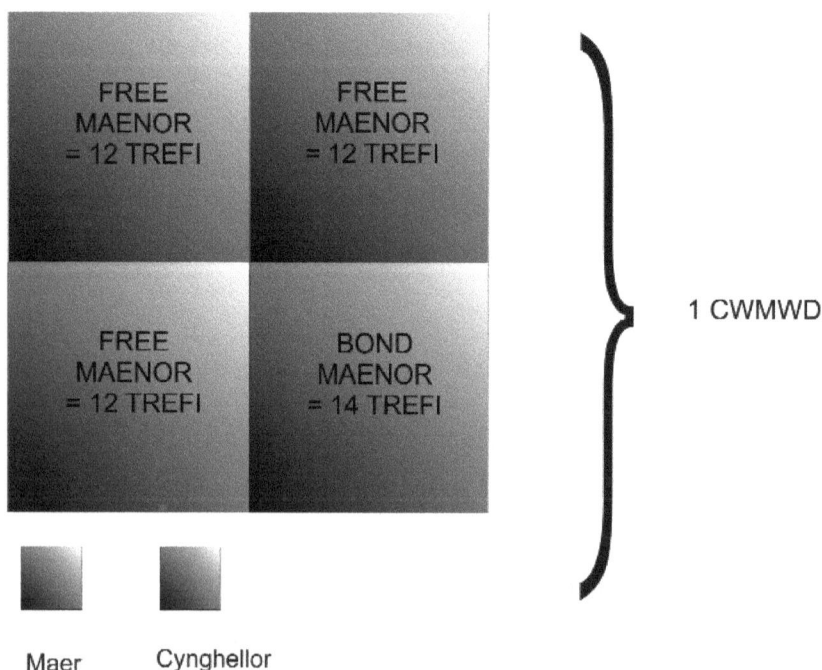

1 CWMWD

Figure 14. The south Wales models in diagrammatic form for comparison.

however, record groups of 13 and 14 vills in Gwent:

"Under Wasric the reeve there are 13 villages, under Emwy 14 villages, under Bleio 13 villages and under Idhael 14 villages. These pay 47 sesters of honey, 40 pigs, 41 cows, and 28s for hawks. The value of the whole £9 190s 4d"

(Rippon, 1996: 65).

Other maenorau with ancient origins were to emerge from research in Carmarthenshire. The earliest known reference to a maenor in south Wales occurs in the 9th century Lichfield marginalia as *mainaur med diminih* and, with the aid of the perambulation, Jones (1972b: 308-311) was able to identify its bounds around the early farmstead of Meddyfnych, its boundary largely coextensive with the modern parish of Llandybie. He was able to add this newly identified maenor to Maenor Llansawel, Y Faenor Isaf and Maenor Rhwng Twrch a Chothi giving Cwmwd Caeo a total of four maenorau (fig. 15). But although the identification of a maerdy or reeve's house near the church confirmed the bond status of Maenor Meddyfnych he was only able to identify seven, not 14 trefi, somewhat conflicting with his own hypothesis above. Again though, Domesday (Jones, 1976: 12) described a unit comprising a grouping of 7 vills, a pattern Jones (1972b: 304, n.3) also observed for Llandysul parish with its group of 7 hamlets.

For Jones the evidence for early, complex hierarchical estates was strong. The treatment by Domesday of vills in 4 separate groups may also preserve the 4-maenor cwmwd and as the work of both Rees and Jones has demonstrated, evidence for the 4-maenor cwmwd in Carmarthenshire is strong. Jones Pierce (1959b: 281, app. 1) had tentatively observed that a south Wales maenor usually occupied a quarter or a third of their cwmwd as at Maenor Meibion Seisyll in Ystrad Tywi. Thus the 3 or 4 maenor cwmwd is evident and is fundamentally different from the 12 of the north.

This chapter has introduced the evidence supplied by the Law codes that are a schematic and mathematical attempt by medieval lawyers to explicate an administrative landscape. The Laws make explicit statements about the nature and extent of the units, cantref, cwmwd, maenor, tref, rhandir and tyddyn but the south Wales evidence is less full although Glanville Jones and Rees have both been able to demonstrate some links between the information given in the texts and reality on the ground. This highlights the usefulness of combining historical and physical data. Rhys Jones's model fails to do this, proposing instead an immature and unsophisticated landscape organisation and, as such, must be challenged.

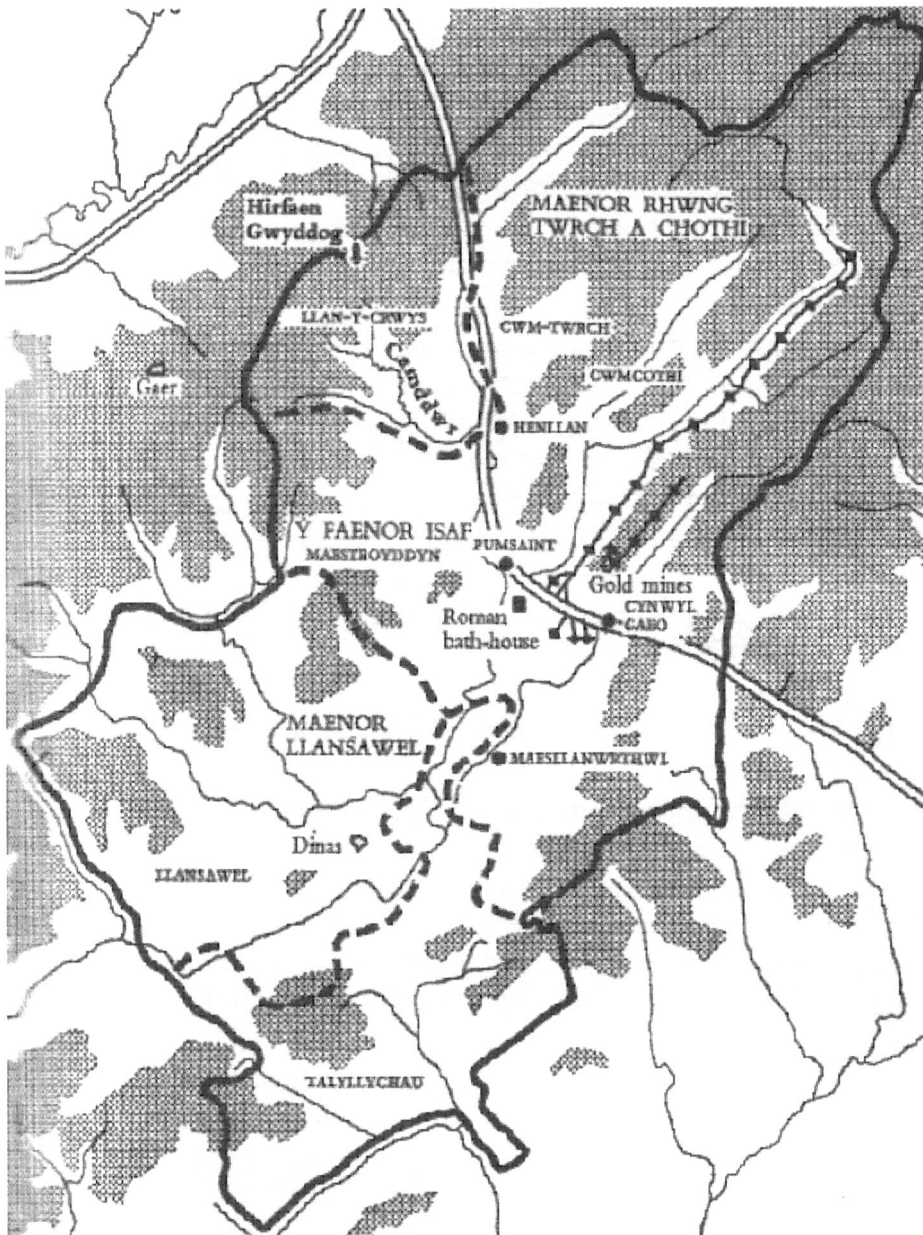

Figure 15. The four maenorau of Cwmwd Caeo, Carmarthenshire identified by Glanville Jones (Jones, 1972b: 315).

FOUR: THE LANDSCAPE OF LORDSHIP

Introduction

This chapter draws on a wide range of historical sources in order to recreate the lordship structures for southern Ceredigion. It will establish that the uniquely modernising vision of Lord Rhys resulted in vast tracts of Ceredigion coming under the ownership of new monastic houses by the end of the 12th century. It will recognise that the vision of a single leader had profound effects on the landscape that have hitherto gone unrecognised. It will also demonstrate that the cwmwd was a familiar administrative unit that was utilised by Rhys as a way of apportioning estates and will highlight the significance of the middle Teifi valley estates centred on Llandysul. The emphasis is on a complex ancient landscape that survived the impact of early Norman military activity.

Grants to Religious Houses

The turmoil and wars of the 12th and 13th centuries emphasises that the conquest of west Wales was protracted and difficult. The Normans could not take major towns nor blockade ports or major routes. The landscape was dispersed with peripatetic leaders highly mobile within their territories. This does not preclude a simple landscape however. When Roger de Montgomery marched through the entire length of Ceredigion in 1093 there was little to hinder him until he reached Cardigan. He had travelled the entire length of the county through a landscape devoid of towns and other nucleated settlements and with few military centres. The creation of so many castles here reflects the fractured, dissected nature of the campaign within the dispersed rural landscape. Norman castle building was an attempt at territorial expansion not consolidation (Longley, 1997: 43).

This upheaval meant changes to patterns of ownership and with the return of Welsh rule under Rhys ap Gruffudd. Jones Pierce (1959b: 278) suggested that this presented an opportunity for Rhys's fresh start, that he effectively wiped the slate clean and generated new forms of governance. For example, the late survival and artificial regularity of the gwestfa is explained as the recreation of an ancient render in an attempt to stabilise and maximise the returns from his administration. The recreation of patterns of ownership here will, demonstrate that elements of an ancient system were retained and formed the basis for Rhys's reorganisation.

The main source that enables the analysis of territorial structures is the grants that Rhys made to monastic institutions. We know of grants from others surviving in written form from the mid 12th century onwards when Cadell ap Gruffudd for example granted SVancti Petrie de Mabonio, the church of St Peter at Lampeter, to Totnes Priory (Pryce, 2005: 165). Most grants, however, were to new Norman foundations in Wales. The Savigniac house at Neath, established in 1130 was followed by the first Welsh Cistercian house at Tintern in 1131. These formed the basis for a network of rich abbey estates in the south-east but it was not until the foundation of Whitland in 1140 by Bishop Bernard of St David's that a mother house for the rest of north and west Wales was provided (Williams, 2001: 5-6). Endowed with a new site in 1155 by John of Torrington, the abbey was later patronised by new grants of lands, including some in Ceredigion by Lord Rhys. In 1164 a small cell from Whitland settled near Ystrad Fflur provided for by a grant of Robert Fitz Stephen and the following year Rhys gained control of Deheubarth and assumed the patronage of this house that subsequently moved to its present site at Strata Florida. Rhys personally founded the Cistercian nunnery of Llanllyr in the Aeron valley. He also founded the Premonstratensian house at Talley in Carmarthenshire which was endowed with estates in southern Ceredigion and he confirmed other grants in Ceredigion to the Knight's Hospitallers.

These landholdings became known as granges, manors and estates. But it will become increasingly clear that these holdings functioned in different ways to the classic grange farms of the great English monastic estates and the precise extent of some of these holdings will be analysed in order to identify Welsh, pre-Conquest landscape units. The precise purpose behind princely grants of this type has long been debated. It is generally assumed that the grants were of surplus, unused or unimportant land perhaps coinciding propitiously with the 'remote' wilderness favoured by the monastic orders. In the Rhys Jones (1998a and 1999) model (fig. 13) for example, land at a certain distance from centres of administration becomes 'unowned' waste. We can challenge this when we look at the map produced here (fig. 16) that reconstructs ownership patterns for southern Ceredigion where other, complex and structured mechanisms are clearly at play.

The broad brush-stroke of Anglo-Norman administration in Ceredigion also recorded many native institutions that relate to territory that will be analysed more closely in chapter five below. Administrators sometimes pasted new terminologies on top of local systems, but where unfamiliar language and practice was encountered they often retained original forms. Minister's Accounts for 1301 to 1303, in west Wales mention the cantref and cwmwd structure from which complex tenurial rentals were rendered (Rhys, 1936). Information supplied by an extent of 1303 details the geographical sub-unit known as the gwestfa (Dodgshon, 1994). This survey, essentially a valuation of rents and returns compiled for Edward I demonstrates the close association of the cwmwd-gwestfa structure that directs us to a pre-conquest system, a system that was to be used into the 16th and 17th centuries as the basis for the 'chief rent'. In order to reconstruct the territories represented by these ancient practices and customs it is necessary to construct this coherent picture of ownership for the first time. It has become increasingly obvious that these grants were not arbitrarily constructed, nor were they plucked out of thin air in order to generate spiritual prestige for the donor.

As will be demonstrated many of the estates were former royal holdings based on an essentially Welsh framework and institution. The landholdings of Strata Florida, Whitland and Talley reflect a specific agenda put in place by Rhys that suited his needs in the turbulent 12th century but what, if anything, can the distribution of holdings tell us about the pre-Conquest landscape?

Mapping the Patterns of Ownership

The primary source for the evidence of lordship in 12th and 13th century Ceredigion is the ownership of vast swathes of the county by monastic houses. The holdings of the Cistercians in Wales have been broadly mapped by Williams (1990 and 2001) but holdings by other monastic bodies have not hitherto been analysed and the results combined. This analysis will examine the evidence for all the monastic landowners in Ceredigion and place them together to recreate lordship patterns for the 12th to 13th centuries. It will emerge that the holdings of Cistercian Strata Florida dominate the upper Teifi valley and upland regions of the Cambrian Mountains that stretch northwards and, with the exception of the small holding on the coast at Blaensaith (that was a later re-apportionment), the estates wrapped themselves around the abbey core. But the holdings of Cistercian Whitland, with some Premonstratensian Talley lands are confined to the mid-Teifi valley westwards, with a few scattered holdings in northern Carmarthenshire and Pembrokeshire.

Lying intermixed with these are the holdings of the Bishops of St David's that seem to have two core areas. One centred along the lower reaches of the Teifi valley as far upstream as the centre of Llandysul parish, the other, a looser clutch of holdings stretching from the coast at Aberarth and Llanllwchaearn, north-eastwards to Llanddewibrefi. As a foundation with 6th century origins, it is perhaps not surprising that the Bishops represent the most prolific proprietors in the region. However, the further north we go, the less influence they have. In fact Lledrod in the centre of northern Ceredigion, whose tithes they collected during the early 16th century, represents the most northerly of their Diocesan holdings at this time. This may be because until sometime before the Norman reorganisation of the church by Bishop Bernard in the early 12th century, the Diocese encompassed only the early medieval kingdom of Dyfed with the southern fringe of Ceredigion and it only 'acquired' the rest of Ceredigion in a gradual push northwards.

The Bishops of St David's

Documentary evidence for pre-conquest holdings in Ceredigion is best inferred from texts written in the 12th to 14th centuries, often using earlier, but now lost exemplars. The seven Bishop-houses of Dyfed listed in five separate redactions of the south Wales Law texts are assumed to reflect practice as early as the late 9th - early 10th century but the creation of these specific redactions are attributed to the rule of Rhys in the late 12th century (Charles-Edwards, 1971). The ancient kingdom of the Demetae tribe represented the former Roman administrative civitas of Demetia which provides the modern 'Dyfed' comprised in modern times the three counties of Carmarthenshire, Pembrokeshire and Ceredigion. In the post-Roman period, the early church was arranged around the tud or tribal territory and presiding over the tuath or people was the secular tudyr or ruler. Charles-Edwards (1971) suggests that each of the tud would have had a 'bishop' and that the tud, not surviving much beyond the 8th century was superseded by the cantref. Charles-Edwards assumed that seven bishop-houses would relate to the seven cantrefi within Dyfed and he was able to identify five of them as follows:

Bishop-House	Cantref	Modern Place
Mynyw	Pebidiog	St. David's Cathedral
Llan Ismael	Rhos	St. Ishmaels
Llan Degeman	Pembroke	Rhoscrowther
Llan Vssyllt?	Pembroke?	St Issel's?
Llan Teilaw	Daugleddau	Llandeilo Lwydarth
Llan Telydauwc	Gwarthaf	Old Carmarthen
Llan Geneu?	Cemais and Emlyn?	?

Table 2. The Seven Bishop houses of Dyfed

Llan Geneu remained unidentified whilst both Llan Degeman and Llan Vssyllt were both assigned to Pembrokeshire, leaving the two cantrefi of Cemais and Emlyn without a house and Pembrokeshire with two. Llan Geneu was later identified by Heather James (2006) in the vicinity of Llangenau Fawr and Llangenau Fach farms near Tegryn in Cantref Emlyn where subsequent field work by Neil Ludlow has identified earthworks within an enclosure. She postulated that the cantrefi of Emlyn and Cemais would have shared this Bishop house.

A different redaction merges Llan Teilaw and Llan Telydauwc together as a single house so that it can add Egluyss Hwadeyn 'Llawhaden', further complicating the premise of seven houses for seven cantrefi but it seems reasonable to revisit the hypothesis that Pembroke had two Bishop's houses. Llan Ismael is described in another redaction as Lan Yssan in Ros, Pembrokeshire, and can be fairly certainly identified with St Ishmael's church in Rhos, a common dedication in the south west (Charles-Edwards, 1971: 248). Llan Vssyllt has been more tentatively identified with St. Issel's in nearby Tenby but is more tenuous and William of Worcester says of Ussylt, 'Sanctus Vssoldus confessor anglice Seynt Vssile plures ecclesie in Wallia' (ibid: 252). Different redactions provide different spellings; Vssyllt, Ecclesia Ussilt, Egluyss Hussilt, Eclesia Ussult and Yssyl is given by Blegywryd, the Deheubarth text (ibid: 250 and n. 5). Without any other supporting evidence it is difficult to make a case for Llan Vssyllt at St Issels. More likely is that Llan Yssyl refers to Llandysul, either as the llan of the hypocoristic ty as the 'house of', 'ty'

Figure 16. 12th century southern Ceredigion (see inset for location). Lord Rhys was the first Welsh lord to found his own monastic estates at Talley and Llanllyr and he granted vast tracts of southern Ceredigion to the new European monastic houses in order to consolidate and modernise his lordship. Many of Llanllyr's holdings were later taken over by Strata Florida, as happened for example at Morfa Bychan, and the Rhuddlan Teifi estate belonging originally to Talley eventually came under the control of Whitland Abbey.

–Yssul, that is, the 'llan of the house of Tysul'. Early renderings of Llandysul give; Llandessel in 1253, Lantessul or Lantesull in 1259, Llan Dussyl in 1535 and Lhan Dyssul in 1600 (Wmffre, 2004: 227-228), and it is possible that it is the unidentified Llanvessil referred to in 13th century grants to Strata Florida (Pryce, 2005: 193, 198 and 217). Llandysul was clearly an important early medieval focus and James (2006) places significant emphasis on the Bishops' substantial estates on the Ceredigion bank of the middle Teifi valley arguing for "an early association of lands and churches with the cult of St. David, since it is hard to see how such a bloc of land could have been built up in the late tenth, eleventh or twelfth centuries". Llandysul is also closely associated with St David's during the 13th century when it is recorded in a Diocesan schedule book of 1259 (Wmffre, 2004: 227).

With the exception of the ancient clas church foundation at Llanbadarn whose enormous parish encompasses the entire north of the county, Llandysul was the richest church in Ceredigion in 1291 as the Taxatio (Record Commission, 1802) survey shows:

Llanbadarn Fawr	£66 13s 4d
Llandysul (landessel)	£20
Strata Florida	£16 0s 0d
Llanddewibrefi	£16 0s 0d
Penbryn	£16 0s 0d
Cardigan	£13 6s 8d
Llanarth	£6 13s 4d
Llanrhystud	£8 0s 0d
Carmarthen	£9 6s 8d
Llanbadarn Trefeglwys	£8 0s 0d
Llanwenog	£5 0s 0d
Llanfihangel-ar-arth	£5 0s 0d
Lampeter	£5 0s 0d
Cenarth	£6 13s 4d
Ystrad Aeron	£5 0s 0d
Tregaron	£6 0s 0d

Wmffre (2004: 227-228) attributes the dedication of Llandysul church to Tysulio a saint associated with Powys and relating to the brief rule of the princes of Powys in the early 12th century and the tower and font of the present church may indeed date to this period (Hughes & Jenkins, 1967). There is evidence for an earlier foundation, however, and the church in its curvilinear enclosure is traditionally associated with the 6th century saint Tysul and indeed the inscribed Velvor stone at the church is also ascribed to the 6th century (CISP, 2007). Similar status in the early medieval period is evident at Llangenau in northern Pembrokeshire. The early medieval foundation of Clydai church, named for one of the 11th century daughters of Brychan but set within a curvilinear enclosure containing three in-situ inscribed stones of 5th - 6th century date, is located close to the purported site of the Bishop House (James, 2006). James sees Clydai as an early predecessor to St David's with the association continuing into the middle ages with the later Bishop's House and Clydai church supporting a cathedral prebend.

Other early holdings of St David's within Ceredigion can be detected at Cenarth Mawr on the north bank of the Teifi, with other holdings nearby at Cenarth Fychan and Llandeilo Cilrhedyn in northern Emlyn and Cemais respectively (James, 2006). St Llawddog's church at Cenarth had earlier associations with St. Teilo and it was certainly claimed by Llandaff in a dispute (ibid.). Evidence supplied by the late 12th century writings of Gwynfardd Brycheiniog give us other pre-conquest holdings in this region forming a cluster around the lower and middle Teifi valley at Bangor Teifi, Henllan, St Dogwells, Llanychar and Maenordeifi which latter had disappeared from St David's possessions by 1326 (ibid.). Holdings to the north of this Teifi Valley estate become fewer and only Henfynwy, Llanarth and Llanddewibrefi can be dated prior to the 12th century using, again, the list in Gwynfardd's Canu Dewi (ibid.). As Evans (2004) points out, however, there are more churches dedicated to Dewi or David in the Teifi and Aeron valleys than there are around the Pembrokeshire site of St David's and there is strong evidence to suggest that St David's original clas foundation had been sited at Henfynwy, only subsequently moving to its present site in Pembrokeshire near the present Cathedral (see for eg Thomas & Howlett, 2003).

The 16th century Black Book of St David's contains a re-written survey of lands held by David Martyn during his office as Bishop in 1326 (Willis-Bund, 1902). Lands in Gower, Carmarthenshire and Pembrokeshire are detailed along with those in Ceredigion which amount to Lodrepedran, Bangor Teifi, Henllan, Adpar and Llandygwydd, along the lower Teifi valley collectively comprising the Dyffryn Teifi estate, with another block of land stretching along the Aeron valley and its littoral including Llanddewibrefi, Llanddewi Aberarth, Llan-non, Blaenpennal, Nantcwnlle and Gartheli. All the Ceredigion holdings with the exception of the newly created borough of Adpar were predominantly Welsh in tenure describing the owners of the *lecti* or gwely, literally 'bed' or 'resting place'. Other sources describe other St David's holdings. In 1222, Rhys's son, Maelgwyn agreed to restore lands to Bishop Iorwerth which included lands in Llandovery, Cenarth Mawr, Cenarth Bychan (Cilgerran), Maenordeifi, Llanerchaeron, Gartheli, Merthirgci'onant (possibly Merthyr Geler or Llangeler), Penboyr, Clydai, Fishguard, Moylegrove, Monington and the entire cwmwd of Ystlwyf (Pryce, 2005: 185). Llansulnet and Lanechren in Gwinionydd were also included and Lanechren can possibly be identified with Llanllwchaearn on the coast near New Quay with Llansulnet perhaps referring to Llandysulfed chapelry in Llandysul parish. Llandysul church had been in the patronage of Gruffudd ap Maredudd ab Owain but in 1274 he relinquished his claim and recognised Bishop Richard de Carew's rights (ibid: 207-8).

Other holdings are detailed in the Episcopal registers of the Diocese made between 1397 and 1518 (Isaacson, 1917).

The small parish of Llandyfriog is listed next to Treferen that Evans (1922: 93, n. 1) equates with Llanfair Treflygen, a tiny neighbouring parish at the heart of St David's pre-conquest holdings and therefore probably part of the original estate. (Isaacson, 1917: 801-802) Some of the churches only appear in the record for the first time in 1513 and although some of these have early histories, without other supporting evidence a medieval link with St David's cannot be definitely made. They are: Aberanell, Kellan, Bettws-Bledrus, Llanbedr, Ystrad, Lledrod, Llanina, Llangybi, Silian, Bettws, Llanwenog, Verwig, Gogof, Ciliau, Llanarth, Trefilan, Llangeitho, Llanbadarn Odwyn, Lledrod, Llanrhystud, Llanbadarn Trefeglwys, Carroge, Llanfihangel Genau'r Glyn, Rhostie and Llansantffraid.

Thus we have a reasonable pattern of St David's holdings within Ceredigion between the 10th to 16th centuries. In order to establish early patterns the map, (fig. 16 above) shows only those St David's holdings that date with certainty to the pre-13th century period and the resulting pattern captures a moment in St David's gradual expansion into northern Ceredigion. The Ceredigion core is focussed on the Dyffryn Teifi estate in the south-west with another block centred on the Aeron valley spreading out between Henfynwy on the coast and Llanddewibrefi on the lower slopes of the upland Cambrians. Outside these core areas their holdings are few and scattered and these areas are dominated by grants of land made by Rhys to Whitland, Talley and Strata Florida abbeys. The boundary between the holdings of St David's and Strata Florida in particular is significant and may reflect a more ancient boundary between the early medieval territories or dioceses of the clas churches of St David's in the south versus Llanbadarn in the north of the county. Norman incursions and subsequent reorganisation by Rhys had blurred but not totally obscured this division.

Strata Florida

Holding vast tracts of the Cambrian Mountains to the north, Strata Florida Abbey's holdings dominate the upper Teifi valley and central Ceredigion between their coastal granges at Morfa Bychan where the monks exploited the coastal fish traps at Aberarth to the collection of holdings that came to be collectively known as the Hafodwen grange neatly forming the western boundary of Mabwynion. The Strata Florida Landscape Project has begun produce evidence to suggest that the abbey's enormous upland granges representing the former clas territories of Llanbadarn, also reflected in the lack of Dewi holdings or dedications in northern Ceredigion (David Austin pers. comm.). James (2006) noted the early importance of Llanbadarn that, until re-granted to St Peter's in Gloucester by Gilbert Fitz Richard in the 12th century, was a major ecclesiastical site with the traditions of a diocese and bishop, and the *Vita Paterni* c.1200 highlights the "saint's territorial sway with aspirations to the whole of Seisyllwg".

The Strata Florida holdings have been mapped (fig. 16 above) using information supplied by Williams (1990 and 2001) who has identified most of the grange locations and Pryce (2005) who has supplied a translation and analysis of the surviving charters and inspeximi made by the Welsh rulers. All the places listed in the Strata Florida grants have been collated in table 3 (below) in the chronological order that they appear in the documentary record. Those lands that lie away from Strata Florida's immediate domain lie close to the Aeron valley and it is proposed that some of these formed the original Llanllyr estate, and the premise that this in turn was based on an early St David's estate is explored below.

Llanllyr

Llanllyr was founded by Lord Rhys around 1191-6 as one of only three religious houses for women in Wales, few when we compare this to around 150 in England, 64 in Ireland and 15 in Scotland (Cartwright, 1997: 21). The site has an early history hosting the 7th century Latin inscribed stone that records the grant of land that Ditoc son of Asaitgen gave to Modomnac, presumably a priest of the local church (Nash-Williams, 1950: 100). Although regarded as a rather modest estate (Cowley, 1977: 38), Llanllyr was accorded the status of abbey and in 1291 was valued at a modest £7 10s (Record Commission, 1802). The returns recorded in the later Valor Ecclesiasticus are complex and difficult to analyse however. The figures were supplied by the heads of the houses themselves and are sometimes regarded as unreliable and conservative. Elizabeth Baynham, the last Abbess of Llanllyr originally refused to make the valuation so it was arbitrarily assessed at £40. The Valor notes that the nunnery subsequently sent a valuation of £18 and Williams (2001: 168) suggests that these two figures were mistakenly added together to give an artificially high value of around £57 compared to average of an annual average of around £25 supplied by ministers' accounts of the few post-suppression years.

The cell of Stratflere was noted by Leland in 1532 (and is taken to mean Ystrad Fflur or Strata Florida but could also refer to Ystrad Llyr where 'llyr' is hypocoristic 'Fflur' - the name of the nunnery's mother house) along with the village of Talesarne Greene, Talsarn (Jones, 2004: 173). Outside this virtually no historical evidence concerning Llanllyr survives and as a result practically nothing is known about the extent of Rhys's original endowments.

The original holdings of Llanllyr appear to have been overwhelmed by the mother-house of Strata Florida at an early date and there is enough evidence to suggest that Llanllyr would have made an attractive target for Strata Florida. We know that Maelgwyn ap Rhys died at Llanerchaeron that lay downstream of Llanllyr (Jones, 1955a: 230), and it is possible that he was receiving treatment for illness or injury from the sisters at nearby Llanllyr, some of whom would probably have been relatives. The cloistering of nuns who were to be apart from society to avoid charges of impropriety and indecency meant that farming and trading would have taken place through intermediaries on their behalf. Llanerchaeron is detailed in a minister's account between 1298 and 1300 which describes the income of 2s 4d from burgesses "having the liberty to buy and sell in the vills of Felindre and Llanerchaeron in the Michaelmas term" (Rhys, 1936: 80). Between 1304 and 1305 these licence holders were referred to as *censarii*, residents of the hamlet paying a rent to freely buy and sell there. Censarii were known from elsewhere in south Wales and have been equated with the "burgess de vento" at Newcastle Emlyn in 1304 for example (Weeks, 2004: 14). At Aberavon in 1313, the distinction is made between 'English burgesses' and the 'still greater' numbers of censarii operating in the town indicating a that a Welsh form of tenure unfamiliar to the record makers existed alongside the ordinary burgesses (ibid.). Weeks calculates that at the close of the 13th century in Wales, the rent *per censer* would have been one penny per annum allowing the calculation of a modest 28 *censarii* or tradesmen operating in Felindre (unlocated) and Llanerchaeron in the early 14th century. A more detailed look at the *censarii* indicates that they would pay a rent for the privilege of trading in a borough or market; a practice that can be related to the demise of demesne farming but which may indicate the important trading status of Llanerchaeron, standing on the routes to the nearby ports of Aberaeron, and Aberarth. Recent archaeological excavations to the landscaped lawn in front of the 18th century Nash villa at Llanerchaeron have revealed substantial medieval settlement including a metalled road between the house and St Non's church, structures associated with significant smithing and metal working activity and domestic buildings of some status dating to around the early-mid 14th century (Evans, 2003). Llanerchaeron then represents an early church site centred on St Non's but a later settlement developed that may have been exploited by the nuns at nearby Llanllyr in order to provide a dependant hamlet and trading centre for their produce.

A significant number of grants to the powerful Strata Florida made after Rhys's death concerns lands away from the core Strata Florida holdings but which surround the Aeron valley and the immediate Llanllyr demesne and some of these may represent former, possibly original, Llanllyr holdings. Giraldus Cambrensis certainly described the Cistercians as bad neighbours, accusing Strata Florida of despoiling the nuns of their Hafodwen grange to the south of Llanllyr (Brewer, 1873: 152-153). This can be supported when it is observed that all of Rhys's original grants to Strata Florida are contained within the cymydau of Mefenydd and Penardd, with only a small, contained group of holdings within Anhuniog, well to the north of Llanllyr. Only with later grants made after Rhys's death do we see Strata Florida's possessions start to creep southwards towards Llanllyr into Mabwynion. The Cistercian order was clearly given to the "competitive accumulation" of land (Cartwright, 1997: 38), in this instance at the expense of Llanllyr Abbey.

Most of Strata Florida's northern upland granges were described within a perambulation along with a further list of other places of significance within this area. All the places are listed in table 3 for the sake of completeness though it is only the latter that fall within the area relevant to Llanllyr. These places have been mapped (in fig. 16 above) and combined with the evidence supplied by Dissolution and post-medieval surveys in order to propose the extent of the original Llanllyr estate at the close of the 12th century. A further association between the recreated Llanllyr unit and the very early Aeron valley holdings of St David's holdings has also emerged.

Giraldus's observation that Strata Florida's Hafodwen Grange originally belonged to Llanllyr suggests that a more detailed study of the grant documents for Strata Florida may be productive and these have been detailed in table 3 (cf. Pryce 2005) in order to identify the date at which new holdings first appear in the documentary record. Hafodwen is not mentioned in any of the surviving charters by Rhys ap Gruffudd and it is only after his death in 1197 that a group of holdings just to the northeast of the Hafodwen grange centre are mentioned for the first time and these are early components of what later became known as the Hafodwen estate. These holdings are described in an Inspeximus document of Edward II dated to 1320 when Rhys's son, Maelgwyn in an act dated to the 22nd January 1198, confirmed Rhys's original charter and went on to grant Marchdy Mawr and Marchdy Bychan (which probably equates with Rhys's previous grant of Marchidi in 1184 (Pryce, 2005: 173), Pencoed, Rossan, Esgair Mayntemull, Riu Annum, Blaen Pistyll and Celli-gwenyn (ibid: 183). These were essentially new grants and this is the first time that they had appeared in the documentary record. Wmffre (2003: 452, 478, 492 and 493) was able to locate four of these at: Pencoed Uchaf (SN 580 524), Tynrhos (SN 578 533), Rhiwonnen (SN 570 546) and Celli-gwenyn (SN 571 524). Marchdy Mawr and Marchdy Bychan remain unidentified as do Esgair Mayntemull and Blaen Pistyll though the other holdings form a group just to the south of the Aeron with Rhiwonnen only just under two miles south east of Llanllyr itself. It is clear then that the appropriation of Hafodwen described by Giraldus must have been a bold move, taking land immediately adjacent to Llanllyr from under the nuns' very noses. By 1198, however, this state of affairs seems to have been generally accepted, sanctioned by Maelgwyn's grant and in any case, apart from Giraldus's obvious indignation at the general behaviour of the monks, there remains no evidence of petition for return of their land by the nuns.

It remains possible then that other Strata Florida holdings in the immediate vicinity of the nunnery may also have formed part of the original Llanllyr estate. The same Inspeximus document of 1320 also records other grants by Maelgwyn of holdings that also appear for the first time. Sometime between 22nd January and the 14th December 1198 he grants Fynnaun Mebwyn 'Ffynnon Mebwyn' to Strata Florida (Pryce, 2005: 183). Known as Tir Ffinnon

Capell Ebwen *ysha* and *ucha* (upper and lower) in 1704, this holding is known today simply as Capeli farm and is located 4.5 miles south of Llanllyr (Wmffre, 2004: 407). Also attributed to Maelgwyn is the grant of Morua, and another grant of Treff Bryn, both made sometime between the 22nd January 1198 and 1202 and recorded in a charter made by Rhys Ieuanc ap Gruffudd ap Rhys in 1202 (Pryce, 2005: 183-184). Morua is generally identified as the coastal grange of Morfa Bychan north of Aberaeron (ibid.) and Tref Bryn is part of the Hafodwen estate to the south located at Pontmarchog which had been known as Trebennith in 1634 (Wmffre, 2004: 444).

After his death, Rhys's heirs struggled for power over their father's former kingdom. The attacks by Maelgwyn on Tenby castle for example damaged Rhys's accord with the Crown but this anti-Norman sentiment made Maelgwyn popular with local chroniclers who described him as the "shield and bulwark of all Wales" (Jones, 1955a: 73). The authors of the annals of the Brut Y Tywysogion based at Strata Florida would certainly have recognised Maelgwyn as their lord who had retained control over much of Ceredigion after Rhys's death, an arrangement recognised in Llywelyn's partition in 1225 between Rhys's heirs (Maund, 2000: 123). Had Maelgwyn capitulated in the demise of Llanllyr's lands as an act of revenge on the foundation made by his father whom he resented? He had sold Cardigan castle, the symbol of Norman power within the county to King John to deny his brother Gruffudd and one can only imagine that he held similar negative feelings

for his father. "Impetuous and hotheaded" (Turvey, 1988: 103), he was certainly in a strong enough political position to be able to make new grants.

Although Maelgwyn had made at least ten new grants to Strata Florida his siblings also granted other new holdings and sometime between the 14th December and 1202, again mentioned in a later charter of Rhys Ieuanc ap Gruffudd ap Rhys, the holding of Coyt Maur or 'great wood' was granted to the abbey by Maelgwyn's younger brother, Rhys Gryg ap Rhys (Pryce, 2005: 191). This has been located in the upper Aeron valley, just south of the village of Llangeitho (Owen, 1936: 501) where the southern part of the small parish of Gwynfil is dominated by farms with 'coed' place names such as Cefn Coed, Coedmawr Isaf and Coedmawr Uchaf. Nantcwnlle parish on the northern flanks of the valley opposite contained Fforest Nantgwnllau, one of the Aeron valley holdings of St David's during the 14th century (Willis-Bund, 1902). A 19th century survey describes Nantgunllo as comprising the holdings of Frongoch, Gaer, Hafod-fawr, Lon, Pantcyfyng, Pengaer, Tir-bach and Tynrhos at around 200 acres (Wmffre, 2004: 656) and hints at the former exploitation and management of the steep wooded valley slopes along the Aeron valley.

Rhys Ieuanc ap Gruffudd's charter of 1202 confirmed all of the above holdings but also included Keuen Guarthauarch and Torchwynt two more properties also making their debut appearance (Pryce, 2005: 194). Torchwynt also appears as Gudh Wynt in a confirmation

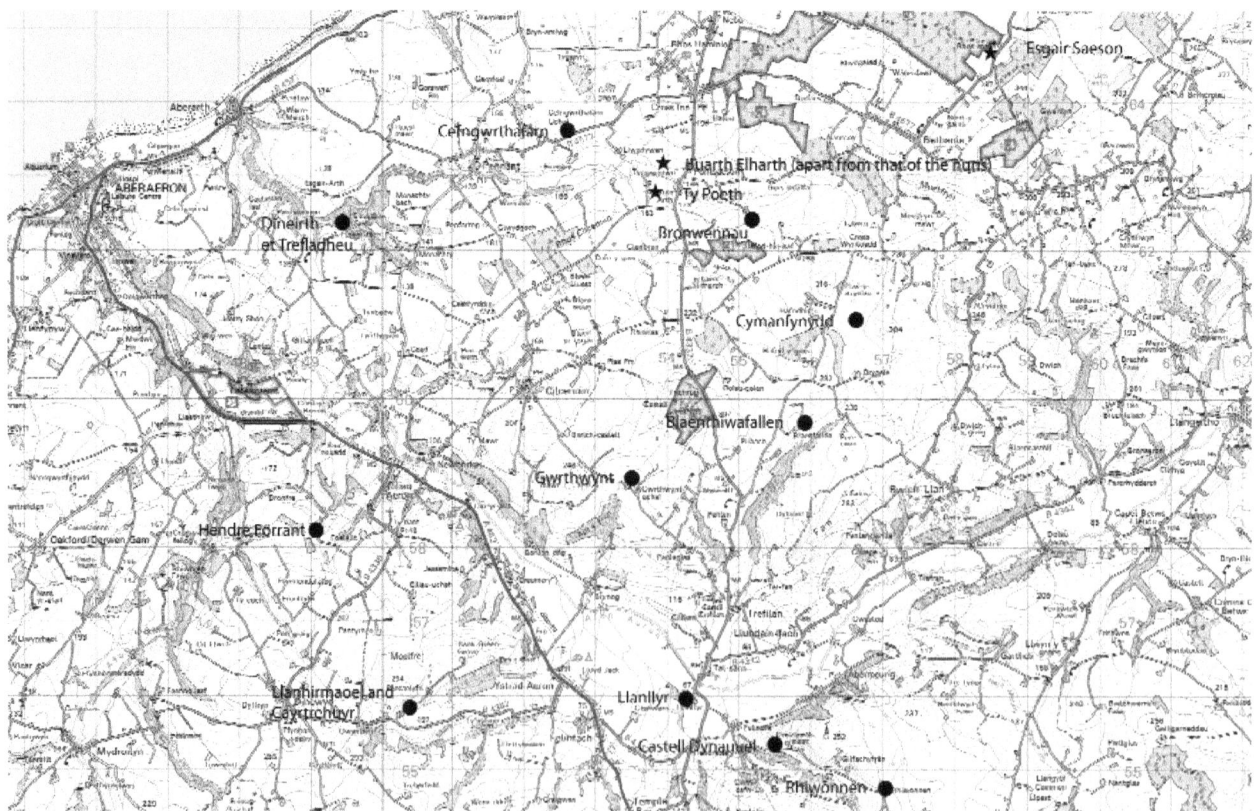

Figure 17. Holdings of Llanllyr (circles) and Strata Florida (stars) in Anhuniog. Only Ty Poeth was granted by Rhys Ap Gruffudd and Buarth Elharth is clearly defined as 'apart from the part of the nuns. Maps Crown Copyright/database right 2008. An Ordnance Survey supplied service.

made by Maelgwyn's son, Maelgwyn Fychan, sometime between the 22 January, 1198 and 1227 (ibid: 197-198) and the farm of Gwrthwynt Uchaf is situated on the edge of Trefilan parish overlooking the Aeron valley and Llanllyr from the north. The close proximity of this valley and overlooks Llanllyr to the south. Here, an Iron Age promontory fort, the 'Gaer' of Pencaerlyfri farm is set overlooking a trackway that forms part of the bwlch, 'pass' or routeway, from the valley floor at Llanllyr, uphill to the early church of Llanwyddalus at Dihewyd. This defended enclosure may also be an alias of the unidentified Caertreuhyr 'tref of the long fort', made in an earlier grant by Maelgwyn Fychan (Pryce, 2005: 191). Forming a small settlement at the head of this pass are Bwlch yr Yrfa, Bwlch Bychan and Bwlch Gwynt (1891 1st ed. OS) and the later but suggestively named Mynach (monk's) Villa. The Bwlch Dihewyd of 1716 was below the Allt y Person and became Bwlch y Person or 'the Parson's pass' (Wmffre, 2004: 416). The principal place name and farm along this prominent ridge now is Bank Green Grove, named for the gentry house of Green Grove on the valley floor below that also formed one of the principle holdings of the post-medieval Llanllyr estate (Jones, 2004: 138-140).

The Glanruallen of the Taxatio is in the vicinity of Nant Rhiwafallen, possibly at Blaenrhiwafallen neighbouring Cymanfynydd to the north (Williams, 1975: 167). Crutseyson has been identified as Pontsaeson in Anhuniog by William Rees (cited without reference in Williams, 1990: 46) and this puts us in the vicinity of Pontsaeson and it may be the half of Bronwennau "beyond Esgair to the Arth" belonging to Llanllyr. Figure 17 (above) maps these complex Anhuniog holdings and demonstrates the further investigation necessary in order to untangle the complex interchanges between Strata Florida and Llanllyr.

Date of Grant Date of document Grantor Name
1165 x 3rd Mar 1182 May 27 1285 Rhys ap Gruffudd
Hendref Kynuaunden to Buarthegre
Teifi to Hirgarth to Fflur
Lanhereth Hedegen
Pistruth to Kelly Agaret to Teifi
Lispennard
Ystrad Fflur
Keuencastell
Kellyeu Anau
Mais Glas
Blaen Pennal
Afon Ddu to Camduuor
Kennenperuet
Kellieu Wremdeuoy
Maisbre
Fennanoyr
Ritheuelin
Derspoith
Riwardh
1184 May 27 1285 Rhys ap Gruffudd
Nanneirth

Nant hi Wleidast
Guy to Hedirnaul
Blain Ystuith
Tauaologeu to Marchnant
Meuric to Teywy
Camdur Wechan to Pant Gueun
Camdur Waur to Hirwein
Cadaithin
Airon to Tref Coll
Brinnit
Nant hi Gellyhir
Vuarth Caraun
Dinas Dritwir
Castell hi Flemis
Mais Glas
Trebrith
Mais Tref Linn
Blinnbuden
Nant Llin
Llannerch hi Guinthwa
Gelly Hagharat
Tiwy
Arban
Calarwen
Elan
Groen Gwinnion
Tal Lluchint
Riscant
Llam hi Vnben
Moil Gediau
Nann Elmer
Nann Eyrin
Nann Morauc
Brithun
Abercoil
Abermethen
Stratgimurn
Kelly Camgoit
Priskieu Enniaun
Stratflur
Ryt Wendigait
Dol Waur
Lluingos
Tref hi Guydil
Finnaun Oyer
Kellieu Brinn Deuy
Esceir Perweith
Castell Flemis
Mays Glas
Cewyn hi Rit
Esceir Saisson
half of Branwennau
from Esceir to Arth
Tref Boith
from Meylyr to Arth to
Bleydud to Pant Gweun
To Marchidi et Brinn Lende et
Ardiscinkiwet

Date (start)	Date (end)	Grantor	Place	Grant date	Grantor	Date	Place
			to Aeron				fossam Bilenyt
		Rhys ap Gruffudd dies April 28 1197					Pant Gweun
							Marchdi et
22 Jan 1198	10 Nov 1320	Maelgwyn ap Rhys					Brin Hlenlde
			Nanneyrth				Ardiscinkywet
			1st appearance of Penweddig				dyke to Aberarth, Haber
			Nant hi Bleidasti				Meiller, Ayron
			Gwy to Hedernaul				Penweddig
			Estuid to Tauologeu	22Jan X 14 Dec 1198	10 Nov 1320		Maelgwyn
			Marchnant to Meuric to Teyui	ap Rhys			Marchdi Mawr
			Camdur Bechan to Pant Guin				Marchdi Bychan
			Camdur Maur				Pencoed 1st appearance
			Hirwen Chadaythuy to Ayron				Rhossan 1st appearance
			Tref Coll				Esgair Mayntemull 1st
			Brynbyt				appearance
			Nanet Herthelthli Hir				Rhiw Onnen 1st appearance
			Buarth Caraun				Blaen Pistyll 1st appearance
			Dinas Deretwir				Celli-Gwenyn 1st appearance
			Castell Flemis	22 Jan 1198 X 1202		10 Nov 1320	
			Pant Gwin	Maelgwyn ap Rhys			Ffynnon Mebwyn 1st
			Mahys Glaas				appearance
			Trebrith	22 Jan 1198 X 1202		10 Nov 1320	
			Mays Tref Linn	Maelgwyn ap Rhys			Morua 1st appearance
			Llinbuthen	22 Jan 1198 X 1202		10 Nov 1320	
			Nanthlyn	Maelgwyn ap Rhys			Treff Bryn1st appearance
			Hlannerch Chundena	1184 X July 25 1201		10 Nov 1320	
			Ghelli Angaraut	Gruffudd ap Rhys			Ystrad Ffin 1st appearance
			Thewy				Y Groen Gwennon
			Arban	14 December 1198		10 Nov 1320	
			Clarwen	Rhys Gryg ap Rhys			Marchdi Maur
			Helan				Marchdi Bichan
			Groen Gwuynnion				Penncoyth
			Tahlluchint				Rossan
			Riscant				Escheyr Mayntemull
			Lhaam her Vnpenn				Riu Annum
			Moyl Gediau				Blain Pistill
			Naant Eylmer				Kelly Gwenyn
			Naant Eyrin	14 Dec 1198 X 1202		10 Nov 1320	
			Naant Morauc	Rhys Gryg ap Rhys			Coed Mawr 1st appearance
			Brithcum	1202		10 Nov 1320	
			Abercoyl	Rhys Ieuanc ap Gruffudd			Rid Bendigeyt
			Aber Methen				Finnaun Oyr
			Stratgenmurn				Castelh Flemys
			Kellhi Cham Choyt				Ryuaunhun
			Prisheu Enniaun				Fynnaun Mebwyn
			Stratflur				Coyt Maur
			Bur Wendigeyit				Morua
			Dool Maur Hluin Gog				Dau Marchty et de Marchty
			Threef he Guidel				usque Caledan
			Fennanoir				Ardischyn Keuet
			Kelheu Brinn Deuy				Keuen Guarthauarch 1st
			Escheir Perueth				appearance
			Chastell Fleymis				Torchwynt 1st appearance
			Mays Glaas				Branwennau
			Cheuen he Reet				Morua Bichan
			Escheyr Sayson				Treff Mays
			Branwenneu				Sauan y Ky
			Tref Boyth				Y Twyarchen
			Aber Meiller				Lan Vessyl

22 Jan 1198 X 1227
Maelgwyn Fychan

Argoyt y Gwenneyn
Baucharn
Tafflogeu
Pullh Peyrant
Bothcoll
Treff Bryn (carta Mailgonis)
Stratfyn
y Groen Gwennon
Keuenoly
Aberdehonoy
Abercoyl
Lanmaude
Nant Mora et Nannheyrth
Cum Goybedauc
pasturam Cantrefmaur et
Cantref Bichan et
quatuor
cantredis de Cardigan
(especially) Penwedic
Tywy to Yruon to Pullh
Ydrach
to Trosnant..Camdour
Helenyt

10 Nov 1320

Rit Vendikeit
Henvanchloc
Brin Hop
Keuen Castelh
Lwynhoc et Dol Maur
Tref y Gwydel
Duy Tafhologeu
yr Eskeyr Perueth
Esker y Prignant
Bot Kolh
Heruyt Lwyacrh
Ritnant y Meryn
Kylmedwyn
Kefryn
Fynnaun Oyr
Brin Merlich
Kelliheu Bykeyn
Kelheu Brin Deuy
Castelh y Flemmis
Y Mais Glas
Treflyn
Dynas Drigwyr to Aeron
Tref y Cholh
Brin Yrich
Esker y Sayson
Kelhy yr Guenyn
Kelhheu Eskarat
Buarth Elharth
Fynhaun Mebvyn
Hauot wen 1st appearance
Tal Pont Gloyued 1st appearance
Hen Voryon 1st appearance
Tref y Benny 1st appearance
Meudyn 1st appearance

Castelh Dynauuel 1st appearance
Tref y Geudu 1st appearance
y morva
y Tref Poith
rhandir o Nant y fin to
Bleydud
Ardis Kyn Keued
Brin Lhaude
Marchty Bychan
Keuen Guardhauarth
Cayrteuhyr 1st appearance
Marchty Mawr
Morua Menhehith
Blay(n) Sayth
Branwenheu
Kyman Vinyd 1st appearance
Gudh Wynt 1st appearance
Dyneyrd et Tref Ladheu 1st appearance
y Morua Bychan
Tref Mays
Sauyn y Ky
Tywarchen Penwedic
Ban Caru
Lhanvessilh
Argoit y Guynweyn
Tal Pont Cuculh
Castelh Gugaun
Castelham
yr Henlhan
Nant Eyrin
Cum Gwybedauc
Nanneyrd Guy
Edernaul et Treanil Guyn
Elenyth
y Bridcum
Ryu Afwanaul
Abercoyl
y Groen Guynnion
Lhanvadauc
Ytsrat Fyn
Nant Bey
Groen Gwynnion et totam
pasturam de
Keredygyaun
except monachos Cumhyr

1280 X 25 Mar 1282
Maredudd ab Owain
(new charter, confirmation and 1st appearance
for some)

20 October 1380   Cynan ap
Ystrad Fflur

Henwynatloc
Bryn Hhop
Keuen Castell
Lloen y Goc
Dol Vaur
Tref Ygoydhell
Kylmedvywe

Trefvnwe
Strat Meuric, (except acres of
lepers.)
Dwe Tafflogev
Pull Peran
Bot Coll
Trefvaes
Yclafdy
Fennaun Oyer
Kellyev
Esgeyr Perueth
Ynys Vorgan
Castell Flemmys
Mays Glas
Dynas Drigwyr to Aeron
Dricwyr to Airon
Treflyn
Tref Ecoll
Trefigoidhel
Blain Airon
Esgeir Saisson
Riwe Anhvn
Kelliev Arwnviwe
Bryn Perueth
Vayn Teuill
Pencoet
Rossan
Kelliev Gwonyn
Kelliev Ygarad
Buarth Elath (except part of
nuns) 1st appearance
Fennaun Vebbwyn
Hauotwen
Castell Dynauel
Tref Ywedu
Tref Yberennyth
Hen Voryon
Meudyn
Morva Maur
Dev Marchdi to Kaledan
Ardiskyn Kyveth
Keuen Guarth Auarth
Blayn Saith
Bryn Llauden
half of Browennev
Keman Vynnyd
Gurthwyn
Dynerth et Trefflatheu
Morva Bichan
Allwen
Guerglaudhallt
Dro Ecapell
Pant Kendelo
Treffuaes
Sauen Eky
Tywarchen Penwedhic
Bancarv
Llanvessil
Argoit Egvenyn

Talpont Cucull
Castell Gugan
Castellan
Aberclaragh
Llechwedlloyden
Keven Ywanvrreth
Driffryn Elan
Nant Moraut
Nant Elmer
Nant Eyrin
Cumgoybedauc
Driffryn Edernawl
Treanill Gwyn
Goletyr Maen
Nan Nerth Goy
Abercoill
Brithen
By We Avanaul
Llanvadauc
Enerllyn
Talluchynt
Aberde Hony
Keuenoly
Elenyth
Nantvey et Trefflath
Pullburwe

Post-dissolution documents detail the extent of the Llanllyr estate which by the late 16th century had come into the hands of the powerful Lloyds of Castell Hywel in Llandysul parish (Jones, 2004: 174). An inquisitions post-mortem of Morgan Lloyd in 1605 gave a detailed description of the estate as it emerged in the early post medieval period with land in Ciliau Aeron, Ystrad, Dihewyd, Llanwnnen, Trefilan, Llanarth and Lampeter. Sixty acres of arable and 40 acres of meadow in Llanbadarn Trefeglwys with property in Nantcwnlle and Cilcennin may have been the scant remnants of their original Anhuniog properties. The estate continued to contract into the 17th century when it passed to John Lewes of Llysnewydd but several of the valuable valley floor holdings had emerged as important gentry properties in their own right. Lewes's third son married Mary Jane of the neighbouring Brynog estate and Colonel John Lewes (1860-1931) married Louisa Hext and their home at Llanerchaeron, downstream from Llanllyr on the Aeron, became one of the principal gentry estates of southern Ceredigion.

Whitland and Talley

Dominating the central Teifi valley are the holdings of both Whitland and Talley abbeys (fig. 16 above). The relationship between the Whitland and Talley granges is a complex one however. Some of the central Teifi valley estates were apparently new grants to Whitland added by Lord Rhys between 1189 and 1195: Penffos, Penfai, Cefnllechclawdd, Darren-Fawr, Fadfa, Blaenbedw Fawr, Blaensaith, Esgairsaith, the larger holdings of Maesycrugiau, Caerwedros, Manorforion, Manor Crug-

Whil, Rhuddlan Deifi and Tir Newydd, plus a carucate of land at Llanborth (Pryce, 2005: 175-177). But the church, or llan(borth) of St Michael's had already been previously granted by Rhys to Talley Abbey sometime between 1180 and 1197 (ibid: 171). Similarly, Rhys's new grants of Blaensaith and Esgairsaith, again to Whitland Abbey sometime between 1189 and 1195, appear to be re-granted by Maelgwyn Fychan ap Maelgwyn sometime after Rhys's death between 1198 and 1227 but this time to Strata Florida Abbey. On the face of it, these are straightforward regrants reflecting shifting alliances and undoubtedly complex tenurial claims in the aftermath of the 12th and 13th centuries.

There is further evidence for dispute and conflict over the patronage of other granges. Between 1193 and 1202 the Cistercian Abbot Peter of Whitland attempted to convert the Premonstratensians of Talley Abbey, managing to influence the Abbot and canons of the house (Cowley, 1977: 74-5). This resulted in disputes over the ownership of some of Talley's granges and after an appeal in Rome most of the lands were restored to Talley save the rich estate at Rhuddlan Teifi that was retained by Whitland in exchange for an unknown holding. Accusation and grievance were common as we have seen with Giraldus's condemnation of the appropriation of Llanllyr's estates.

Although Rhys was to become the foremost patron of Strata Florida, Talley Abbey had been actually founded by him and benefited from generous grants of land. Rhys's eldest son, Gruffudd had married Matilda daughter of William de Breos, also an early benefactor of Talley (Cowley, 1977: 37, n. 108). The Premonstratensian order was an austere one with a consequently cheap outlay, although it is also possible that the foundation was an attempt at spiritual reparation after Rhys's wife had been able to dissuade him not to take the cross offered by Baldwin as part of his Crusade recruitment (ibid: 36, n. 107).

All the contemporary medieval evidence relating to the Talley grants come from a single document; an Inspeximus of Edward II in 1324. The earliest grant was made by Rhys sometime after 1180 where he grants St Michael's church in Penbryn on the coast which was described in a perambulation (Pryce, 2005: 171). After this the Rhysian lineage including Rhys Gryg ap Rhys (ibid: 189), Maredudd ap Owain ap Gruffudd (ibid: 203) and Rhys Fychan ap Rhys Mechyll (ibid: 228) are recorded as confirming the original grants with the addition of a variety of new holdings. Rhys Gryg confirms a number of holdings in Carmarthenshire but Ceredigion's holdings only appear for the first time with Maredudd ap Owain ap Gruffudd which dates to between 1235 and 1265. He lists Mayrdreui Guin nouit Maerdref Gwinionydd at Faerdre near Llandysul (for identification of the place names see Evans, 1878: 60-72 and see further analysis in chapter five below), *Brin Yron* 'Brynaeron', *Rit Ywein* 'Rhydowen', *Nant Kediuor* 'Nant Cadifor' and *Kynbit Ysalld* all contained within a perambulation (Pryce, 2005). He also adds the holding of *Moylehaedauc* 'Moelhedog', *Potthoni* 'Aberporth' and the granges of Gwyddgrug and Brechfa in Carmarthenshire. Although these have appeared for the first time, it appears to be a confirmation of earlier grants made by "his great-grandfather Rhys the Great, his grandfather Rhys Gryg, his uncles his cousins or kin or nobles" (ibid: 203).

Despite these complexities of ownership, the units of land themselves appear to have a longevity. Many of these central Teifi valley holdings are described by perambulations that use landscape features and other, eponymously-named lands in a formula familiar from early Saxon charters suggesting that written grants may have replaced earlier oral testimonies. The swathe of Whitland and Talley grants across the central portion of the Teifi valley to the coast represents land that would have become available to Rhys after the hiatus of war and perhaps represented former secular or royal estates. Mapping Rhys's grants to Talley (in fig. 16 above) and including the former grange of Rhuddlan Teifi it is evident that the Premonstratensian house originally held the eastern portion of Gwinionydd upstream of Llandysul. These grants were significant ones and the motives of Rhys and the former royal status of this central Teifi area will be discussed in chapter five below. Before the appropriation of Talley's important Rhuddlan Teifi estate, Whitland's holdings had been confined to a loose scattering along the southern bank of the Teifi in Pembrokeshire and Carmarthenshire but in Ceredigion remained largely confined to the western portion of Cwmwd Caerwedros.

Discussion

The mapping of these princely grants along with the estates of the Bishops of St David's during the 12th and 13th centuries clearly indicates the cwmwd as the primary territorial framework at this regional level. The cymydau are clearly comprised of smaller units however. Some of these exist simply as place names in the grants and records but others are described with more detailed perambulations and an analysis of Talley's Gwinionydd holdings in particular will aid the identification of the maenor and tref in chapter five.

The estates of St David's dominate the lower Teifi valley and have been shown to have strong early medieval foundations. Until the 9th to 10th century, St David's sphere of influence is reflected in their Aeron and Teifi estates with a significant focus at Henfynyw. These lands stretched along the Aeron valley inland as far as Llanddewibrefi and it is this that may have formed the geographical basis for Rhys's foundation grants to Llanllyr. The rising supremacy of St David's and Llandaff had begun to eclipse Llanbadarn in the north of the county, a process accelerated by the gift of Llanbadarn to an English house. In a similar way, the newly created administrative seat at Cardigan eclipsed activity at the former secular, elite holdings centred around the central Teifi valley and, as an act of consolidation, Rhys granted these lands to Talley Abbey. At the same time he granted a vast swathe of central and upland Ceredigion to Strata Florida that represented the former estates of the ancient diocese of Llanbadarn.

A long history of female association predates monastic Llanllyr. Significant is the unidentified Dau Marchty, the 'two women's houses' granted to Strata Florida by Rhys and appearing in a charter of 1184 (Pryce, 2005: 172). This remains unlocated but a perambulation describes a dyke between Marchdy and the vill of Ardiscinkiwet, also unlocated, but which had been granted to the monks by Rhys's wife Gwenllian (ibid.). Owain Gwynedd (d. 1170) had also provided for his wife Angharad by way of a dower with the entire cwmwd of Anhuniog (Beverley Smith, 1983) and this is probably the Kelly Agaret that first appears in Rhys's grant to Strata Florida made sometime between 1165 and 3rd March 1182 (ibid: 167). This is only part of an early pattern of early female influence focussing on female dedications in Anhuniog and the Aeron valley in particular and complementing the Dewi cult and a swathe of other female dedications can be identified along the Aeron catchment; Llansantffraid, dedicated to Brigit or Ffraid, Ina, daughter of Ceredig at Llanina, Hilary or Ilar near Trefilan, St Non's at Llan-non and again at Llanerchaeron adjacent to Llanllyr in the lower Aeron valley and Gwynlle, Leucu and Gwenfyl in the upper Aeron. The links between St Non and St David in the histories may be a medieval attempt to explain the links between their lands and settlement here, and James (2006: 41) also makes the link between the Irish Bridget or Bride and the cult of David in Pembrokeshire. Links between the Llanerchaeron estate and St David's are also evidenced when St Non's was appropriated to Llanddewibrefi in the 13th century by Bishop Bek as part of his collegiate foundation (James, 2006: 38). The original and core holdings of the Llanllyr estate therefore correspond to the early Aeron valley St David's holdings. This discrete estate or group of estates is exclusively defined by the cymydau of Anhuniog and Mabwynion and is identifiable with the early female/David saint's cults. Rhys was able to gift this entire holding and in so doing he was able to maintain a link to its former identity by granting it to the women's house at Llanllyr.

This chapter has emphasised the politically intelligent

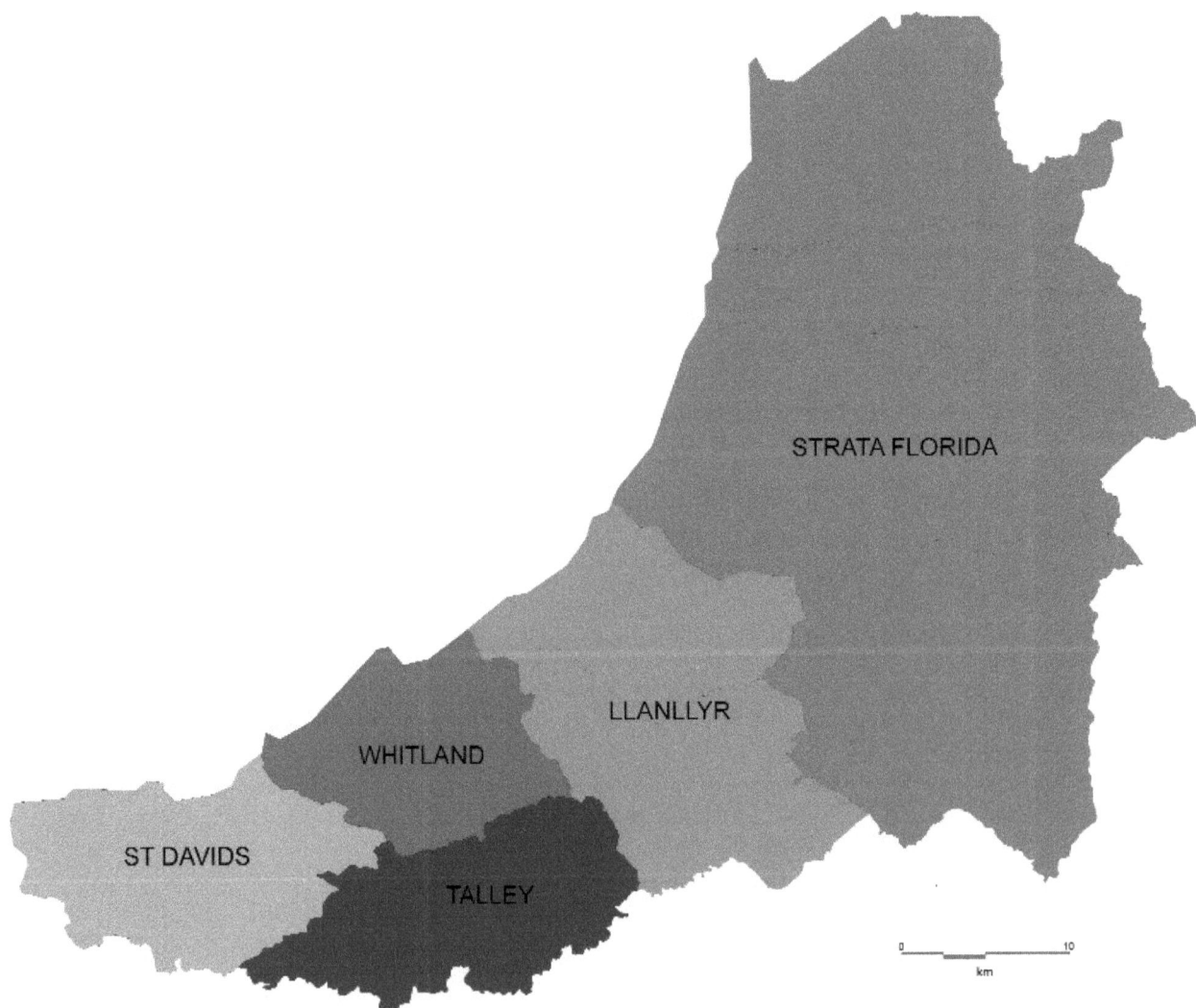

Figure 18. Rhys's vision for Ceredigion was based on the allotment of cymydau to various monastic lordships in order to consolidate and modernise his kingdom.

nature of Rhys's lordship, a factor that undoubtedly contributed to his relatively peaceful reign for over 30 years. The cwmwd was the dominant unit of territorial administration and he used it as the framework for donations of estates to monastic houses but based on the framework of smaller estate sub-units contained therein. The links to earlier holdings of St David's and Llanbadarn indicates the continuity of these estates that survived the turmoil of the earlier 11th century.

Rhys's reign was groundbreaking in many ways, being the first recorded ruler to mimic the Norman construction of castles in stone and the first Welsh ruler to found his own monastic institutions, but by providing them with ancient Welsh estates and by staffing them with Welsh ministers he found a new way to assert their Welsh identity. It has been argued that the popularity of European monasticism by Welsh rulers was as a rejection of anything 'English' but the majority of Cistercian foundations in Wales were Norman ones originally and in any case the earliest abbots of Whitland for example were Welsh (Pryce, 2007) and political motivation beyond the mere "symbolic capital" described by Bourdieu (1991: 112-121) is evident. Demonstrative of this is Rhys's foundation of the nunnery at Llanllyr which he endowed with some of the best estates in the county. Fossilised in this 12th century landscape is an earlier pattern of ownership that highlights the link with the great upland granges of Strata Florida and the former clas estate of Llanbadarn (D. Austin pers. comm.).

In the aftermath of Norman incursion during the early 12th century, St David's were dispossessed of many of their estates and evidence has been outlined that indicates that they were repatriated with some of their property. The primacy of Llandysul as an important Bishop house of (not in) Dyfed highlights the longevity of their links to the Teifi valley. What has also emerged are the original intentions underlying Rhys's grants. Figure 18 shows the trend of ownership that Rhys was aiming for and largely achieved. The political and cultural influence of the pre-conquest Welsh clasau of St David's and Llanbadarn must have been present in Rhys's mind and by granting estates to European monastic houses he was deferring to the church, albeit a new one. However, his warring neighbours were a potential threat and cause for concern, Gwynedd to the north and Normans to the south. But the in-fighting that developed amongst his own sons was a greater threat close to home and by granting vast swathes of their inheritance to monastic houses he may have been attempting to neutralise the military potential of these estatese central Teifi valley, particularly Gwinionydd has emerged as a focus of particular importance with half of the cwmwd belonging to St David's and the eastern half of significant value to be appropriated by powerful Whitland. These intricacies of ownership and sub-division were acted out along smaller territorial units and the next chapter examines the survival of these in more detail.

FIVE: RECONSTRUCTING MEDIEVAL GWINIONYDD

Introduction

This chapter analyses the evidence for survival of the maenor and the tref in the present landscape. Key to this analysis is the evidence supplied by monastic granges and estates and the proposition that these holdings represent a continuity of territorial geography will be examined. Although the maenor as an administrative unit had disappeared by the 12th century in Ceredigion, two previously unidentified examples from neighbouring areas will be considered in order to form a framework for investigations north of the Teifi. Murphy (2007b) had speculated on the pre-Norman origins of Manordeifi parish which borders the southern banks of the lower Teifi in Pembrokeshire and place name elements within Manordeifi have highlighted the parish's former significance and possible maenor status. Some ten miles upstream, on the southern flanks of the Teifi, this time in Carmarthenshire, the extent of Llangeler parish combined with post-medieval rentals allowed Williams (1990) to reconstruct one of Whitland Abbey's former granges known as Manorforion (see fig. 19 below for the location of places mentioned in chapter five). A more detailed analysis here has allowed a reconstruction of the former maenor upon which the later monastic estate was based. These analyses have allowed the identification for the first time of a pre-conquest maenor within Ceredigion at Rhuddlan Teifi, a territory which formed the basis for a grant to Talley Abbey by Rhys. The political and cultural significance of this location becomes even more evident when historical evidence pointing to its former royal status is examined and geophysical survey has identified the site of a possible pre-conquest llys enclosure.

The constituent unit of the maenor, the tref, is much more readily identifiable in the present landscape and in some instances survives into the 19th century as the chapelry served by a chapel of ease. These are analysed in detail for Llandysul parish and in particular, historical evidence has Vallowed the medieval antecedent of the modest gentry estate at Llanfair to be reconstructed. Formerly a grange of the Premonstratensian abbey at Talley the boundaries of the original grant are recreated using a detailed perambulation. A strong correlation between Llanfair's medieval extent and the 19th century chapelry bearing the same name is noted and the premise that other chapelry units may have also their origins in the medieval tref is explored, allowing the tref units for the whole of Gwinionydd to be proposed. A more detailed examination of Llanfair's relationship to the neighbouring chapelry of Maerdref has clarified the political status of this central Teifi valley area.

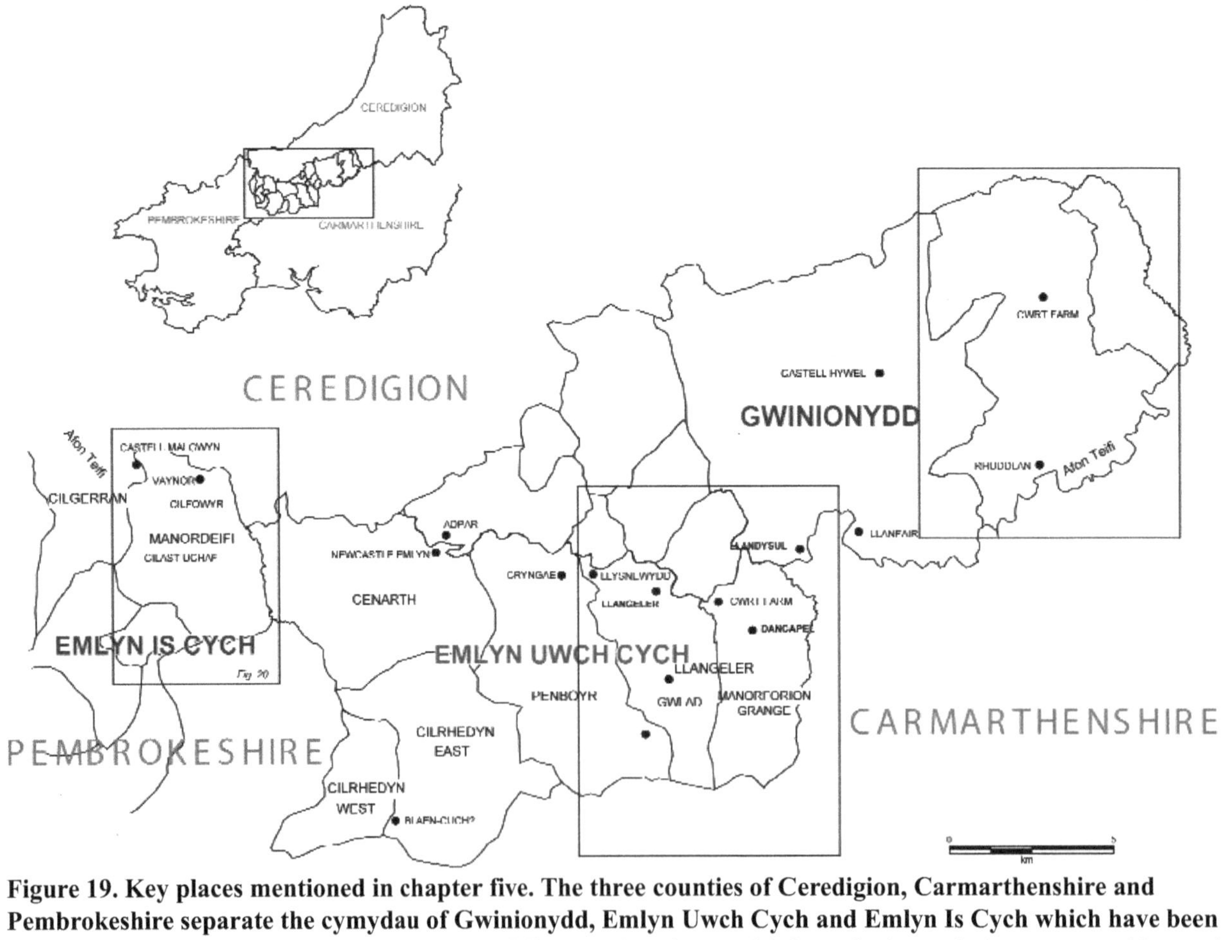

Figure 19. Key places mentioned in chapter five. The three counties of Ceredigion, Carmarthenshire and Pembrokeshire separate the cymydau of Gwinionydd, Emlyn Uwch Cych and Emlyn Is Cych which have been reconstructed by Rees (1951) and Richards (1969), largely using parish boundaries and place name evidence. As will be demonstrated, many of the parish units comprise a number of chapelries and these will be related to the medieval tref or township.

Maenor Teifi

The northernmost extent of Norman control around 1100 saw the establishment of Cilgerran castle in the northern tip of Pembrokeshire. The subsequent carving of cwmwd Emlyn in two along the line of the Afon Cych created the new border between the counties of Pembrokeshire and Carmarthenshire in the east. Manordeifi parish (fig. 20) sits on this border and is the focus for a particular concentration of significant gentry estate centres at Pentre, Clynfyw, Ffynone, Fforest, Rhosygilwen, Cilgwyn and Cilwendeg. Castell Malgwyn mansion sits just inside neighbouring Cilgerran parish but its home farm and estate centre are situated inside Manordeifi. This is neighboured by St David's church and Vaynor farm, from 'maenor' and taken together this valley floor group indicates a site of significant pre-Norman status.

Figure 20. Manordeifi parish and other places mentioned in the text (see fig. 19 above for location).

Further south and uphill along the Morgenau valley stands the site of a former medieval chapel of ease at Cilfowyr (PRN 304131) and further to the southwest the gwestfa payment is preserved in Westfa Kylvaur which was recorded in 1500 (Charles, 1992 : 386). Gwestva Kilast also survives at Cilast Uchaf which formed the focus for a group of farms strung along the Morgenau valley which included Cilast Isaf and Penalltyfelin (Jones, 1996a: 30). It is probable that Manordeifi parish was once the core of a larger pre-conquest maenor and that Emlyn Is Cych became the Lordship of Cilgerran perhaps representing extent of the former maenor.

Maenor Forion

The fracture of the cwmwd along the lines of their constituent units can be further studied at Llangeler parish. Situated on the southern, Carmarthenshire bank of the Teifi opposite Llandysul, Llangeler is within the eastern half of

Cantref Emlyn; cwmwd Emlyn Uwch Cych. Manorforion (fig. 21) comprised a grange of Whitland abbey and its boundaries are preserved in the western 'hamlet' of the parish called Grange; the eastern hamlet being known as *Gwlad* or 'countryside' (Williams, 2001: 204). The Cistercian house of Whitland had been originally founded with the assistance of grants by John of Torrington, with later gifts by Hywel Sais (Pryce, 2005: 175). Rhys ap Gruffudd subsequently became its most important patron and between 1189 and 1195 he confirmed the original grants and made numerous new ones, Manorforion being one of these. These new lands were outside of Torrington's lordship and had been held by Rhys since 1165 so it is possible that he may already have granted some of these holdings at an earlier date or that he may have been confirming an earlier, unrecorded donation of land previously been held by the sons of Maredudd of Cilrhedyn (Evans, 1922: 77).

The monastic grange of Manorforion comprises the eastern half of Llangeler parish and its extent has been described by Williams (2001: 204, fig. 21). The element forion from Manorforion is a now-obsolete deriving from fawr meaning largest, greatest or superior and is an indication of the former political importance of the estate which has hitherto remained unexplored. Today the area comprises a dispersed landscape of farms improved in the 18th and 19th centuries and these are loosely dotted within grazing land gently rising to the late-enclosed uplands to the south. The present village of Pentrecwrt, 'village of the court' is just outside the northern boundary of the former grange though it developed largely during the late post-medieval period in order to service the growing woollen industry of the 18th and 19th centuries. Upstream from Pentrecwrt and within the grange boundary, former monastic activity is demonstrated at the large modern farm of Tanycoed which is named in an estate map dated to 1796 as Dan Coed Mynach, 'below the monk's wood'. Between this and the village, and also within the grange's boundary, lies Cwrt farm. Known as Court Manorvorion sometime before 1768, it was described as the homestead of Harry Evan and around the same time, a Rees Prydh of Glanrhyd in Court Manorvorion had a son, Tomos Prydh who married Elizabeth Thomas, also of Court Manorvorion (Carmarthen, Carmarthenshire Record Office, MS I:31 [Golden Grove Books]). Lhuyd (1909-11) noted at the turn of the 18th century that the Abbot (of Whitland) had "a place of residence for diversion in the summer time" at Cwrt farm which probably represented the administrative focus of the monastic grange. A large enclosure surrounding Cwrt farm is named Parc-y-Brenin, the 'King's Park', possibly referring to the reversion to the Crown of the estate after the dissolution or may even be a remnant of the estate's pre-conquest royal status. Cwrt farm is a currently a modest 18th to 19th century farmhouse but is still connected to the farms of Llwynffynnon Uchaf, Llwynffynnon Isaf and Dancapel by a series of sunken trackways and it is along this trackway that a spring is described by the HER as one of the possible locations of

Figure 21. Eastern Emlyn Uwch Cych (see fig. 19 above for location). The monastic grange of Manorforion was carved from the larger Maenor Forion (shaded) and granted to Whitland Abbey in the late 12th century.

holy Ffynnon Fair, St Mary's Well (PRN 32241).

Just northeast of Cwrt farm, corn and fulling mills formerly sat within a loop of the Teifi where the level floodplain is known as Ddol Abbas, 'Abbot's meadow'. Oats, wheat and corn provided the staple arable crops and were processed at the grange's mills (Williams, 1990: 67). Murphy (2007a) suggests that the presence of medieval woollen mills here may be an early precursor to the thriving post-medieval woollen industry and certainly the agricultural character of

the medieval grange was defined by wool production with sheep grazing the unenclosed uplands above Dancapel farm at 200 metres. Cheese was also produced in some quantity and cattle would also have accompanied sheep in the uplands when they were not required to graze and manure the dolau or valley meadows after cutting. The grange was staffed by lay brothers alongside secular occupants whose pedigrees describe the families of Maynorvoreen in 1214 and Maynorvoreon in 1447 (Jones, 1987: 52) while the roll of the Court of Emlyn in 1303 records that "brother

56

Aygloth" of Maynovoryon withdrew a complaint against Madoc ap Madrun who also appears to have been a brother of the grange (Evans, 1922: 83).

The estate's agricultural focus appears to have been at Dancapel farm (fig. 23) which, adjacent to the only church building within the grange, Capel Mair or 'St Mary's chapel' is suggested as a possible former grange nucleus by Williams (2001: 204). Although Williams does not elaborate on this proposition there is sufficient evidence to suggest the considerable status and antiquity of this location which also comprises Pencastell motte and bailey castle some 200 metres south of the church.

Figure 22. Manorforion grange (see fig. 21 above for location). The view from Dancapel Farm overlooking Pentrecwrt and Cwrt Farm on the floor of the Teifi Valley.

Pencastell motte is just one of a string of medieval fortifications along the central Teifi that bears out the turbulent history during the 12th century. The fortified site commands a view of the Teifi valley approach from the east, whilst guarding the significant upland bwlch, or pass connecting the central Teifi valley with the Tywi valley and, eventually, Carmarthen. This north-south upland route is reflected in the late village settlement at Bancyffordd, which translates as 'bank road', and upland routes of this type are similar to those found to the north of the Teifi where they connect the central Teifi valley with its hinterland and the coast. Pencastell motte is described by Lhuyd (1909-11: 77) at the beginning of the 1700s as "a heap of earth of about 100ft in diameter and 30ft high ye entrenchment 10ft deep & as many over, The outworks are defaced & very near made level by frequent ploweings". Lloyd (1935: 271) remarks that "the bailey is frequently absent from Wales, but in some cases it has been obliterated by the plough; this has happened at Llangeler" and the 18th century estate map clearly indicates the enclosure that represents the former bailey and this can be traced today as a slight linear rise in ground levels. The date and nationality of the builders of many of the defended earthworks in this area is poorly understood although we know for example that Maelgwyn ap Rhys built the impressive motte at Trefilan very late in 1236 reflecting the renewed Norman threat in the area (Jones, 1955a). The existence of

Pencastell motte on a monastic grange implies that the motte predated the granting of the holding to Whitland in the late 12th century. Emlyn Uwch Cych had remained in Welsh possession until the late 13th century but skirmishes across this part of the border were common. In 1145 Gilbert de Clare, penetrated deep into Deheubarth and may have constructed the motte and bailey known as Castell Mabudrud at nearby Pencader. In 1159 Rhys ap Gruffudd attempted to take Carmarthen Castle and in 1162 he took Llandovery. Henry II retaliated and drove Rhys into the uplands where a battle took place at Cefn Rhestr Main, the 'ridge of the stone row'. Dubé (pers. comm..) places the scene of this battle at an earthwork known as Caer Rhys, situated on the uplands roughly halfway between Pencader and Pencastell. He refers to the nearby prehistoric standing stones and cairns that also retain the place name Blaennantrhys and describes the defences as 'thrown up in a hurry'. In fact, Caer Rhys is a classic inland promontory fort, of a type commonly dating to the Iron Age with an earthen ditch and bank securing the neck of a steep isthmus (PRN 303803). Common in west Wales there is insufficient evidence to assess the degree of reuse of these features in the medieval period although the possibility remains. More likely is that Rhys retreated to Pencastell just over a mile distant where a defensive motte had already been constructed, perhaps by the Welsh lord, Maredudd of Cilrhedyn.

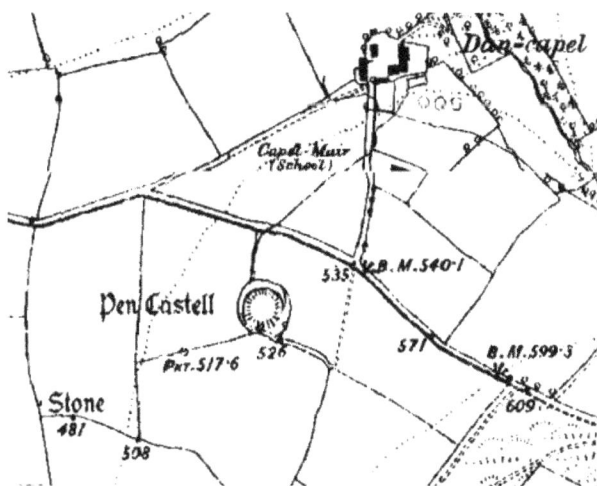

Figure 23. The Dancapel 'complex' acted as agricultural management centre of the monastic grange but a 7th century Latin and ogham inscription indicates a significant pre-conquest religious foundation (see fig. 21 above for location). © Crown Copyright and Landmark Information Group Limited 2008. All rights reserved 1891.

It was, however, to the Norman-built Castell Mabudrud that Henry II subsequently came in 1163 to receive his homage from Rhys. This location was significant, chosen perhaps in order to reinforce Pencader as a Norman counter to the obvious rival status of Welsh-held lands nearby and to the west, particularly the important centre at Manorforion which reflects the importance of this estate prior to the monastic activity. The political and strategic significance of Manorforion is also reflected in earlier periods. The north-south routeway through Bancyffordd is marked by a significant concentration of late prehistoric monuments (see fig. 21 above), including a Neolithic chambered tomb, a rare monument in this non-coastal location (PRN 303800), a concentration of elaborate Bronze Age mounds and cairns (eg PRNs 402918, 303796 and 402919), some used as parish boundary markers and several late Neolithic and Early Bronze Age standing stones (eg PRN 303797), including a small cluster around the Dancapel complex (eg PRN 303799). A linear earthen dyke, Bwlch Clawdd runs north-south along part of the western boundary of the parish. Features of this type are poorly understood in this area but recent dating evidence from similar features in Powys known as short dykes have provided dates ranging between the early 5th and late 8th century AD where at least one, Clawdd Mawr, is thought to have been constructed as the boundary marker of Cantref Mechain sometime between 630-710 cal. AD (Hankinson & Caseldine, 2006: 266-267).

Other evidence for significant pre-monastic activity exists at Capel Mair. The present chapel was built in 1899 on a new parcel of land carved out of the field in which it currently sits. The construction included a generous donation of £100 from Dancapel farm, a considerable sum for a tenant farm when this area formed part of the Llysnewydd estate in the 18th century (Rhys, 1907). An estate map for Dancapel dated 1796 describes the enclosure adjacent to the church as *Hen Capel & Fynwent*, 'former chapel and cemetery' indicating the former location of the medieval graveyard enclosure. This enclosure now contains the early 20th century Sunday school building which is aligned east-west perhaps occupying the footprint of the medieval chapel building. The dedication to Mary suggests a Cistercian grange chapel built sometime after the late 12th century grant but there is further evidence to suggest that this church replaced a much earlier, pre-conquest religious foundation. The western part of its enclosure forming the access track to Dancapel curves around it and the close proximity of the farm to the graveyard is highlighted by the discovery of "burials found by cowshed and in field to the south" (Williams, 1990: 67). The date of this event remains unclear but must refer to the field to the immediate south east of the farmyard directly adjacent to the graveyard where a leat supplying water to a small reservoir above the yard was constructed, probably during the late 18th century when the yard and house were also 'gentrified'. The spring supplying water to the farm and the chapel lies some 200 metres upslope and is one of several springs along this contour but the proximity suggests that this is in fact the site of the unlocated holy well of Ffynnon Fair. Thomas (1971: 30-32) has suggested that large, circular or sub-circular churchyards are an indicator of early sites and indicators of a larger enclosure can be seen at Capel Mair in the two fields to the west of the original chapel enclosure named, ca wrth cefen fwnwent, 'field by the rear of the cemetery' and ca fwnwent, simply 'cemetery field'. The church itself contains a simple 'font' of Norman date that resembles a rough, plain holy water stoup similar to

examples known from Llangelynin and St. Non's chapel at St David's. More significantly, the church also houses the important 7th century Deccabar stone (fig. 24) inscribed with Latin and ogham which is said to have stood in the (old) churchyard c.1828 (Rhys, 1907: 295). Thomas (1994a: 75) records the inscription as DECABARBALOM FILIUS BROCAGNI, "Deccabar, son of Broking" (lies here) and links with Brecon have been made where there is an unusual inland cluster of ogham inscriptions. This inscription is one of 19 known inscriptions within Carmarthenshire and are of a type proliferate along the coastal areas of south and south west Wales, especially Pembrokeshire which contains over 30 known inscriptions compared to only 12 for Ceredigion (CISP, 2007). The antiquity of the churches in this region is poorly understood but is paramount to developing an understanding of the medieval landscape. The church of St Tysul at Llandysul contains early inscribed stones and is a 'classic' early llan site albeit truncated on the north by the Teifi. Set within a curvilinear enclosure, this is one of the primary Christian sites which also contains the ubiquitous llan prefix derived from the Latin *lann landa* or *lant* from which the English word land also derives (Roberts, 1992).

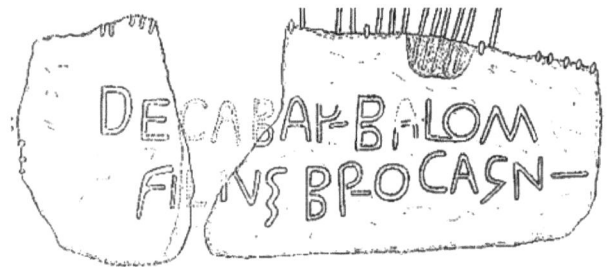

Figure 24. The Deccabar stone, Capel Mair, Llangeler (Macalister, 1945). Many of these 'late medieval' chapels demonstrate evidence of earlier activity.

Seen in per*llan* 'orchard' and yd*lan* 'rickyard', the prefix in ecclesiastical association originated in a preaching site with monastic functions and eventually came to describe the enclosed cemetery which later developed church buildings (Thomas, 1994a: 101). These enclosures are one of the oldest extant features in our landscape and the "uinndilantquendi" mentioned by Rhigyfarch in the 11th century are postulated to date to a 6th century foundation (ibid: 103). These llanau often share similarities with secular enclosures, for example the raths of Pembrokeshire. Many more 'prehistoric' curvilinear enclosures are discovered every year by aerial photography and some must be associated with medieval activity perhaps reusing an earlier site by enclosing with banks in order to fortify like the Cornish ker or caer, 'fort' of Wales (ibid: 318).

Llangeler parish church was known as the Ecclesia de Martir Keler or Merthyr Celer in 1291 when it was valued at £4.13.4 (Record Commission, 1802). Its outer circular enclosure is evident on the 1st edition OS (fig. 25) and is indicative of its pre-conquest origins. Ann Preston-Jones (1992: 118-119) has also noted the circularity of early church sites in Cornwall and has linked this to the possible reuse of rounds. Elsewhere a radiocarbon date at Capel Maelog (known as Landemaylon in 1291) has given a date of cal. AD 776-1020 (CAR-936, 1100+60bp) for the circular enclosure bank (James, 1992: 98). Merthyr meaning martyr, in the context of ecclesiastical establishment is a term with early medieval associations often indicating the presence of the grave of a saint which may well be in a satellite chapel building known as a capel-y-bedd or saint's chapel (Thomas, 1971: 89). At Llangeler, this may have been situated 150 metres to the northeast of the churchyard where a well chapel was sited. This healing well attracted those seeking cures and a lively fair ensued during the middle ages. Llangeler church had also been gifted to Whitland Abbey, the grant of which was confirmed by King John between 1199 and 1216 (Murphy, 2007a). Thus we have in Llangeler parish two early church sites; Merthyr Celer serving the western gwlad and those travelling east-west along the Teifi valley, and Capel Mair or its predecessor serving the eastern grange and those travelling the north-south route to the early church at Llanpumsaint on the other side of the upland ridge, reminiscent of James's (2006) liminally-placed trans-montane church sites.

Sufficient evidence exists therefore regarding the antiquity and significance of Manorforion to suggest that it was a pre-conquest maenor, perhaps the royal maenor of Emlyn Uwch Cych and probably comprising the entire parish of Llangeler. It will be referred to as Maenor Forion in order to distinguish it from the 12th century monastic Manorforion which preserved the earlier designation. Likely to have been based on the llys and maerdref model, Llysnewydd, 'New Court' outside the grange boundaries south of Henllan only emerged into the late medieval period as part of the substantial holdings of the Lewis family who had acquired Manorforion during the 17th century. It essentially replaced the earlier secular caput at Cwrt farm that would have been the secular administrative focus or llys of the Maenor and would have been served by a demesne settlement or tref, administered by the reeve or maer. The maerdref may have been have centred on the important Dancapel-Pencastell-Capel Mair complex that would administer the extensive tir bwrdd or demesne grazing and arable areas. In adjacent Gwlad, Llangeler church would have formed the nucleus for tir corddlan or nucleated settlement which had small, shared quillets, lleiniau or garden plots, gerddi, of the type described by Jones (1972b: 338), the vestiges of which can be seen in the field and garden boundaries in fig. 25). On rising land to the south of this, a loose group of holdings or tyddynod girdled the upland common land known as Mynydd Llangeler, Llangeler Mountain (PRN 13776); Hendre 'old settlement', Mountain Hall, Penyrallt Mansion and Hengae 'old enclosure' farm (fig. 21 above).

However, there is other evidence that Manorforion was in fact liable for gwestfa payments which, as a bond maenor (and a monastic grange), should have been exempt. An

extent dated to 1328 records that 6½ gwestfau were to be rendered on cwmwd Emlyn Uwch Cych but without actually identifying the individual gwestfau districts by name. Evans (1922: 99, n. 2) speculated that the constituent parishes of Emlyn Uwch Cych, Llangeler (including Manorforion), Penboyr and Cenarth may have related roughly to the former gwestfau areas and would therefore have paid two gwestfau each with the half-parish of East Cilrhedyn paying only half. This supposition led Evans (ibid.) to propose that -orion from Manorforion derived from wyrion, the 'descendants of', a phrase familiar from descriptions of individual holding land by gwely tenure and one liable to gwestfa payments. The Bishop's of St. David's Dyffryn Teifi estate records Gwely Orion Redewyth, the 'descendants of the gwely of Redewyth' and Gwely Orion Cuelyn, the 'descendants of the gwely of Llywelyn' holding land in the vill of Bangor for example (Willis-Bund, 1902: 215). However, as monastic-held land, Manorforion would in any case have been exempt from the gwestfa payment, a phenomenon that is visible for example, in a an early 14th century gwestfa survey of Gwinionydd which omits the monastic granges of Faerdre, Tir-Newydd and Rhuddlan (Wmffre, 2004: 1319).

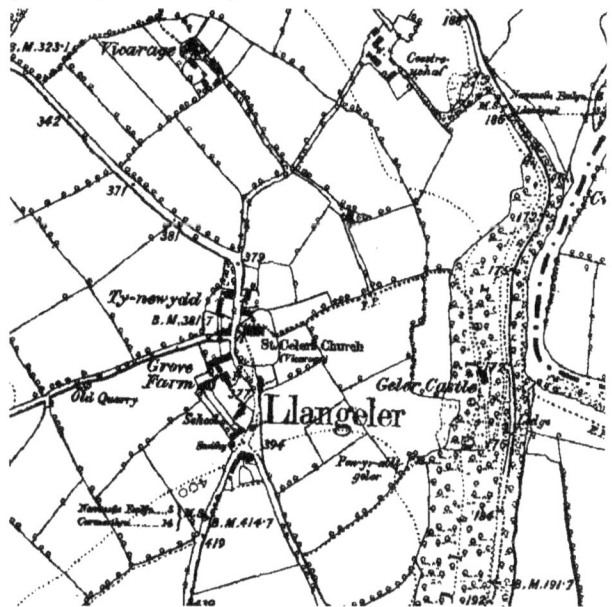

Figure 25. Llangeler parish church and its circular outer enclosure preserved in hedge-lines. Note the small radial plots on the eastern edge of the graveyard indicating tir corddlan or nucleal settlement (see fig. 21 above for location). © Crown Copyright and Landmark Information Group Limited 2008. All rights reserved 1891.

The identification of Maenor Forion makes Evan's (1922: 99, n. 2) allocation of 6½ gwestfau amongst the three parishes of Llangeler, Penboyr and Cenarth and part of Cilrhedyn erroneous. The early history of the parish of Cilrhedyn is complex and often contradictory. James (1997: 3) places the now-lost caput of Blaen-Cuch in west Cilrhedyn, just outside Emlyn Uwch Cych in the neighbouring cwmwd of Emlyn Is Cych. This pre-conquest centre is attributed to the lordship of Cadifor Fawr (d. 1091) who was lauded by the *Brut* as "supreme lord over the land of Dyfed" (ibid: 4). This powerful pre-conquest dynasty would have held considerable influence over the whole region and the 'splitting' of Cilrhedyn into two perhaps reflects a fossilisation of complex ownership patterns prior to the eclipse of this dynasty by the house of Deheubarth during the late 11th and early 12th centuries. It is possible that the portion of Cilrhedyn outside the cwmwd was included at a value of ½ gwestfa by virtue of its patronage as part of the Cadifor dynasty, more likely, however, that the ½ gwestfa had been rendered on the gwlad portion of Llangeler parish whose status as a bond maenor had been lost when the eastern half was granted to Whitland Abbey.

Maenor Forion can be added to the other maenorau that comprise a steadily growing group identified from elsewhere in south Wales, demonstrated by Domesday and Liber Landavensis in the south-east, and by the work of Glanville Jones (1972b), Rees (1924: 203) and Jones Pierce (1959b: 281, app. 1) in Carmarthenshire (see above, chapter three). The turbulence of the late first millennium had ensured the decline of the maenor as an administrative unit, especially within Ceredigion but its constituent element, the tref survived and continued to be the territorial unit upon which the gwestfa assessment was based. In some parts of Carmarthenshire the maenor had been preserved in administrative language but with an Anglo-Norman overlay as at Kidwelly, Perfedd, Is Cennen, Mabelfyw and Mabudrud. Glanville Jones's (1972) reconstruction of Maenor Meddyfnych serves to demonstrate the deep antiquity and complexity of this institution and there is evidence for similar antiquity at Maenor Forion.

The identification of Maenor Forion has demonstrated that the monastic grange preserved much of the earlier maenorial territory. Although the grant is attributed to Rhys, there is evidence to suggest that the original donors where the sons of Maredudd of Cilrhedyn (Evans, 1922: 77), a rare example of free holders or uchelwyr making such a grant. Pryce (2007) points out that that the Welsh ruler would have been entitled to the renders from the land of freeholders within their territories and may have been reluctant to lose this right but the proximity of Maenor Forion to Norman-held lands to the south and the previous skirmishes in this region may explain his necessary consent to the original grant in order to consolidate the ownership of territories along this turbulent border.

Maenor Rhuddlan

The identification of the maenor within Ceredigion proves more difficult. An analysis of place names shows that 'maenor' survives at Maenor Gogouan and Maenor Gorwydd in Llanddewibrefi but with little other evidence for early origins (Wmffre, 2004: 1329). Likewise Maenor Llanio on the site of a Roman fort north of Lampeter and Maenor y Mynydd near Tregaron. It is possible that in these cases the name may have been applied in the post-medieval period in the same way as the English 'manor' to

simply mean a discrete estate, but what of the specific maenor of the pre-conquest Welsh laws? Maenor Lampeter appears in Minister's accounts for 1298 (Rhys, 1936: 204), Maenor Sulien in 1301-2 (Lewis, 1923: 67) and Maenor Crug Whil in 1214 (Evans, 1878: 73-75).

Crug y Whil formed part of a suite of holdings within Gwinionydd originally granted by Rhys to Talley Abbey that were later appropriated by Whitland. This grant describes three holdings that came to collectively represent the Rhuddlan Teifi Grange in Gwinionydd; and together Maynar Cruchyl, Crug y Whil; Rudelan, Rhuddlan Teifi and Dinenwyn, Tir-Newydd form the major part of the present Llanwenog parish (Pryce, 2005: 175-177, fig. 26 below). That these three immediately adjacent holdings are granted as separate holdings demonstrates their significance as discrete units prior to the grant. Lloyd (1911: 260) describes Rhuddlan Teifi as the caput of the legendary rulers of the early kingdom of Dyfed. Rudelan is described in the 13th century Mabinogion where the royal court of prince Pryderi of Dyfed was entertained with mythical tales told by the bard Gwydion (Breeze, 1994: 64). The administrative functions of the royal residence of Rhuddlan Teifi may have been eclipsed by the monastic occupation and any remaining office may have been moved downstream to the medieval fortified ringwork at Castell Gwinionydd (Lloyd, 1911: 260) sometime in the later middle ages and this premise is explored further below.

The present tiny hamlet named Rhuddlan is mainly comprised of 19th century estate buildings lodges, a mill and a former smithy. These are associated with the estate of Highmead whose substantial gentry mansion lies one mile to the east. The present house was built in 1777 by the descendants of Dafydd Llwyd (Lloyd) Gwyon (d.1611) of the neighbouring Llanfechan estate, descendants in turn of the ubiquitous Lloyds of Castell Hywel. The estate was visited by Meyrick and Fenton who described it as a desirable place to visit on the journey from Carmarthen to Lampeter (Jones, 2004: 153). The valley is very broad and gentle here and the mansion is located on an elevated, open plateau commanding views along the valley east and west and recent aerial photography has recorded linear features in the vicinity of the house (Toby Driver pers. comm.).

A faint, irregular earthwork near Cefn Rhuddlan farm, just to the north of Highmead, is likely to relate to Kaer Dyron, 'land of the fort', described in a will dated to 1648 (Jones, 2004: 165). Elevated above the floodplain on a large level plateau, Highmead itself is a compelling site with views across and along the valley. But the site is relatively recent, originally part of the nearby Llanfechan farm which was occupied by Lloyd family since the 16th century at least (ibid: 164). Highmead and the adjoining meadows must have been prized for their fertility and were described as Dolau Mawr, Dolau Canol and Dolau Uchaf in the 1838 tithe.

The farm of Crug y Whil to the northwest of Highmead also

Figure 26. Maenor Rhuddlan (see fig. 19 above for location). The monastic grant to Talley Abbey (bold) largely preserves the former Maenor (shaded). The grant comprised the three tref of Maynar Cruchyl, Rudelan and Dinenwyn whilst Llanwenog was omitted. The extent of each tref can be identified using hamlet and chapelry divisions.

lies elevated above the valley floor on a low-lying river terrace and is just east of a prominent glacial hillock on the floor of the valley, also known as Crug y Whil. This rises approximately 20 metres from the surrounding farmland and is close to the Teifi in the east. The summit is circular in shape and is only some 30 metres in diameter. Meyrick (1810: 187) described the former chapel that stood atop this mound where the impressive ogham and Latin inscribed

Trenactus Stone, was unearthed amongst the 'ruins' of a building on the mound and was subsequently taken to Llanfechan house but is now part of the collection held at the National Museum, Cardiff. Described by Murphy (Murphy et al., 2006) as the site of archaeological excavations, none have actually taken place here although geophysical survey on the mound during the spring of 2005 returned disappointing results, the glacial deposits proving resistant to magnetic survey.

The extent of the monastic holdings of Crug y Whil, Rhuddlan Teifi and Tir Newydd have been proposed by Williams (2001: facing pg. 212) and these are reproduced in figure 26 below. During the early 19th century, Meyrick (1810: 213-217) recorded the division of the parish into four chapelry units. The chapels serving these areas are described by him as Cappel Whil, Lanfechan, Capel Santessau ascribed to an earthwork site near Llanfechan but without authority, and Capel Bryn Eglwys presumably near a farm of that name near the village of Cwrtnewydd, although recent aerial survey failed to pinpoint its location with any greater accuracy (Driver, 2002: 123). The chapelry boundaries can be confirmed using a further subdivision evident from the 1838 tithe survey where ten hamlets are indicated (Kain & Oliver, 2001) and these are also shown on figure 26. It is likely then that Capel Whil chapelry represented the Maynar Cruchyl granted by Rhys and comprised the single hamlet of Rhyddlan Issa, Rudelan grange developed into Llanfechan chapelry comprising Rhyddlan Ucha, Alltyblacca and Rhiwsion hamlets and Dinenwyn became Cwrtnewydd comprising Court, Fawnog and Brynhaugh. The fourth chapelry unit remained ungranted and was served by the parish church at Llanwenog comprising the hamlets of Llechwedd, Gwilim and Bryn Llefrith. It is reasonable to suggest that the chapelries correspond with former tref units and the hamlets perhaps representing further rhandiroedd subdivisions.

Indicators of significant monastic activity place an upland grange centre at Cwrt farm, near Cwrtnewydd village. An aerial survey located a complex of earthworks (fig. 27) on the slopes below this significantly named farmholding (Driver, 2002: 123). These have been interpreted as the proposed site of Whitland's upland Tir Newydd grange (ibid.) and Jack (1982: 192) describes the lease of a fulling mill at Tir Newydd to Einion ap Dafydd in 1539. The large rectangular earthwork shown below Cwrt farm is described as a probable enclosure containing a leat, pond and other features.

Field-inspection of these features in the summer of 2003 however indicated that the rectangular enclosure actually runs diagonally across a slope at a relatively steep gradient and seems more likely to be a lyncheted trackway. The complex earthworks at the foot of the slope indicate the route of a possible holloway but the rest is attributable to disturbance made during drainage of this boggy area by the present owner's father in the early 20th century.

Figure 27. Aerial survey at Cwrt Farm, Cwrtnewydd (see fig. 26 above for location). Earthworks somewhat obscured by early 20th century drainage but notice the defensive ditch and bank to steep isthmus in central foreground (Driver 2002).

Figure 28. Broncwrt facing southeast towards the plateau edge (see fig. 26 above for location).

More prominent on the ground are the remnants of an apparently bivallate earthwork feature defending a short promontory to the northeast. The earliest document recording the grant of 'Tir Newydd' or 'new land' dates to a confirmation by King John dated to 1214, not long after the assumed original date of the grant made sometime between 1189 and 1196 (Pryce, 2005: 175). Named as Dinenwyn, however, it contains *din* from the root dinas meaning fortified place or settlement which can also be seen for example at the hilltop enclosure north of Llandysul at Dinas Cerdin for example. Alternatively Dinewyn is a now obsolete term meaning wealthy and abundant and enwyn is often used as llaeth enwyn to describe buttermilk or rich milk and is a place name associated with dairying as at Llygad Enwyn farm near Llanybydder (Richards,

2007). Perhaps the name of the defended promontory site below Cwrt farm preserves the original name of this upland estate, one of the functions of which would have been to provide upland grazing.

There is other archaeological evidence to suggest significant medieval activity within the parish, and a level plateau forming a large, steeply defended plateau adjacent to Crug y Whil farm is known as Broncwrt, 'slope' or 'bank of the court' (1838 tithe). Meyrick (1810: 213-217) described a mound that formerly stood in the southeast corner of the field (fig. 28) but the corner of this steep bank has been quarried since the late 19th and any trace of a former earthwork is lost.

Geophysical survey (fig. 29) along the southern edge of Bron Cwrt was conducted in order to locate possible features associated with this mound and the results indicate at least two separate phases of significant activity over a wider than anticipated area. Two substantial ditched enclosures can be seen arranged on the edge of the plateau. The smaller, irregular enclosure is enclosed by a substantial negative feature, probably a ditch some 2.5-3 metres wide which encloses the very edge of the plateau. Although the degree of erosion, if any, to the edge of the escarpment remains unknown, the features have been truncated by a substantial hedge that is revetted with herringbone stonework that runs along the break of slope and which appears on the 1st edition Ordnance Survey map.

This irregular enclosure would have been perfectly defended on the south and east by the steep escarpment and the river with the substantial ditches protecting the west-

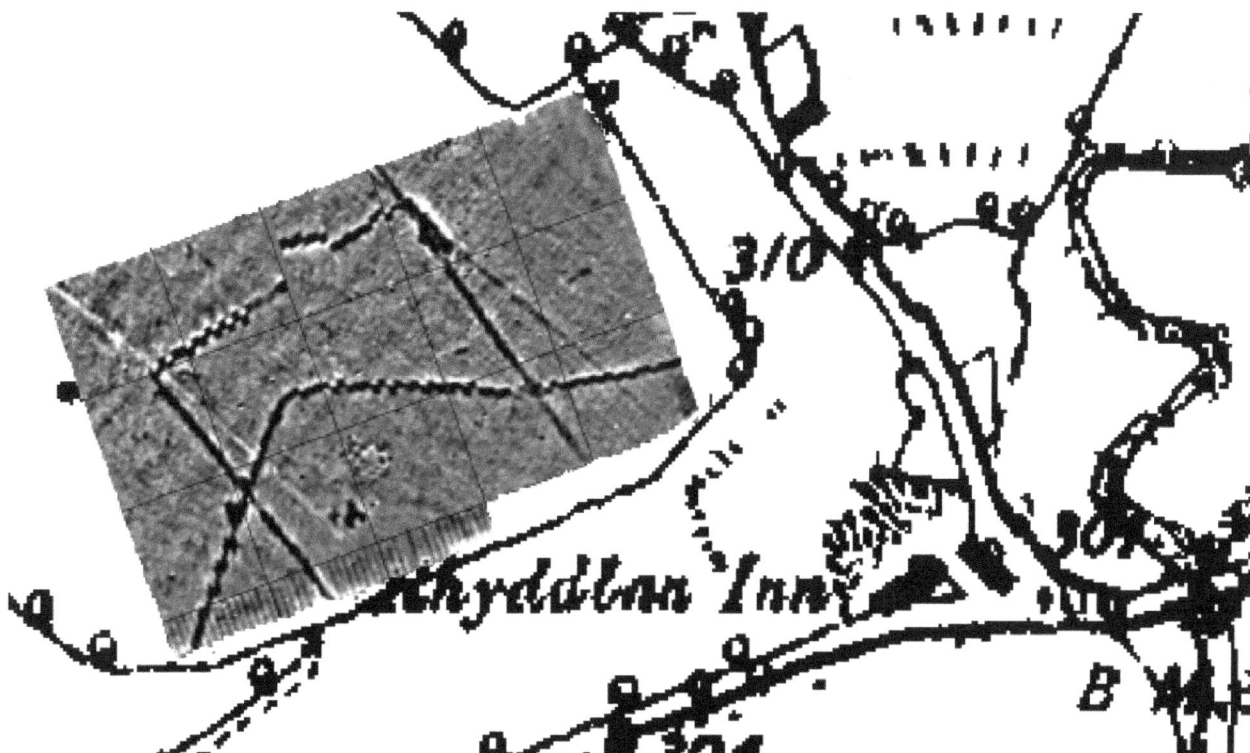

Figure 29. Geophysical survey at Broncwrt, Rhuddlan Teifi. At least two distinctive phases of ditched enclosure situated on the edge of an elevated plateau above the valley floor (values clipped to + 6 nT.). © Crown Copyright and Landmark Information Group Limited 2008. All rights reserved 1891.

facing edge. Over 140 metres long and enclosing an area of just under 1.5 acres it is impossible to date precisely without excavation. This could be an Iron Age enclosure but in this region are mostly circular or sub-circular to rectangular in shape (Murphy et al., 2006) and, as such, is unusual and may even be early medieval in date. Its relationship to the other, more regularly-shaped, enclosure is unknown. At 80 by 82 metres it is roughly square with ditches of 2.5 to 3 metres across enclosing an area of just over 1.5 acres. A fourth enclosing ditch is missing from the survey, either on the very edge of the escarpment outside the survey area, eroded away or never present. The two visible corners are very slightly rounded, reminiscent of the classic 'playing card' shape of Roman constructions. Known forts in Wales are larger than this with the fort of Loventium at Llanio at 150 x 134 metres enclosing an area of around 5 acres (Wilson, 1970: 269). But a 'fortlet' south

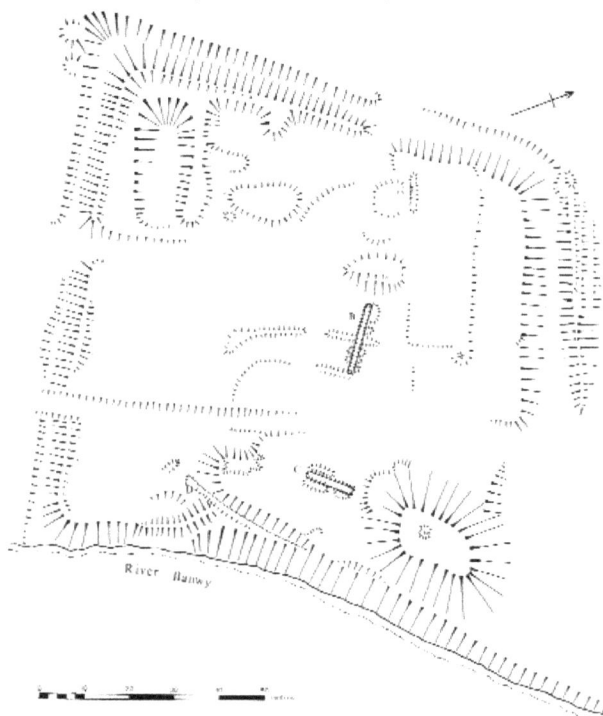

figure 30. Mathrafal (Arnolfd and Huggett 1986: 483).

of Coelbren in West Glamorgan is much smaller at 23.5 x 23 metres (St. Joseph, 1961: 126), a small fort at Erglodd measures 51 x 47 metres (St. Joseph, 1977: 152), two practice works to the south of Llanfair Clydogau measure 32 x 26 and 26 x 18 metres (Nash-Williams, 1969: 128-130) and a fortlet near Tedstone in Worcester measures 70 x 67+ metres (St. Joseph, 1956: 88). These smaller forts and practice works are characteristically situated either on a well-established Roman routeway or are ancillary to a larger fort, often nearby and the level plateaux long this area of the Teifi valley may repay further investigation. The Highmead estate lies exactly halfway between the Roman town of Carmarthen and the fort at Llanio and the presence of a Roman marching camp somewhere halfway between the two has long been postulated and is often ascribed to the site of a defensive earthwork at nearby Llanwnnen

although Castell Ddu (PRN 303863) is probably medieval in date. Other linear features run through the corners of this enclosure which may be yet another, even larger enclosure also with wide ditches. Areas of magnetic 'noise', perhaps reflecting occupation activity or buildings can be seen near the edge of the plateau although it is impossible to say which enclosure phase this activity may belong to.

A similar rectangular ditched enclosure is also evident from surviving medieval earthworks at Mathrafal near Welshpool, originally dating to the 9th century and the reputed royal llys of the princes of Powys (Fig. 30, Davies, 1993). Although poorly represented in the archaeological record, Longley (1997) proposes the increasing fortification of llys sites at this time in north Wales as a late development in the continuum from the highly visible Iron Age sites and continuity with early high status sites is implied. Broncwrt also bears close comparison to other proposed llys enclosures in north Wales identified by Glanville Jones (Jones, 2000a). At Ystrad Owain in Denbighshire (fig. 31) for example, lying within the angle of two rivers a rectangular ditched earthwork indicates a possible former llys enclosure and at 100 yards in length is comparable to the rectangular Broncwrt enclosure at around 80 metres. Mathrafal and Ystrad Owain lie in protected but open valley positions, well placed to provide access both along, and across riverine boundaries; both are immediately adjacent to a bond demesne or maerdref and a small motte stood within the enclosure at Ystrad Owain. Likewise, Broncwrt is a defended, enclosed site rectangular site on an elevated fertile valley position with excellent views along and across the valley. The nearby Capel y Whil has early medieval associations and the nearby small hamlet of Rhuddlan with mill and smithy may have been the maerdref

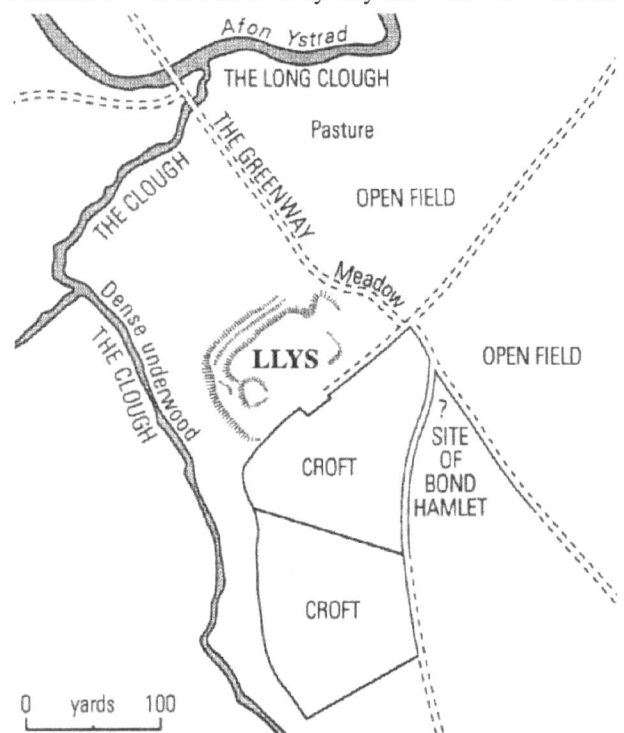

Figure 31. The llys enclosure at Ystrad Owain, Denbighshire, (Jones, 2000a: 305).

settlement. The mound destroyed by quarrying may have been a small motte, one of a suite of medieval defensive sites, common along the Teifi valley.

That Rhuddlan represents an important early site is evident and there are strong indications of royal patronage from an early date. The creation of Seisyllwg in the 8th century saw Cantref Mawr added to the former kingdom of Ceredigion and this led to the establishment of the royal house of Dinefwr at Llandeilo in Carmarthenshire (Lloyd, 1911: 257). The royal status of Rhuddlan Teifi may have been eclipsed at this period and there is evidence that will be outlined below to suggest that the surviving administrative functions under the responsibility of the reeve shifted upstream to the estates of Maerdref and Llanfair near Llandysul. These cwmwd-level administrative functions must not be confused with the more localised duties of the maer y Biswail that would have overseen the immediate demesne farm of the royal estate that would have been centred at Crug y Whil. It was this llys and maerdref estate that formed the basis of the grant to Talley and later, Whitland.

The Tref

The association between the holdings granted to Talley and Llanwenog's chapelries are evident and represent tref units fossilised through into the modern landscape. The large neighbouring parish of Llandysul also contained smaller sub units that emerged into the historical period as chapelries and the boundaries of these provided the lines along which the parish and indeed the whole cwmwd was divided. Gwinionydd Is Cerdin to the west was centred on the early church of St Tysul standing on the valley floor at the nexus of east-west, north-south routeways and with early links to the clas church of St David's. Gwinionydd Uwch Cerdin was located in the eastern half of the cwmwd with its secular medieval centres at Rhuddlan Teifi and Castell Gwinionydd in Maerdref. As a parish, Llandysul may have fossilised in its present form as a grouping of smaller trefi during the later medieval period perhaps when the more powerful church based on the newly emerging parish system began to eclipse the former royal Welsh secular centres after the 12th century.

Two of these smaller chapelry units, Maerdref and Llanfair are studied below in greater detail and have allowed the identification of the trefi upon which they were based. As a former monastic grange known as Maerdref, historical evidence supplies information about the extent and character of the grange and its possible antecedents. This has allowed the creation of a narrative concerning local and regional practice during the 12th to 13th centuries and has allowed the reconstruction of Gwinionydd's political status and the operation of its trefi.

Tref translates today as town or settlement and is an abundant place name in all areas of Wales. Shortened to -dre in Felindre, Pentre and Hendre the term once had more specific meaning in terms of settlement. Jones Pierce (1959b: 281, app. 1) states that that the term tref had "several shades of meaning"; a large administrative district, a subdivision of that district or even an isolated settlement. Gresham (1987) claimed that the trefi or townships of Gwynedd were created in the 12th century alongside the parish system as part of deliberate policy by Owain Gwynedd in order to strengthen his kingdom against Norman attack. Analysis of the gwestfa system established by Rhys in 12th century Ceredigion will establish the complex and ancient territorial framework that he used as a basis for the better exploitation of the gwestfa. An ancient render was being administered but in a new way and indicates only a loose link between parish and tref in this area.

In Gwynedd, 12th century documentary evidence indicated that a parish would have contained one or more townships (or trefi) of varying sizes and number and that a township would never have been never larger than a parish (Gresham, 1987: 141). Gresham (ibid: 142) describes this phenomenon as the result of the creation of new boundaries observing two overlapping systems in existence at this time. For him the larger territorial units, the cantrefi and cymydau, were the 'simplest' and the earliest. Their boundaries would have followed topographically recognisable features such as rivers to enable those that lived there to easily recognise them and remember them, thus reinforcing them. The 'reservations' created for bondsmen inside the lord's demesne were also ancient in order to define the demesne and but there is confusion when he equates bond land with gwelyog tenure when the opposite is generally the case. The origins of townships in Cornwall are equally opaque but may relate to a version of the Welsh tref and for example 'township' is a term occasionally used for tref in Ceredigion as at Llanfair Clydogau parish in the 19th century tithe. Hadley (1996: 12) succinctly defines the problem by stating that "the flaw in many attempts to reconstruct early-medieval estate structures lies in the underlying assumption that there was a point in time at which the landscape was uniformly divided into neatly segmented territories". Kain and Oliver's (2001) mapping of the British parishes has demonstrated the complexity of organisation at a sub-parish level, especially in Wales where terminologies for sub-parish divisions use both English and Welsh, essentially local derivations and terms for a number of different territories. For example there are a number of 'divisions' inside Llanerchaeron parish, 'townships' inside Llanina, amlwdau or 'hamlets' within Llanwenog whilst Lampeter town contains a 'division' and a 'hamlet'. Some of Gwinionydd's parishes are small, Henllan, the smallest at 466 acres in contrast to the largest, Llandysul at 17,640 acres. It will become apparent that these confusing terminologies obscure a relatively stable small community unit; the tref of the laws. Groups based on extended kin communities collectively formed together to make the pre-conquest tref that survives as townships, hamlets, chapelries and small parishes and these represent a stable unit as part of a modular landscape.

Cwmwd Gwinionydd

This section will reconstruct Gwinionydd's constituent trefau units and define their geographical extent. It will become apparent that ancient trefi units are fossilised in 19th century parishes, hamlets and chapelries but also that they significantly predate the 14th century origins suggested by Hughes (1957). This network of community units was managed through lordship at a larger scale using the maenor, an institution that had apparently vanished from this region by the 12th century but it will be the premise that Lord Rhys regularised the gwestfa institution along new lines within Ceredigion thus transforming the ancient maenor but that he did so by utilising existing tenure and territory, preserving the tref within this new system. This enabled him to exploit these ancient renders much more efficiently in order to finance the consolidation of his powerful lordship.

Cwmwd Gwinionydd described by Lloyd (1911: 260) as "one of the most desirable commotes of the land of Ceredig" commands the Ceredigion side of the central Teifi valley, essentially controlling the fertile valley floor and flanks but also movement inland along the valley and the routes crossing the river southwards towards Carmarthen or north towards the coast. A number of highly visible prehistoric hilltop enclosures along the valley reinforces this impression of control and are an essential component of Jones's discrete estate model (Davies, 1982: 43). Likewise, Longley (1997: 47- 48) considers the prehistoric defended hilltop and promontory sites in north Wales at Tre'r Ceiri, Bryn Euryn and Carn Fadryn for example as the antecedents of elite secular settlement during the pre-conquest period. Davies and Hogg describe eighteen Iron Age enclosures within Gwinionydd alone including the prominent hillfort of Pencoedfoel where a bronze half-collar dating to the first century BC was discovered (Davies & Hogg, 1994). Pencoedfoel overlooks the Teifi from the north at the point where the valley narrows and similarly, Dinas Cerdin to the north guards the Cerdin valley with a smaller promontory enclosure just downstream. On the southern bank of the Teifi and opposite Pencoedfoel is the imposing Craig Gwrtheyrn with its impressive chevaux de frise which nevertheless faces away from the river crossing at Llandysul and was perhaps more to do with posturing and display than defence. The prehistoric and medieval routeway along the Teifi valley floor was thus well guarded but was superseded during the post-medieval period by the ridge-top turnpike routes that parallel the valley running east-west.

This concentration of early status sites is paralleled by a particular concentration of medieval ring-works, mottes and castles that cluster along this part of the valley with a number of smaller earthwork and crop mark sites which remain less well understood. The precise relationship of the hilltop enclosures, the fortified medieval sites and the territories in which they are embedded is poorly understood. The use of prehistoric sites during the medieval period has been little-explored but Hughes (1957) records a battle between the 'men of Bangor' in Gwynedd and Dafydd ab Cadifor that took place below Pencoedfoel in 1250. Whilst this tale was originally recounted from a lost document and cannot be verified it nevertheless reflects the cultural significance ascribed to the complex which includes Pencoedfoel and the fortified medieval site situated on its lower flanks named Castell Gwinionydd. The castell was the defensive 'ditch' dug as part of the recounted battle whilst further fortifications were supposed to have been erected upon the summit of Pencoedfoel. The story is not repeated by other sources although it perhaps serves as an explanatory mechanism for the fortifications and their constructors. The site of Castell Gwinionydd itself is described as a motte on the second edition Ordnance Survey map but displays more complex properties. Described in the HER (PRN 303830) variously as an Iron Age hillfort, a defended enclosure or an early-medieval occupation/settlement site the site is scheduled by Cadw as a medieval ringwork. It is this feature that is traditionally believed to have been the royal llys of Gwinionydd (eg. Davies, 1896: 36 and Hughes, 1957: 106) and two farms nearby are named Faerdre Fawr and Faerdre Fach preserving the maerdref element. This premise has remained substantially unchallenged until now where the identification of a pre-conquest royal llys and maerdref in neighbouring Maenor Rhuddlan indicates a more complex sequence of events. Both Castell Gwinionydd and Rhuddlan Teifi lie in the upper or westernmost portion of Gwinionydd Uwch Cerdin contrary to Richards' assertion that the caput or court of the cwmwd should lie in the Is or lower region. By way of explanation for this, Richards (1964: 14) claims that the obvious importance of the church at Llandysul may have influenced the naming, Is in this instance meaning 'closer to' or 'nearer'.

The complex genealogical and property matters of the numerous Tivyside gentry characterised the progression of the uchelwyr into the post medieval period. A branch of the Lloyds of Castell Hywel came to prominence in the lordship of Gwinionydd Is Cerdin when they held the major estate of Cilgwyn at Newcastle Emlyn and Gilfachwen near Llandysul. The neighbouring cwmwd of Is Coed Uwch Hirwen was also claimed by the Lloyds, then (Baker-Jones, 1999: 110) of Coedmore, inherited from Sir John Lewis of Abernantbychan. The complexity of title and estate is illuminated when a survey of 1651 states that the manor was in the occupation and tenure of Sir John Lewis "by what right and title he holds the same wee know not for that noe evidence was produced to us" (Richards, 1960b: 399). The consolidation of post-medieval estates into contiguous land holdings allowed the lucrative enclosure of common land and in 1878, W.O. Brigstocke of Blaenpant bought the manor of Gwinionydd Is Coed for £1000 from the commissioners of Woods and Forests, surveyors of Crown land, probably representing a remnant of the former forest of the Bishop's of St. David's Dyffryn Teifi estate (Baker-

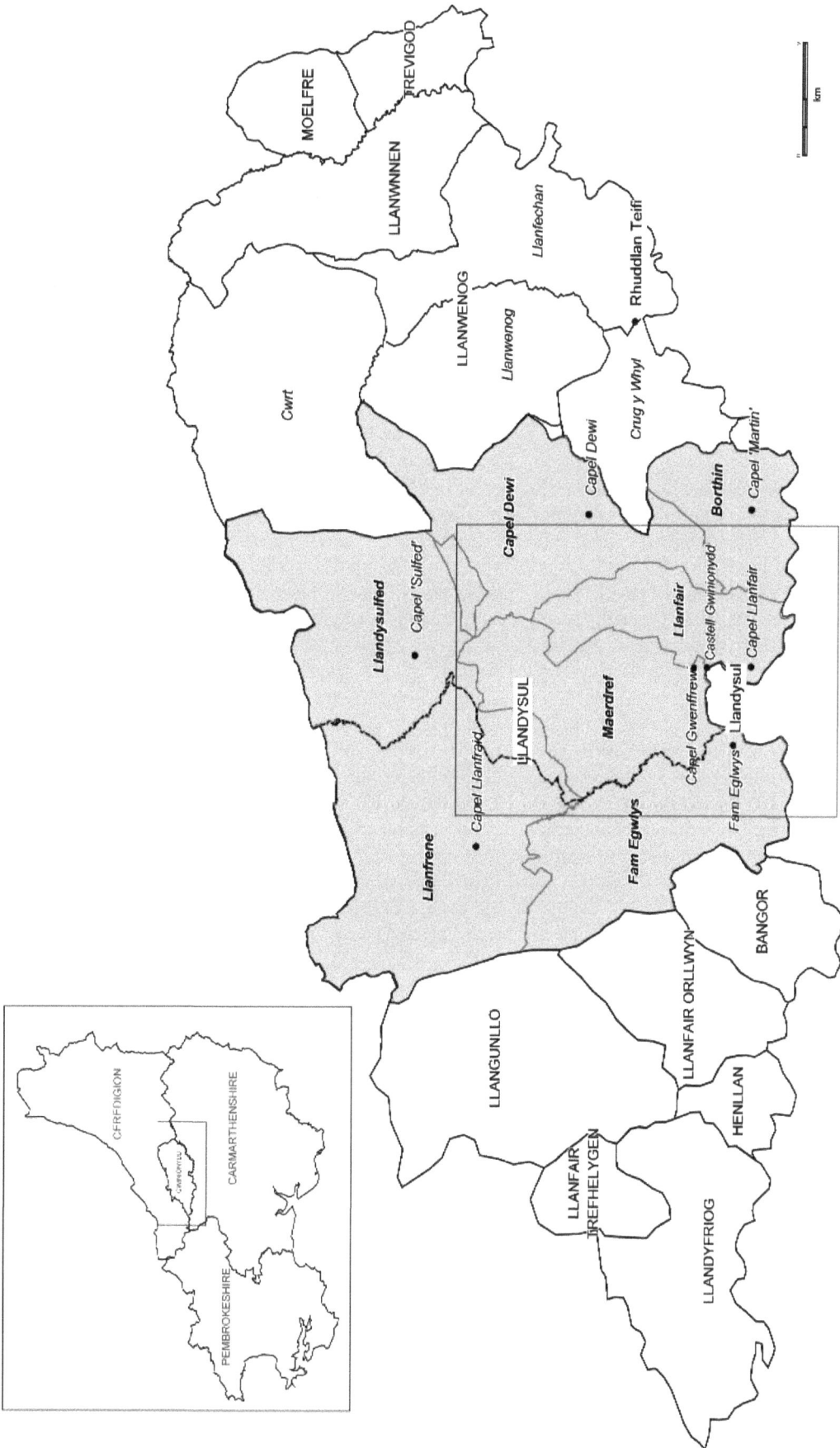

Figure 32. The nineteen medieval trefi of Cwmwd Gwinionydd (inset above left for location). All land east of the Cerdin was known as Gwinionydd Is Cerdin; to the west, Gwinionydd Uwch Cerdin. A huge variation in parish size is evident with Henllan at only 600 acres and Llandysul the largest at over 17000 but Llanwenog parish is further subdivided into four chapelries and Llandysul into seven.

Jones, 1999: 11). It is likely that this 'manor' also included much of both Is Coed Uwch Hirwen and the half of Gwinionydd known as Is Cerdin but its precise extent is not clear because some 20 years later in 1897, B.E. Hall's grandson at Cilgwyn wanted to purchase Dyffryn Teifi Manor, possibly as an attempt to raise the status of the borough of Adpar. Local government reform in 1880 had removed the jurisdiction of the lord of the manor but tolls exacted for the right to trade at a fair or market led to disquiet but continued until the 1880s in Newcastle Emlyn, Llandysul and Lampeter. The convoluted ownership patterns and consolidation of these separate lordships had long influenced the development of the hundredal system and was felt into the 18th and 19th century, but the Cerdin as a boundary remained as an ancient one.

Llandysul

Although complex, the post medieval patterns of ownership clearly preserve earlier structures, and this is especially evident in the parish of Llandysul. Despite the large and elaborate parish church, Llandysul town is small with a population of only 1,500 and is centred on two parallel streets leading to speculation that it might originally have been a planned town (Neil Ludlow pers. comm.). But the character is predominantly 19th century and there is very little evidence for medieval settlement beyond the 14th century fabric of St Tysul's church (Hughes & Jenkins, 1967). The parish is very large at nearly 18,000 acres and covers a large stretch of the valuable Teifi valley between Newcastle Emlyn in the east and Llanwnnen that borders Lampeter parish to the west. The parish runs north onto the upland watershed that separates it from the coastal plain some ten miles distant.

In 1291, the parish church was assessed at £20 which is exceptional when one considers it to be the most valuable parish church outside the main monastic establishments and provided the focus for the Dyffryn Teifi estates as one of the Bishop's houses of Dyfed. Llandysul is one of a network of other important early religious church sites along the Teifi valley that formed part of a dispersed, but highly organized medieval landscape. The neighbouring parish of Llanfihangel-ar-arth to the south in Carmarthenshire also centres around an early medieval church overlooking the bridge documented unusually early during the 13th century (Lloyd, 1935, 316-7). Richards (1974, 119) identifies the correct name of Llanfihangel Orarth meaning gorarth or great hill and just two miles west at the small hamlet of Maesycrugiau the early parish church of Llanllwni, St Non's, is set on a rocky knoll where a motte also guards a river crossing. Activity here probably predates the medieval period considerably and the remarkable rectangular Iron Age enclosures around the lower Teifi valley are currently being investigated as early 'farm' enclosures by Cambria Archaeology.

Meyrick (1810: 140-141) describes the division of Llandysul into seven chapelries named Vairdref,

Glandysilved, Llanvair, Llanfrene, Capel Ddewi, Borthin and Llandissel and he describes their chapels as being in a "most dilapidated state, scarcely any vestige of them remaining". The extent of the chapelries is also appears in the enumerator's notes of the 1851 census where they are described as hamlets. This, and the information produced for the tithe in 1841, enabled Evans (1960) to map the extent of the chapelries. Hughes (1957 and Hughes & Jenkins, 1967) speculated that the chapelries had been established during the 14th century in order to ease parochial administration. Likewise, Owen (1979) proposed that churches other than the chief, Minster or foundation parish churches of Kesteven in Lincolnshire occupied a later, secondary role as private estate or field chapels. Although there is little information to the suggest the origins and dating of these foundations, Owen (1979: 40) indicates that these chapels were situated on marginal, narrow or constricted areas and that they would have been established by communities on "newly opened land". As will become apparent however, there is significant evidence to suggest pre-conquest origins for many of the lost chapels within Gwinionydd, perhaps with a long-established hierarchy with the 'mother church' of Fam Eglwys serving as an important central focus.

As early as 1926, Bevan (1926: 69) had speculated that the hamlets within the parish of Llanarth on the coast north of Llandysul may represent former tref units but this hypothesis gained little further attention. Glanville Jones (1972b) later speculated that the seven hamlets within Llandysul parish may reflect the seven trefi required of a bond maenor described within the text of the Llyfr Blegywryd. This proposition only appeared in a footnote to a more general assessment of the evidence of the medieval Lawbooks (ibid: 304 n. 3) and the links between parish, chapelry and hamlet with former tref units has not yet been investigated and the precise status of Maerdref and Castell Gwinionydd in light of the identification of the royal maenor at Rhuddlan Teifi needs revision. Details of the chapels (see fig. 32 for location) were summarised by Evans thus:

Llanfrene. (or Llanfraed). St Bridget, St Bride, an early saint associated with the cult of Dewi and supposedly sited in a field named Cae Capel, near Dyffryn Llynod farm at SN 40564552.

Llandysulfed. -fed from 'fedd' or 'meddu' – to 'possess', the 'church possessed of St Tysul'. A chapel apparently stood below Penrallt, one mile north of the village of Pontsian between Nantremenyn and Castell Hywel. There is a group of three buildings (now lost) indicated on the tithe map (SN 43144701) all aligned northwest-southeast, probably representing later structures (but see Gwestfa Bedwyt below that suggests a different location for the original chapel building at St. John's church, Pontsian.).

Maerdref, St Winifred's, Gwenfrewi in Welsh, a 7th century saint associated with a healing well at Holywell. St

Winifred's is in the vicinity of the Afon Gwenffrwd near Faerdre Fawr and Faerdre Fach farms. A 9th to 10th century cross-incised slab recovered from the vicinity is now used as an altar in the Lady chapel at Llandysul church (Thomas, 1994b: 415). It was reputed to have stood in a field above Tancoedmawr (SN 43304180) on the valley floor, directly above the medieval fortified enclosure at Castell Gwinionydd.

Capel Dewi. The remains of a chapel building that can be seen at Gwarcoed Einion (SN 46774409) farm two miles northwest of Capel Dewi village (a field visit in 2004 confirmed these are post-medieval agricultural and domestic buildings dating at the earliest to the late 18th century).

Borthin. Capel Martin. Site remains unknown but possibly near Blaenborthyn farm (but more likely to be on site of the Calvinistic Methodist chapel (SN 46524142) which was constructed by Thomas Bowen of Waunifor in 1760. Apparently dedicated to St Martin, Ffair Fartin was held here on 21st November. More likely is Borthin rendered by mutation from porth meaning 'door' or 'gateway' and a commonly used place name for harbour at Aberporth on the coast for example; and see below for Gwestfa Arborthen).

Llanfair. Evans suggested that the location of Llanfair chapel was to be close to, or incorporated into the major dwelling of Llanfair (SN43304095), a modest estate to the west of Llandysul (excavations have subsequently located the church-site along with significant medieval activity on the meadow below the present house and will be discussed in chapter six below) (cf. Evans 1960, my parentheses).

Figure 33. Left: St John's, Pontsian. A later construction on an early circular raised mound? Right: The church is just south of Castell Hywel (beyond the trees on the left) which guards the narrow north-south route through the Clettwr valley.

Using the information supplied by Evans and the Enumerators notes, the chapelry boundaries and probable locations of their chapels of ease have been mapped and presented in figure 32. Some of the chapels exhibit early characteristics. Besides the important early centre at Llandysul, the llan name element is present at Llandysulfed and Llanfrene and the dedication of St David at Capel Dewi is also an indicator of probable pre-conquest origins. The medieval chapel formerly serving Llandysulfed is presumed to have stood near Nantremenyn farm with St John's in nearby Pontsian replacing it in 1854 when John Lloyd Davies of Blaendyffryn and Alltyrodyn built the

church (Baker-Jones, 1999: 242). The HER (PRN 400334) reputes this to have been on a new site but the reference is vague and cannot be verified.

Typologically the church site demonstrates some convincingly early features, being substantially raised above the valley floor and retained by an almost circular upright stone revetted wall elevated some 3 metres above the valley floor in places (fig. 33). Only some 500 metres to the north is the 12th century caput of the medieval estate of the important Lloyd family at Castell Hywel where a modest gentry house replaced a motte and bailey castle. Lord Rhys had confirmed this estate to Cadifor ap Dinawal in the late 12th century (Jones, 2004: 45-47). General hospitality and care was provided for the traveller in northern Ceredigion by the Knight's Hospitallers of St John and Rhys granted property to them in Ceredigion at Ystrad Meurig and Llanrhystud (Pryce, 2005: 166) with Rhys Ieuanc granting Llansantffraid to them sometime between 1215 and 1222 (ibid: 196). Rhys (or Cadifor previously) may have done the same at St John's in Pontsian which probably originated as an estate chapel to Castell Hywel. Cule (1977) suggests that Ystrad Meurig's origins had been in the care of travellers and that the nursing of lepers here may have been licensed to the Knights Hospitallers at Ysbyty Ystrad Meurig by the Cistercians of Strata Florida Abbey. The Commandery at Slebech in Pembrokeshire provided the headquarters for the Welsh Hospitallers and grants of land and churches throughout Wales followed. Those that survive include Spittal from *ysbyty* meaning 'hospital', in Haverfordwest, Ysbyty Ifan, St John's hospice near Nantgaredig in Carmarthenshire, and two early hospitals in Tenby, one dedicated to St. John the Baptist which was founded by the Earl of Pembroke (Cule, 1977). In Ceredigion, the parish church at Ysbyty Ystrad Meurig is dedicated to St John, and it is likely that they held property at neighbouring Ysbyty Ystwyth and further north at Ysbyty Cynfyn whose churches are also dedicated to St John. St John's at Pontsian may also be one of these early dedications and may be where the -sian of Pontsian or 'John's bridge' derives.

Ysbyty is a fairly widespread name and other links to the Hospitallers remain to be made in order to push back the chronologies of these poorly understood chapels and their territories. Capel Iwan, 'John's Chapel' stands some two miles south of Newcastle Emlyn and some two miles to the north of the Cych valley. The present village is typically late in character, the nonconformist chapel forming the hub of a dispersed community. At around 200 metres the large rectangular fields surrounding the village indicate mainly late enclosure whilst the older farms generally lie below the village in a girdle pattern taking advantage of the natural spring line and access to the sheltered river valleys of the Mamog and Cych. The HER (PRN 1069) locates a medieval chapel, for want of anywhere more convincing, on the site of the present 18th century chapel. But the name Parc-Yr-Eglwys 'church park' (PRN 12629) survives within the vicinity of Glan Dwrog farm under a mile north of the village. A loose girdle of farms here spread themselves along the Dwrog stream, a farm to the west called Hendy, 'old house' and its neighbouring major dwelling of Dolybryn. To the east a farmstead named Carne or Carnau defines the location of Bronze Age barrows nearby and, significantly, Spite farm that is named on the 1st edition Ordnance Survey map. A medieval mill stood at nearby Rhydyfelin on the Dwrog and Parc Y Beili survives as a field name to the north at Penrherber which is located just to the south of a defended enclosure at Pencelli. The village stands on a routeway over the upland zone that separates the major river valleys of the Teifi and the Cych. Newcastle Emlyn and Adpar lie on the Teifi to the north and the river Cych to the south forms the junction of the three counties of Ceredigion, Carmarthenshire and Pembrokeshire. This settlement based around the ysbyty at Spite would have contained the church of St John for which the later village was named and the links between St John dedications and the Knights Hospitallers at Pontsian, Capel Iwan and elsewhere deserves consideration.

In a similar fashion the proposed medieval chapel at Gwarcoed Einion farm in Capel Dewi was ostensibly replaced by a 'new' building on a new site within the nearby village. The village church however sits on top of a significantly raised, circular enclosure which may well be the site of the lost Castell Abereinon. The Brut Y Tywysogion recorded the building of a motte by Maelgwyn ap Rhys in c. 1203, the location of which was proposed to be on the steep spur of Cil Graig that overlooks Capel Dewi village and some few hundred yards from the church. But a survey conducted by Thorburn (1987) suggested that the earthworks here were the result of recent quarrying and he recommended looking to the valley floor for remains of the actual site. The mound on which the church sits fits the description perfectly and is situated above a crossing of the river Clettwr on an important valley routeway that connects Rhydowen with Llanfair and the Teifi. There are other church sites locally that incorporate a defensive fortification. The impressively situated motte within the graveyard of Maesycrugiau church, on a tall rocky mound that bears the remnants of Iron Age defensive ditches and which also guards an early river crossing.

Llanfair

Emerging from the analysis so far is the significant status of those trefi fronting the Teifi in Gwinionydd Uwch Cerdin between Llandysul in the west and Trevigod in the east. Rich agricultural land, politically and strategically significant, large chunks of it had been granted to Talley Abbey and these grants survive in the form of a 14th century inspeximus and can be recreated from their boundary clauses. They include the trefi of Maerdref and Llanfair and a separate grant for the tyddyn or homestead of Moelhedog which will be analysed in chapter six.

Some two miles to the west of Llandysul is the small, privately-owned estate of Llanfair (SN 43154090) situated on the narrow valley floor on the northern banks of the river Teifi. The mansion operates at the centre of the chapelry of Llanfair and although a medieval chapel once stood "ar y ddol islaw plas Llanfair", on the meadow below the plas, Davies (1896: 13) states that there are "no remains to be seen now" and practically nothing is known of the pre-18th century estate.

Llanfair stands adjacent to the chapelry of Maerdref and there is evidence to suggest that these trefi units were closely linked at an early period. Both Maerdref and Llanfair were both granted by Rhys to Talley Abbey becoming known collectively as Maerdref grange but preserved their trefi distinctions within their chapelry units. Maerdref grange comprised an estate of over 3,500 acres that extended north to include Pantmoch farm near Pontsian and would have been administered from the maerdy or 'house of the maer' along with at least one small hamlet or vill staffed by unfree tenants or taeogion.

Llanfair was only one of a range of holdings within the Maerdref grange that can be identified historically. Talley Abbey was finally dissolved in 1535. Despite being valued at only £136 9s 7d per annum the abbey was at that moment richer than both Strata Florida at £118 7s 3d and Whitland at £135 3s 6d In accordance with procedure, however, it meant that because it was worth less than £200 per annum the entire estate came under the jurisdiction of the Crown and, in the case of Talley, the Crown retained most of the landholdings well beyond the 16th century. The lands in the immediate vicinity of the abbey were formed into a coherent manor or lordship and rentals still exist for the 17th century. These were administered by Richard Dauncey of the Royal household and some of the outlying lands were sold (Jones, 1972a: 519). In 1557 for example the grange of Pencothy along with other lands was sold to John ap Henry and Doldhe was sold to Griffith Rice in 1562 (Owen, 1894: 207-208). The holdings remaining to the Crown at that time were bringing in an annual revenue of £159 16s 8d but unfortunately there is no list of the individual holdings. There is no mention at all of the Ceredigion holdings of the abbey, namely the small coastal holdings at Aberporth and Blaenannerch, the church of St Michaels at Penbryn or of Maerdref. These outliers were perhaps considered to be remote and unimportant and effort was concentrated on consolidating the immediate demesne lands of the abbey. Fragments of information from Exchequer proceedings (Jones, 1939) however indicate that the Crown retained the core at least of these Ceredigion holdings into the 16th and 17th centuries and a study of the land use and ownership of these holdings will demonstrate the transition from customary rights and usage towards modern forms of documented ownership.

The *Taxatio* of 1291 (Record Commission, 1802) recorded Talley Abbey's holdings itemised by Archdeaconry. Thus for the Archdeaconry de Kardigan we see:

Abbas de Tallaleze habet grang. De Maerdrefe ad firmam

Item habet grang. De Dolhenwel et Brunhes duas caruc.

Terr. Cumaliis commoditatibus	18s 0d
Item Porthenny et Killawen	8s 0d
Summa	2 6s 0d

Maerdref was quite a wealthy holding at the time, poorer only than the extensive grange of Brechfa which included "Oskernant, Kemionez, Breska, et Coytegme, de redd. Un carruc terr, et un molend. Cum alio molend de Trathleneygan" which was all worth slightly more at £1 15s 0d.

The Valor Ecclesiasticus assessments of 1535 valued each of Talley's granges, appropriated churches, chapels and tenancies (Dugdale, 1817-1830: 165). Despite the remoteness of the Ceredigion granges from the core lordship they were valuable. "Grangiam de Vacidre et molendinum" (Maerdref) was valued at £6 and only one grange was more valuable at this time: "Grangiam de Gowithgrege et molendinii" (Gwyddgrug, south of the Teifi in Carmarthenshire) at £6 16s 8d, possibly because this had more than one mill. A valuation made by the Augmentation Office adds some detail to these figures (ibid: 166). The core lands around the abbey had been formed into a discrete estate and were collectively worth £51 19s 7d. Again, Gwyddgrug grange was the most valuable outside the core abbey estate but Mardreff Grang' had also increased slightly in worth at £6 16s 6d. Exempt from gwestfa, the former bond tref would have been liable for other renders and the commortha is recorded here, also worth £6 16s 6d. Gwyddgrug's returns this time were worth £9 0s 5d but the commortha was only valued at £6 10s 0d, perhaps reflecting a range of free and bond tenants within this estate.

Usefully this valuation is broken down into its constituent revenue elements (Owen, 1894: 42-43). Thus for Maerdref we have:

"Redditus tenencium ad voluntatem et per Indenturam infra grangiam de Mardreff: Et de

s	d	
3	6	Griffino ap Rice Gough: ad voluntatem: solvend' (ut supra)
7	0	Arron ap Rice Gough
7	0	David ap Ievan
4	6	David ap Jevan degan
7	0	Moricio ap Jevan ap John
6	4	Ade (Adam) Gitto
3	9	David ap Ievan Gough
7	0	Thome ap Adey
5	3	Lleke (Lleucu) Thomas
0	0	48 b' avenar' price le b' 4d. Hugoni ap Jenkyn
16	0	de redd' 16 agnor super ten' p'd' ut patet per rental'solvend' annuat' ad terminus predictos
10	6	de redd' duorum tenement' jacentium infra grangiam

predictam in Com' Cardigan quorum unum vocat' Tegden Kellnaren alium vocat' Tegden Iowyn dimiss' per Indenturam Likye Lane gough et Thome ap gough sigillo conventuale nuper Mon' de Talley sigillat' quam quidem non ostend', sol' ad terminus predictos

5	3	ter' Kelthy Vaharren Per Indenturam Ievan ap Poell ap Ryce
7	0	Tethen Fees Hesgolde (in Com' Cardigan): Ricio ao Jevan David tege
7	0	Jevan ap Henry
8	11	ter' Iworde et terr' Jevan ap Rice Ll'n gough: Hoell ap Rice ap Powell
20	0	unius tenementi et unum [unius] molendini aquatici Hoell ap Rice ap Powell
5	3	terr' Idowen David ap Powell ap Rice

Summa £6 16s 6d

Commortha: Et de £16 6s 6d de quodem redd' p'ven' de diversis tenementis in grangia predicta vocat' Commortha qou-libet tercio anno et solvit hoc anno quia est annus tercius.

Summa £6 16s 6d"

This lists some 19 tenancies including the mill, molendinum aquatici. Some of the place names can be identified (see fig. 34 below for location of places mentioned). Kelthy Vaharren (and possibly also Tegden Kellnaren) is Gellifaharen, a farm just to the north-east of Fardre at SN 4198 4311. The mill with its tenements is at Rhydowen where a group of later mills sits adjacent to a circular earthwork enclosure, motte and post-medieval plas at Alltyrodyn indicating a high status centre. Terr' Idowen again relates to land at Rhydowen and may be linked with Tegden Iowyn which remains unidentified. Tethen Fees Hesgolde refers to Tyddyn Ffos Esgob, a farm to the west of Rhydowen. The challenge in relation to this document is to see how it can be related to the detailed list of places mentioned in the medieval perambulation which will be examined in detail below.

This valuation serves as a useful baseline in order to reconstruct medieval ownership and the next dated evidence available is Exchequer proceedings for the late 16th century, about a generation after the dissolution. In 1538, Hoell ap Rice ap Powell had leased from the Crown a tenement and water mill in Maerdref grange at a revenue of £20. A 'Grant of Premises' by the Crown in 1595 made the property over to a David Williams for a period of 31 years. He had conveyed this lease to Hoell's descendant, David Lloyd Griffith ap Howel who in any case had inherited the lease by right. By 1602 David ap Howel had died and, Ieuan David Lloyd, possibly a relative, was bringing an action as executor against Thomas ap Ieuan and David ap David who were accused of withdrawing suit at the mill and of encouraging others of the grange to do likewise (Jones, 1939: 97-98).

Sir David Williams was granted the 31 year lease of the tenement by the Crown and described as a Sergeant-at-Law was surely an absentee landlord (Jones, 1955b: 89). Further complex ownership in the wake of the dissolution can be seen at the neighbouring Rhuddlan grange of Tyrenewith. The Crown demise of *ffoes y ffalde* Ffos y Ffald, *Rong y ddwyforth* Rhwngdeufordd, Carn Dd. Lloyd and *Gwern Ridlam* Gwern Rhuddlan, went initially to Gilbert Gerrard, Master of the Rolls, for 21 years and after that to William Whiteman. A new demise went to Sir Arthur Ingram who sold his interest to two London gentlemen, Edmond Sawyer and Thomas Brinley, described as 'strangers' (ibid: 107). Sir David Williams also had interests in Rydlantyvie where the grant of the mill William Wightman of Harowehill, co. Middlesex, Esq., for a term of 60 years. The lease is then conveyed to David Williams, then of the Middle Temple, and now Sergeant-at-Law which was the highest order of counsel. The office was prestigious, only a handful were created every decade or so, most going on to become judges. The Williams are difficult to trace in this area and may relate to the Fitzwilliams of Cilgwyn who were descended from the Lloyds of Gilfachwen, Llandysul. A later branch of the family changed adopted the surname Williams. David Williams held the lease of Rydlantyvie mill along with the grange, divers messuages, lands and tenancies in the parishes of Llanwenog and Llandysul, along with Richard Price of Brecon and Thomas William of Ystrad Ffyne. This lease was then conveyed to Gwyon Llywelyn Lloyd in 1579. In 1602, Gwyons' executor, David Lloyd Gwyon of Llanwenog, brought an action against David Phillip, Ievan David, Lewis Rees, Rees ap Howell of Llanwenog, and a yeoman of Llandissell, Rees David Llywelyn Lloyd, who were all accused of withdrawing their suit from the mill (Jones, 1939: 99).

What is evident is a fairly complex series of grants and leases for the former grange of Maerdref and the neighbouring Cistercian grange of Rhuddlan Teifi making ownership patterns difficult to recreate. The Crown retained ownership of these holdings throughout the early post-medieval period, granting the lease of substantial sub-units in the first instance to English, absentee landlords. The later 16th century however sees the emergence of many of the local families beginning to purchase leases directly from the Crown in their own right. Thus the lease of Rhuddlan Teifi with other lands in Llanwenog and Llandysul is sold to Gwyon Llywelyn Lloyd in 1579 and David Williams conveys Rhydowen mill to David Lloyd Griffith ap Howel in 1558 who in any case inherited it from the former tenant, Hoell ap Rice ap Powell. Similarly, by 1604 the occupation of Kelley Vaharan along with a messuage termed Tir Castell y Vairdre is held by William David Lloid who, by the death of his father is, "now holding by right of survivor" (Jones,

1955b: 89). Thus the tenure of these units appears to remain within family units for several generations and reflects customary patterns of tenancy and inheritance even within these former bond settlements.

Another generation later the situation has changed again. The owner of Rhydowen mill was now Jevan David Lloid, gent. of Llandissell (Jones, 1955b: 89-90). He was the son of the former owner, David Lloyd Griffith ap Howel mentioned above, and an exchequer proceeding for 1604 notes that he has also purchased three tenements from the Crown. This is the first evidence for the outright purchase of land within Maerdref grange from the Crown by a local family and probably reflects a pattern of piecemeal, ad hoc purchase and conveyance that makes the reconstruction of ownership in this region so problematic. Along with the purchase of these elements goes the set of rights and obligations associated with this former bond settlement. Henrie ap Jevan ap Henrie of Llandissell, gent., represented the tenants of Vairdre in the excessive tolls and customs charged on them and these are atypically listed here as part of the official consideration of the case. The customs and suit to the water grist mill called Melin Rhud Owen, Llandissell, grange of Vairdre are listed thus:

Grinding corn grown on their tenements, and payment of accustomed toll.

Carrying timber at the request of the farmer, of repairs; thatching the mill and scouring the pond. Each tenant has a customary portion of the work, known by 'long usage'

The farmer of the mill to find sufficient 'meat, drink and diet' for the labourers working on the mill.

The farmer to grind the tenants' corn before that of any others. (ibid.)

Instead of going to an absentee stranger however, these dues now went to the local Jevan David Lloid whose family had held the tenancy of the mill previously and the are other specific details added to this case, that the portion to be thatched by the owners is that portion "directly over the millstones, hopper and grinding place". A charge of excessive tolls taken by the owner and his miller, Jevan David ap Jevan John (probably a relative) runs thus:

"three toll dishes of every grinding of every measure (called in that country a teale). Sometimes the defendants take ten toll dishes for grinding two teales, sometimes one-ninth, one-eight, one-seventh or one-sixth of the corn. Tenant John Williams paid three dishes for shelling oats into pilcorn and then had to take it away unground. Tenant Jevan ap Henri (probably a relative of the complainant!), a poor man, paid a teale and a quarter for grinding a teale and a half. The defendants also keep, in addition, the meal that remains around the grinding stones which often accounts to five toll dishes full. Defendants, against equity, claim toll on the grain which tenants sell. Defendants have not thatched their customary portion and the tenants corn is damaged by rain"

The defendants answer that

> "there was never any agreed allocation of repairs to each tenant. The tenants did what repairs were needed irrespective of which part of the mill needed them. No excessive toll has been charged – only that which is customary"

This level of detail is invaluable. At first glance it is a fairly standard set of dues and customs. With ownership of the mill, Jevan David Lloid has also acquired the duties and dues formerly due to the lord of the manor. In this case that had been Lord Rhys who then granted this privilege on to Talley Abbey, thence to the English crown after the Dissolution. The new gentleman owner could expect labour and tolls for the privilege of the tenants having their corn preferentially ground even into the early 17th century. But these customs reflect 'long usage' and are highly detailed regarding weights and measures of grain, closely connected with the kinds of traditional payments dating to the medieval period such as commorth and gwestfa. But the lord has to bear much of the upkeep of the mill and sustain the labourers while they work.

The entirely reciprocal nature of these types of agreements is apparent and challenges our notions of ownership and tenancy. The 'new' owners of the mill had in fact held primary rights over the mill, its lease and its tenancy by 'long usage' for generations and buying the freehold of the mill in the 17th century was just part of a long continuum of 'ownership'. Likewise the tenants of the rest of the grange have held their tenancies over long periods reflecting ancient tenurial practice. The new class of 'yeoman' gentry did not yet hold large, rich consolidated estates. Their affiliations were with their neighbours, not the absentee landlords that had begun to loosen their grip on this area. Family ties, behaviours and custom are bound up with long-lived, tenurial and ownership patterns that survive in this area into the 18th and 19th century gentry estate.

The ownership of Rhydowen mill and its messuages continued into the 19th century. Although the fabric of the present Alltyrodyn mansion dates to c.1827, by the middle of the 17th century at the very latest we can see the genesis of the modern house and estate where we see a Ievan Loyd of Alltyrodyn whose son, David had become High Sheriff for 1667-8 (Jones, 2004: 19), continuing the lineage from Jevan David Lloid's ownership in 1604, from David Lloyd Griffith ap Howel in 1558 and Hoell ap Rice ap Powell in 1538. David's will of 1679 lists the manse, Alltyrodyn and Melin y Pandy, not the medieval corn mill but a fulling mill. Other lands in Llandysul parish included messuages and land called Tir Dol Walker along with land near Llandysul bridge. The family had also accumulated land in other parishes at Llanfynydd, two messuages and land in the parish of Llanfihangel Year'th called Tir y Pant Mawr and Tir Blodoyen, two messuages and land in the parish of Talley, one called Kilwoor and Tir Penn bont of Lanrhyd.

When the estate was sold in 1929, altogether some 46 properties amounted to 5,294 acres.

This kind of documentary evidence complements the Crown rental evidence that we have for Gwinionydd Is Cerdin for 1564 and supports the identification of some of the ancient farmsteads made on morphological grounds previously. We can use these two sources to build a picture of the kinds of rents we can expect to see in Gwinionydd Uwch Cerdin. That is, the valuations made in 1538 above are only 26 years earlier than the rental of the manor of Gwinionydd is Cerdin in 1564. When you look at the name of the 1564 rental it is from all of Gwinionydd cwmwd below the Cerdin but includes some outliers. The rental 'is made by' Howel John Lloyd without any further explanation. Was he lord of the manor or just a surveyor – that nonetheless were usually drawn from the gentry class. He is probably from the Bronwydd/ Cilgwyn Lloyds as there is no record of John Howel Lloyd in any of the Uwch Cerdin evidence above. A similar set of rental documents dates from 1651 and comprises a Parliamentary Survey of the Manor or Lordship of Is Coed (Uwch Hirwen) and a Survey of the Manor or Lordship of Gwinionydd Is Cerdin.

The Inspeximus of 1324 (Evans, 1878: 60-72 and Owen, 1894) that details the grant to Talley describes: "the gift, grant and confirmation that Rhys Fychan" (d.1271), son of Rhys Fychan (d.1244), "to Talley Abbey that which Rhys the great" (Rhys Gryg, Lord Of Ystrad Tywi) "and Rhys" (Lord Rhys d. 1197), implying the original grants of Lord Rhys made before 1197. The grants include lands in Carmarthenshire and Ceredigion and a section reads "Apud Keredigaun" (in cwmwd Ceredigion) and "Porthothin in the ancient boundaries". Evans (ibid: 62) describes this as Borthin chapelry but it is actually Aberporth on the coast to the north. Borthin was assessed for the gwestfa in a document dated to 1303 and therefore could not have been either a bond or monastic holding. The grant continues with a list of the following;
> "Y Vardreiv (The Maerdref)
> Ryt Ywein (Rhydowen village)
> Nant Kedivor (Nant Cadivor stream)
> Brin Yron (A hill at the mouth of the Afon Geyron stream near Capel Dewi)
> Kynbyt
> Molehedauc in the ancient boundaries, with the mills and common pasture
> of the whole land of the said Rhys."
(Owen, 1894: 41 my parentheses).

These lands are named again in the same document (ibid.) by confirmation of a charter by Maredudd ab Owen but with different spellings and in a different format as:
> "Mayrdreiv
> Gwinonit (Gwinionydd)
> Brynyron
> Ryt Ywein
> Nant Kedin (Nant Cerdin stream)
> Kynbyt Ysalld"

73

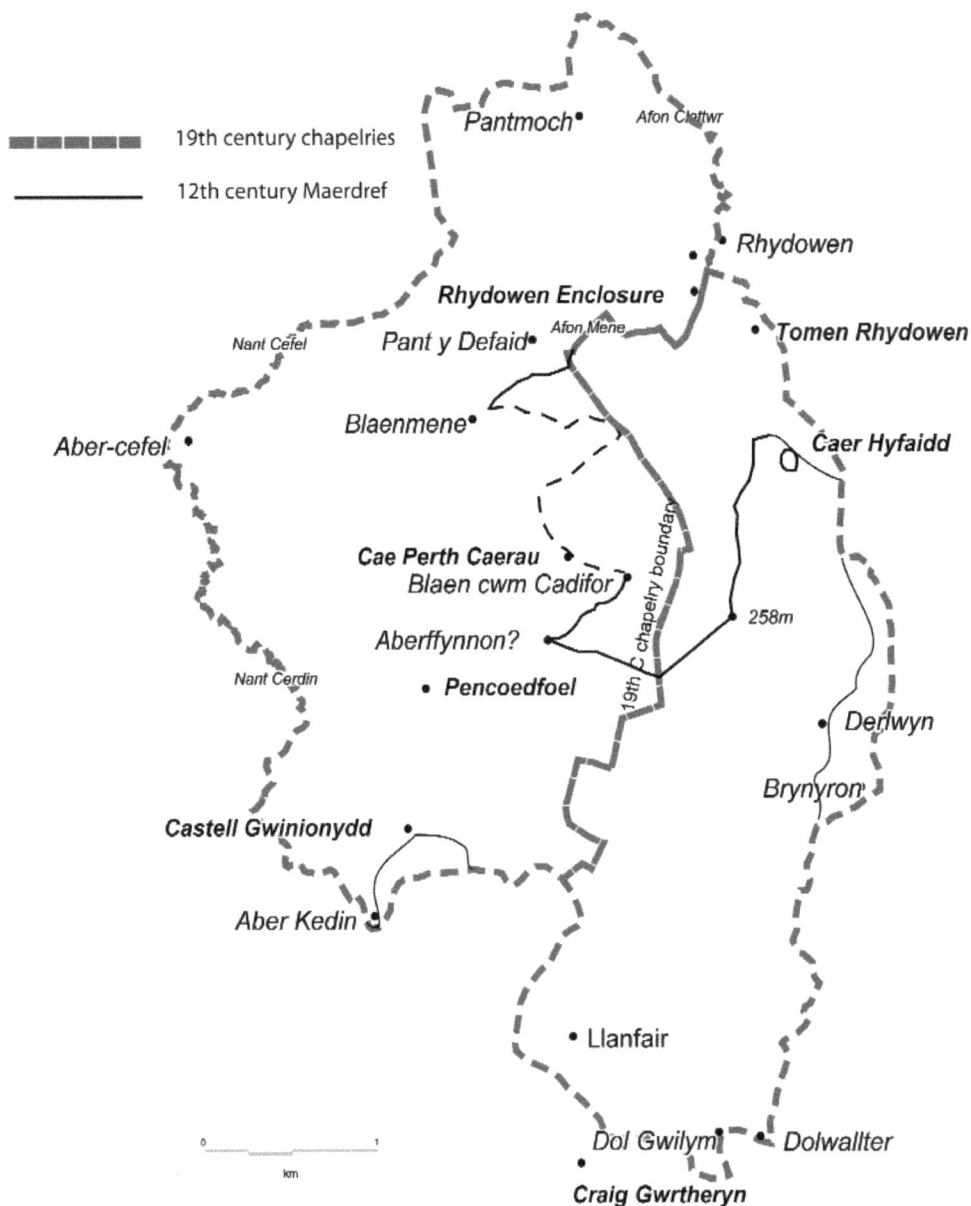

Aber y Ffynaun ab inde rivulo illius fontis in sursum decente usque ad ortum suum, et ab inde versus viam ubi proxima est dicto fonti, et trans viam illam versus lapides magnos jacentes in campo, ab illis lapidibus per transversum usque Cayr Huvid, et a Cayr Huvid usque Corderwen, et ab inde usque ad fontem, fonte illo descendente usque ad pratun in valle, et inde versus Teievi, sicut satis noti sunt fines Teivi usque ad Aber Kerdin ubi cepit prima diffinitio.

As by these bounds they are encompassed: from Abercerdin in Teivi, towards its source as far as Abercevel, along the stream Cevel unto its source, and from its source across unto Blaen Pant y Moch: Pant Moch leading unto the trench: that trench leading to Clettwr; the stream Clettwr unto its confluence with Menai; Menai towards its source at Gwaun Rhydd; thence unto the spring towards the High Way leading from Blaen Nant Cadivor; and from that spring unto that way, and across that way to the little Moor; and from that Moor unto the Wolve's Pool, and from that Pool straight to Blaen y Pantsych; and through that Pant or Dingle leading unto the source of the source of Nant Cadivor; by this stream descending to Aber y Ffynnon; thence along this Ffynnon from its outlet to its source; and thence towards the road nearest the said source; and over that road towards the great stones lying in a field; from those stones across unto Caer Hyveidd; and from Caer Hyveidd unto Gwarderwen; and thence unto the spring: by that spring descending to the meadow in the valley; and thence towards Teivy and as the bounds of Teivy are well known, unto Abercedin where the first boundary began."
(Evans, 1878: 65-67).

Figure 34. The 12th century grange of Maerdref granted by Lord Rhys to Talley Abbey (see fig. 32 for location).

And a perambulatio reads;

"Provt hiis terminis continentur...
Ab ostio Kerdin in Teivi versus ortum suum usque Aber Keveil in longitudine sui usque ad ortum suum et ab ortu ejus per transversum usque Blayn Pant y Moch, Pant y Moch ducente ad fossam, inde desecendatum foss illa ducente usque Kaletur, Kaletur usque Abermenei, Menei versus ortum suum Gwenn Ruth, ab inde usque ad fontem versus viam majorem venientum de Blan Nant Kedivor, et a fonte usque ad viam illam, et trans viam illam usque ad moram parvam, et ab illa mora usque Bleidbull, et a Bleidbull recte usque Blan y Pantsych, et illa valle ducente usque Blan Nant Kedivor, illo rivulo descendente usque

74

The perambulation has allowed the mapping of the grant as follows (Fig. 34): The Afon Cerdin meets the Teifi at Abercerdin Mills along the Cerdin northwards until the mouth of Nant Cefel at Aber Cefel farm, to Pantmoch farm, by the trench (the chapelry boundary here follows a small stream to the north of the farm to its confluence with the Clettwr) to the Afon Clettwr, along the Clettwr southwards

on the upland somewhere, then onto Blayn Pantsych or the top of the dry hollow. These places remain unidentified and the perambulation is shown dashed in fig. 34 (above), but the next place in the list locates us at the source of the Nant Kedivor at Blaen cwm Cadifor. Downstream along this until Aberffynnon, which may be the junction with a small stream that runs eastwards along a sinuous field boundary.

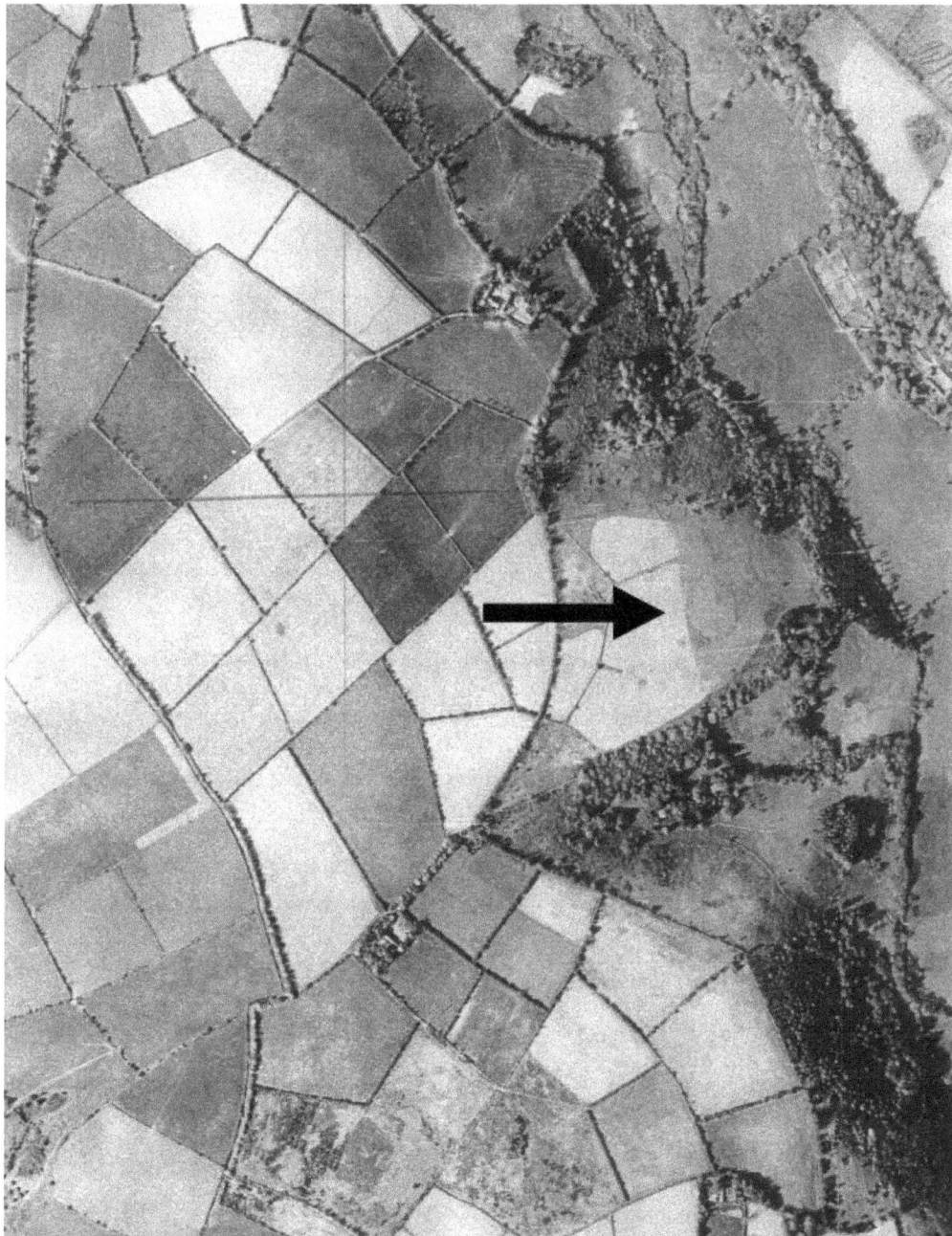

This field boundary leads towards the road over which the boundary passes until reaching the big stones in a field. These are now lost but may have referred to a cairn or field monument near the peak of 258m just east of Blaen cwm Cadifor. From here to Caer Hyveidd. Hyfaid, a 9th century king of Dyfed is generally thought to refer to Pencoedfoel hillfort as the largest visible fortification in this area. Another candidate for Caer Hyfaid however could be the enclosure at Bryngolau identified by a sub-circular crop mark at SN 44564401 (fig. 35). This would allow the boundary to continue easily southwards until Gwarderwen which must be in the vicinity of the hamlet of Derlwyn, both of which contain the root derw for oak referring to the steeply wooded sides of the Clettwr valley. It is here also that Brynyron at Capel Dewi is situated. Although not named in the perambulation it is one of the places said to be contained within the grant. If Pencoedfoel was Caer Hyfaid it is difficult to see how the detailed boundary clause could get from there to Gwarderwen, crossing the intervening valleys, river and trackways that had already been mentioned without mention in this case. From Gwarderwen the boundary descends along the stream (the Clettwr) unto the meadow (partum) in the valley. This section of the valley is characterised its level valley floor

Figure 35. Sub-circular enclosure near Bryngolau farm, possibly the site of Caer Hyfaid (north to top). The Clettwr is to the east and Tomen Rhydowen is marked by a small clump of trees just north-east of the enclosure (see fig. 34 for location)

to the mouth of the Afon Mene, upstream along this to Gwenn Ruth ('gwaun rhudd' or red moor), probably located somewhere in the vicinity of upland Blaenmene near Pant y Defaid farm. Then onto the spring towards the trackway that leads from way that leads to Blaen Nant Kedifor, or Blaen-cwm-Cadifor. From this way to the 'little moor' then to Bleidbull, the wolf's pool, presumably a pond formerly meadows still identifiable by their dol place names at Dolwallter, Dolbantau and Ddol Gwilym. To finish, the boundary runs back along the Teifi to Aber Cerdin where the perambulation. Former river channels show the Teifi to have run closer to the foot of the slope which was guarded by the fortifications at Castell Gwinionydd and this is the likely medieval course of the Teifi. The 1st edition OS map indicates this former course as the county boundary and it would have meant a large fertile meadow at this point but within Carmarthenshire, south of the river.

The perambulation corresponds for the majority of its route with the 19th century chapelries of Maerdref but only partly with Llanfair. The boundary instructions that refer to the upland part after reaching Aber Mene are intricate and detailed. This perhaps demonstrates the complex ownership patterns even in open upland areas away from settlement and the trackway crossing this upland region north-south is telling, suggesting that unenclosed uplands could be traversed using defined routeways. It is probable that the intricacy of this section which is impossible to recreate today reflects the complex shares assigned to upland communal grazing that gradually came to be expressed in physical strips. This part of the grant, however, seems to exclude a parcel of land to the northeast that is centred around Brynclettwr, formerly named Tomen Rhyd Owen. This is named for the motte or fortification on the valley

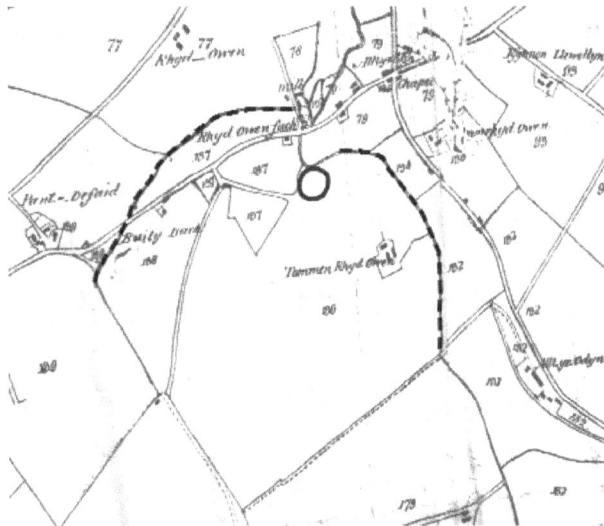

Figure 36. Tommen Rhydowen farm (tithe map 1841) and the circular earthwork enclosure, note 'Baily Bach' farm. An early unit preserved within its outer enclosure.

floor nearby called Tomen Rhydowen.
In 1841 the tithe map (fig. 36) demonstrates the extent of Tommen Rhyd Owen farm which runs up onto the upland as far as the north-south trackway, largely corresponding with the portion omitted from the grant. By this time John Lloyd Davies of Alltyrodyn owned Tomen Rhydowen and most of Rhydowen village as part of the entire Castell Hywel estate. Rhydowen was centred around a medieval mill and was an important river crossing point on the upland routes northwards to the coast. Evidence supplied

by LiDAR survey (fig. 37) indicates a circular banked enclosure that is adjacent to Bailey Bach and is named Dol Willem on the tithe map. This may be an early secular fortified site, probably the antecedent of the nearby motte, guarding this important access route. Hints of a larger outer enclosure are fossilised in field boundaries and the 'bailey', and circles the early banked enclosure, the later motte and Tomen Rhydowen farm. A discrete holding it is likely to have been the early antecedent of the modest Alltyrodyn estate, one of many such units comprising the powerful secular Castell Hywel estate.

One of the holdings contained within the perambulation is Kynbyt Issald that has hitherto resisted identification. A rental for Llanfair of 1758, however, gives Llanfair Perthcynddyn, two years later this is Llanfair Perth Cindin and Llanfair Perthycyndy in 1778 and demonstrates the survival of the cyn or kyn element from Kynbyt (Wmffre, 2004: 228). Perth can be directly translated as hedge and is sometimes used to indicate enclosure as at the nearby earthwork of Cae Perth Caerau situated on the slopes below Pencoedfoel. In this case it may refer to an early church enclosure. Wmffre (ibid.) gives 'stubborn person' for cyndy but it may relate to a topographical descriptor. The *cyn*-prefix relates to 'first' or 'foremost' and *din*- preserves dinas, 'fortified place'. Din and caer are often assigned to quite modest earthworks or settlements with a range of dates and functions. Castell Cenddu farm in Ciliau Aeron parish for example refers to an early enclosure overlooking the Mydr valley. The fiscal and political administration of Llanfair, and all the trefi of Gwinionydd would have taken place from Maerdref and Llanfair might have been referred to as the 'first enclosure (that you come to?) below the allt (wooded slope)'. The inference is that the holding only acquired the Llanfair element after the grant and the influence of the Premonstratensians whose abbey church was also dedicated to Mary, but that an enclosure denoting activity of some kind was in existence at Llanfair prior to the monastic activity.

The Gwestfa

The identification of Gwinionydd's trefi creates a framework that allows the identification of the gwestfau areas that were recorded in 1303 (Dodgshon, 1994). This will allow the relationship between territory and render to be more fully analysed and investigated and support the proposed former trefi areas. The supply of food and hospitality to a king and his entourage whilst on a circuit or cylch was known as the gwest (Jones, 1994: 89). The gwestfa, literally the place, *ma*, of the gwest is echoed in the Welsh word for hotel, gwesty. The southern Law redactions detail the bread, meat and beer that comprise the rent, but give values for each of the items marking the gradual trend towards commutation (Ellis, 1926: 285). In typical schematic manner, the Iorwerth codes state that the gwestfa was rendered equally on all, meaning that a maenol was liable to pay £1 successively divided so that the render on the individual homestead would have been less than a farthing. The medieval food tribute was also common outside Wales. The chief's banquet is described in the Irish Corus Flatha, the 'Code of the King', and communal feasts are recounted in the Senchus Mor. In south-east Wales Domesday book details honey rents from Ewias for 32 acres of land, from the Walenses of Caerleon and in Archenfield the tribute was accompanied by pigs and sheep (ibid: 287).

information actually illustrates the widely varying number of occupants and size of each of the units hinting at a mature, developed system. Jones Pierce (ibid: 317-318) assumed the survival of a pastoral tribal society as late as the 12th century and he saw the gwelyau and gwestfa systems of south and west Wales in their infancy with no time depth. He also noted that the "heirs of each tenant are compelled to receive the inheritance after the death of their

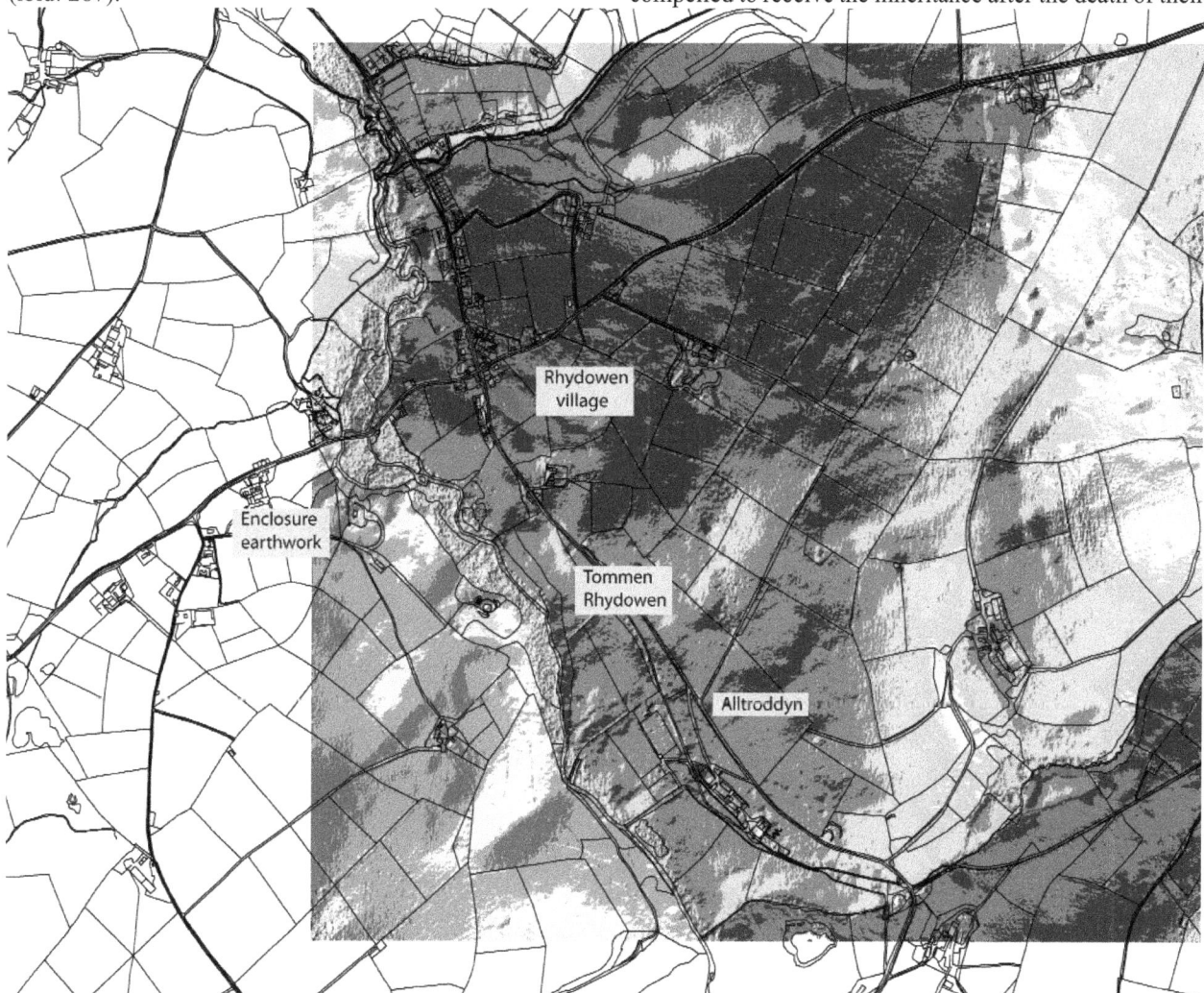

Figure 37. An earthwork enclosure south west of Rhydowen village, the antecedent of Tomen Rhydowen and the Alltroddyn estate. Crown Copyright/database right 2008. An Ordnance Survey supplied service

By the later middle ages it is evident that the gwestfa had developed into the geographical area or district on which the administrative rent was based. Llyfr Cyfnerth for southern Wales states that the gwestfa was to be rendered on the tref (of four rhandiroedd – a free tref), in contrast to north Wales where the maenol was stated as the unit of render (Jones, 1992: 100). Jones Pierce's (1939: 18) analysis of 13th century renders for Caernarvonshire in the north had noted a correlation between parish districts and the tref suggesting a strong link between the tref, the parish boundary and the geographical gwestfa.

In Ceredigion the gwestfa was rendered in equal amounts on each unit prompting Jones Pierce (1959b: 275) to note a certain amount of administrative uniformity that was difficult to correlate with actuality. But the rental

parent" in effect binding them to the soil in perpetuity. He described this as an example of servility not acknowledging the subtle emphasis on the inalienable nature of the freehold, a basic feature of gwelyau holding and one that meant it was able to survive fragmentation over many centuries, not becoming untenable after a few generations as Jones Pierce believed.

By the 13th and 14th centuries the Welsh gwestfa was no longer paid in kind but had been commuted into cash payments. The 1334 Survey of the Honour of Denbigh shows that the twnc payment had replaced the gwestfa in North Wales (Vinogradoff & Morgan, 1914) and by this time the gwestfa survived only within Ceredigion. Here the 13th century 'rent of assize' or gwestfa was recorded, returning equal amounts for each cwmwd. This rent survived into the 16th and 17th centuries where it became the basis upon which all tenancies were assessed and was known as the 'chief rent' (Rees, 1924: 224). Jones Pierce (1959b: 275) was suspicious of the regular nature of the payments at 13s 4d (or 1 mark) per gwestfa unit which were spread evenly throughout the cymydau, and he suggested that it had the uniform appearance of "a system conceived by a single mind and put into effect at one and the same time". For him it was inconceivable that the spontaneous and chaotic appearance of apparently tribal arrangements on the ground could have produced such a regularised system, especially following the disorder and desolation of the preceding centuries. He proposed that Lord Rhys had committed an act of radical administrative reorganisation and that the new gwestfa system paralleled the shaping of parochial and civil boundaries (ibid.). But, as a list of gwestfa regions below indicates, these institutions were not as regular as they appear, actually preserving in many instances earlier, existing systems that owed as much to the pre-conquest situation as did the Demetian Laws, codified as part of Rhys's government.

It is not until a century after the death of Rhys that we glimpse the first documentary evidence for his reorganisation. An Edwardian survey dating to 1303 lists the gwestfau districts (below) for the cymydau of Ceredigion (Dodgshon, 1994: 347-348 with additional information supplied by Wmffre, 2004):

Genau'r Glyn had 5.5?

Gwestfa Oeron Oweyn
Gwestfa Oeron Ynoi Moryddyg
Gwestfa Oeron Gruff. Ab Wyron
Gwestfa Oeron ab ph.
Gwestfa Goythenes

Perfedd had 4

Gwestfa Trefmeyric
Gwestfa Dyffryn Reydaul
Gwestfa Llangwrda
Gwestfa Rhydonnen

Creuddyn had 6

Gwestfa Llanfihangel Upper
Gwestfa Llanfihangel Lower
Gwestfa Llanbadarn Upper
Gwestfa Llanbadarn Lower
Gwestfa Llanafan
'Gwestfa'

Anhuniog had 9

Crown: Gwestfa Kilkennyn
          Gwestfa Ciliau
          Gwestfa Lan Sanfred
          Gwestfa Llyswen

Lay: Gwestfa de Tr[e]fethwal
          Gwestfa Gwascarauke
          Gwestfa Llandewi-Aberarth
          Gwestfa Llan-non
          Gwestfa Morfa mawr Anhuniog

Mefenydd had 8

Crown: Gwestfa Blaenneu
          Gwestfa Rhosdie
          Gwestfa Rodmaed
          Gwestfa Garth Meyt
          Gwestfa Morfa Bychan
          Gwestfa Goyllwyd
          Gwestfa Maes Peydauk
          Gwestfa Lledrod

Penardd had 4

Crown: Gwestfa Llandewi
          Gwestfa Betws Leucu
          Gwestfa Caron
          Gwestfa Gwynfil

Caerwedros had 10

Crown: Gwestfa Arcoed Treflas
          Gwestfa Kylleu
          Gwestfa Drefreyr (in Iscoed cwmwd?)
          Gwestfa Hyscoed K[a]rwedr[o]s
          Gwestfa Ochayaran
          Gwestfa Elychton
          Gwestfa Penarth K[a]rwedr[o]s
          Gwestfa Oryon Gruffth
          Gwestfa Maur

Is Coed had 4

Crown: Gwestfa Blayn Annerch
          Gwestfa Cauros
          Gwestfa de Berwic
          Gwestfa de Lancoydmaur
Tithing: Bettus Ythell   (Wmffre, 2004: 1322
from later rentals)
          Blaen Keri
          Koedcwm
          Dyffrin porth Hoffni
          Hofnant
          Tredroyre
          Wyren Ho[e]ll
          Ystimkoed

Mabwynion had 8

Crown: Gwestfa Betus Lleucu
          Gwestfa Kestyll Bygeyd
          Gwestfa Dyhewyd
          Gwestfa Kelli-Hyr

Gwestfa Lanveyr
Gwestfa Llanerch Ayron
Gwestfa Llugenydd
Gwestfa Treberuet
Gwestfa Estat

Gwinionydd had 4

Crown: Gwestfa Aber Grannell
Gwestfa Vaur
Gwestfa Redwyt
Gwestfa Arborthen & Gwern[ ]bran

Whilst some of these remain unidentified, many of the gwestfa names can be located using modern place names. These have never been mapped before and the premise that the gwestfau districts preserve earlier trefi units will be addressed but if Jones Pierce is to be believed, the pre-conquest system had been swept away by war, political upheaval and the state-forming policies of Rhys.

The number of gwestfau within each cwmwd differed greatly. Anhuniog (33,000 acres) and Gwinionydd (40,000 acres) are roughly comparable in size but contain nine and four gwestfau respectively. In many instances the name of the gwestfa district can be equated with the names of parishes, Gwestfa Lledrod, Gwestfa Dihewyd, Gwestfa Llanerchaeron and Gwestfa Bettws Lleucu for example. The gwestfau were also of widely varying sizes with the large upland Lledrod unit comprising nearly 9,000 acres with the smaller Llanerchaeron in the Aeron valley at only 1,000 acres, making Jones Pierce's 'uniform' appearance less convincing.

The names of other gwestfau survived in farm and river names. Dodgshon (1994: 348) has Gwestfa Kestyll Bygeyd as unlocated but is surely the 'Castell Bugad' just east of Lampeter town. Rees (1932) was also able locate gwestfau Clychton, Sillen and Aberannell for example, but only as far as the location of the surviving place name and without any attempt at territorial reconstruction. Rees (1932) mistakenly locates Trefethwal at the farm of Tryal Mawr in the parish of Llansantffraid. Tryal is a common place name associated with the post-medieval encroachment and enclosure of upland common. More likely is that Trefethwal is the unidentified Tref Ladheu of Dyneyrd et Tref Ladheu granted to Strata Florida by Maelgwyn between 1198 and 1227 (Pryce, 2005: 197-201), a later grant giving Dynerth et Trefflatheu (ibid: 216-222). Trefflatheu has resisted identification but Dinerth is clearly identified as Dineirth Castle guarding the north bank of the Arth just north of the Aeron, and Trefflatheu must be in this vicinity. Figure 38 shows the location of known Strata Florida holdings (stars) distributed in the eastern half of the parish of Llanbadarn Trefeglwys. These are distinct from the holdings of Llanllyr (circles) arranged in the west of the parish. These two distinct blocks may represent the former distinction between two units which is reflected in the 'double' name of Llanbadarn Trefeglwys. Llanbadarn church in the western portion lies just over a mile north-east of Dineirth Castle and forms the western portion whilst the eastern upland portion forms that part of the tref belonging to the church; Trefeglwys. Gwestfa Trefethwal probably relates to this upland portion and as such represents a unit smaller than the present parish.

Less common for the name of gwestfa units are personal names. Genau'r Glyn to the north contained *Gwestfa Oeron Oweyn* 'Gwestfa of the descendants of Owain', Gwestfa

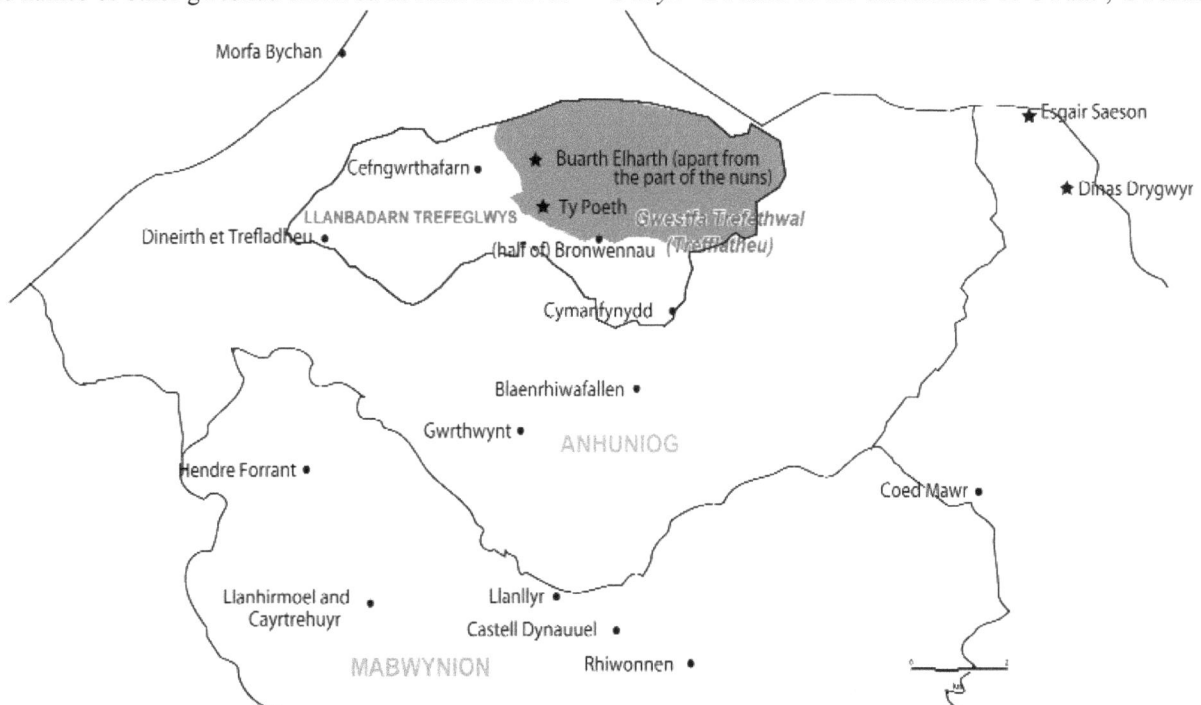

Figure 38. Gwestfa Trefethwal (shaded) as a portion of the larger Llanbadarn Trefeglwys unit. The holdings of Strata Florida (stars) are distributed in the eastern, upland portion whilst Llanllyr (circles) held the western portion containing the church and castle.

79

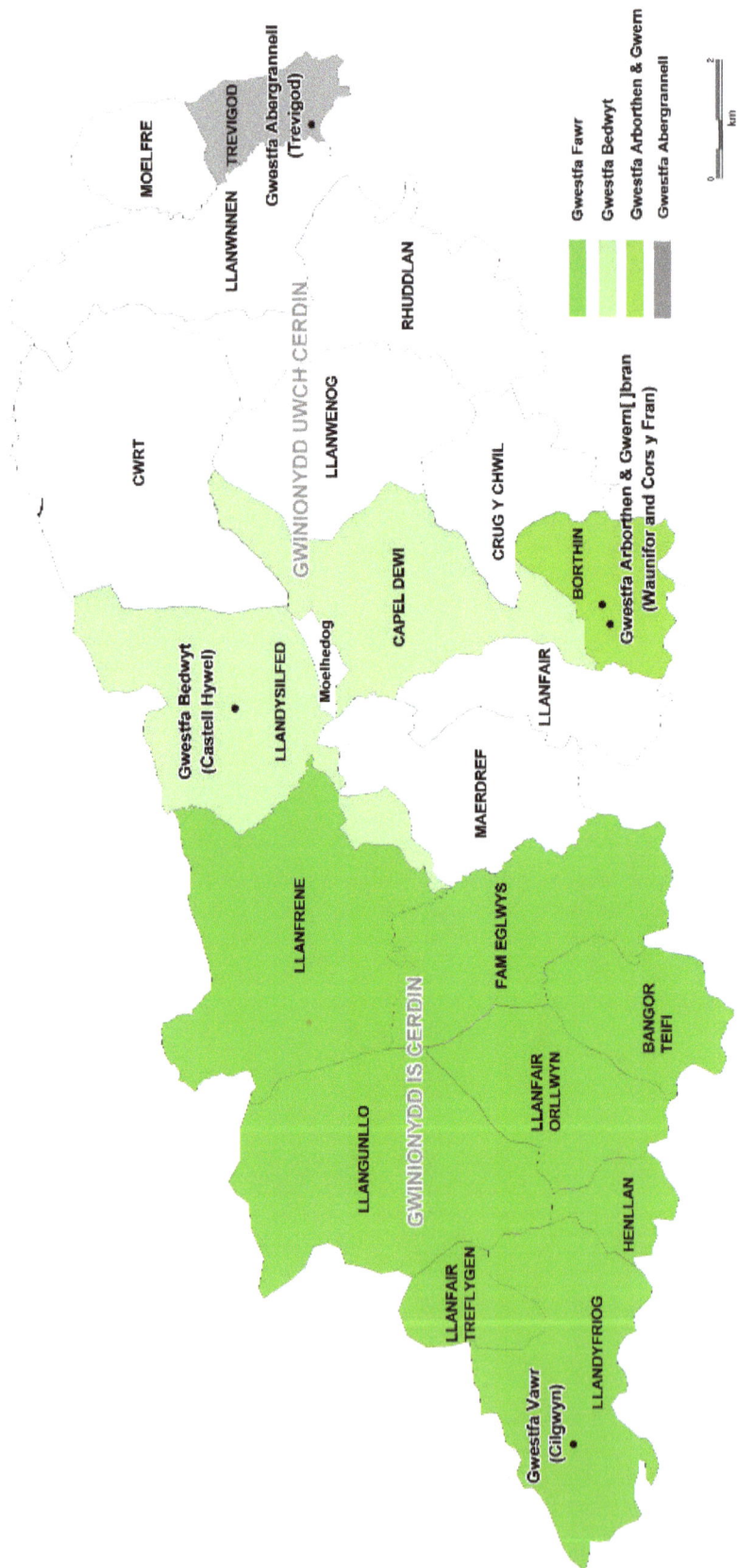

Figure 39. The four gwestfa districts of Gwinionydd. Gwestfa payments in 1303 were rendered on freemen and collected from four areas shown in green. Gwestfa Vawr from Cilgwyn at Adpar administered the whole of Gwinionydd Is Cerdin and corresponded to the Bishops of St David's Dyffryn Teifi estate. Gwestfa Bedwyt from Castell Hywel in Llandysulfed possibly also administered neighbouring Capel Dewi where the Lloyds had the estate of Alltroddyn. Gwestfa Arborthen and Gwern Fran from the tref of Borthin at Waunifor and nearby Cors y Fran. Gwestfa Abergrannell from the farm of that name adjacent to St Mary's chapel. As monastic holdings Moelfre, Rhuddlan, Moelhedog, Maerdref and Llanfair were exempt.

Oeron *Ynoi Moryddyg* 'of Moryddyg', Gwestfa Oeron *Gruff. Ab Wyron* – 'of Gruffudd son of Wyron' and Gwestfa Oeron *ab ph* – 'of the sons of Philip'. Dodgshon (1994: 347) suggests that these are the kindred names relating to the gwelyau or land of the freeholders. In north Wales there is evidence to suggest that the twnc was required of both free and bond communities alike (Ellis, 1926: 288-289) but the insistence of the south Wales codes was that the gwestfa was to be paid by a free tref containing four rhandiroedd. The four rhandir given to William de Knoville and known as Gwestfa Llyswen during the late 13th century was described as the equivalent to a knight's fee and was clearly a free tref liable for gwestfa (Rees, 1932: 35, n. 1). The amount rendered for each of the gwestfau was fixed at 13s 4d but this was regardless of the number of occupants or size of the territory they held. The burden of payment also fell unequally upon the differing-sized gwelyau groups within the gwestfau as the returns from Gwestfa Kilkennyn demonstrates (Rees, 1924: 224, n. 4):

1 group (gwely) of 4 tenants pays jointly a sum of		1s 5½d
1	11	1s 10½d
1	10	1s 11d
1	14	11d
1	14	1s 11d
1	15	1s 10½d
1	12	1s 11d
Acquittances - Gruffudd Goch, reeve		1s. 0d.
Llywelyn, the scholar		5½d.
		1s 5½d
	Total	13s 4d

Whilst one group of 14 tenants paid 1s 11d another group of 14 paid only 11d. The gwestfa unit in question here probably relates closely to the present Cilcennin parish just north of the Aeron valley in Cwmwd Anhuniog but the precise physical nature of the gwelyau holdings and character remains opaque in this instance without supporting evidence. Neighbouring Gwestfa Trefethwal contained only two gwelyau with one group of 16 tenants paying 6s 8d and a larger group of 26 paying the same amount to a total of 13s 4d (Rees, 1932: 35, n. 1). It is evident therefore that the amount of gwestfa paid probably related, not only to the size of territory in question, but also to the quality and productive potential of that land.

Using the newly identified trefi as a framework it has been possible to recreate the likely extent of the four gwestfau of Gwinionydd as follows and these are mapped in figure 39.

1. Gwestfa Vawr. The 'largest' or 'principal' gwestfa probably comprised the whole of Gwinionydd Is Cerdin that lay to the west of Llandysul church, essentially that portion of the Dyffryn Teifi estate that lay within Gwinionydd. It was probably administered from the secular medieval caput of Cilgwyn near Adpar where a branch of the Castell Hywel Lloyds established the lordship of Gwinionydd Is Cerdin in the latter middle ages. It included the trefi of Llandyfriog, Llanfair Treflygen, Henllan,

Llanfair Orllwyn, Bangor Teifi, Llangunllo, Llanfrene, and Fam Eglwys, the latter two being chapelry units within the parish of Llandysul indicating that the framework upon which the gwestfa was based pre-dated that of the parish system.

2. Gwestfa Aber Grannell. This refers to the mouth of the Afon Grannell that runs into the Teifi at Llanwnnen, but the farm of Abergranell is beyond the boundary of the cwmwd as given by Rees (1951) and Richards (1969). The place name may easily have wandered across the Afon Grannell over time but a rental for 1564 includes Trevigod (Trefycoed) making payments as part of the Gwinionydd Is Cerdin Manor and it is likely that Trefycoed originally belonged to Gwinionydd and was served by a chapel at the farm of Llanfair nearby. The northern-most portion of the tref, Moelfre was detached as part of a grant to Llanllyr sometime in the late 12th century. This gwestfa included the trefi of Llanwnnen and Trefigod which is currently a hamlet within the large Lampeter parish.

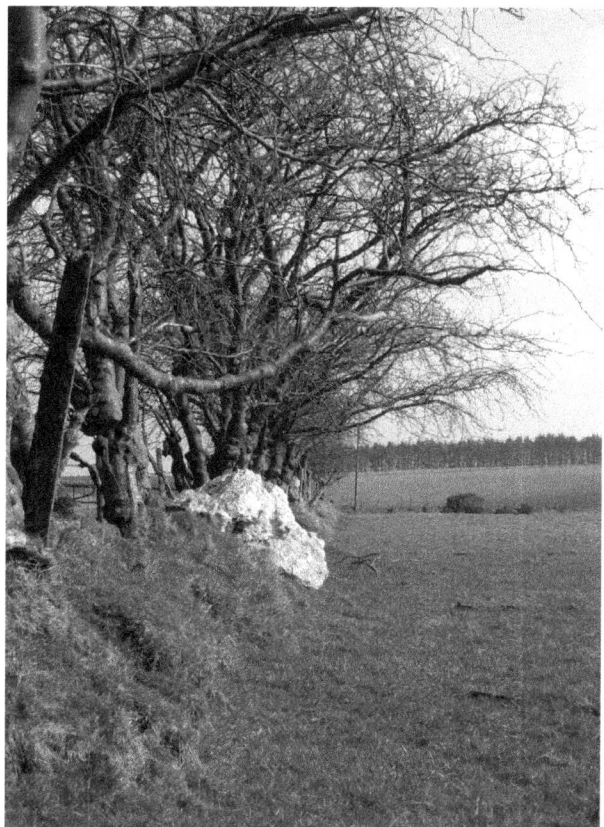

Figure 40. Meini Gwynion, 'white stones' marks the northern extent of Llandysulfed, the direction of a significant north-south route and the meeting of three parishes.

3. Gwestfa Redwyt. Dodgshon (1994: 347) has Bedwyt whilst Wmffre (2004: 1319) translates *Redwyt* as Rhydywain for the village of Rhydowen, but it more likely derives from *dedwydd* meaning happy or blessed and can be seen at Esgair Ddedwydd adjacent to Castell Hywel which formed part of the Castell Hywel estate whose core encompassed the tref of Llandysulfed. Dedwydd rarely

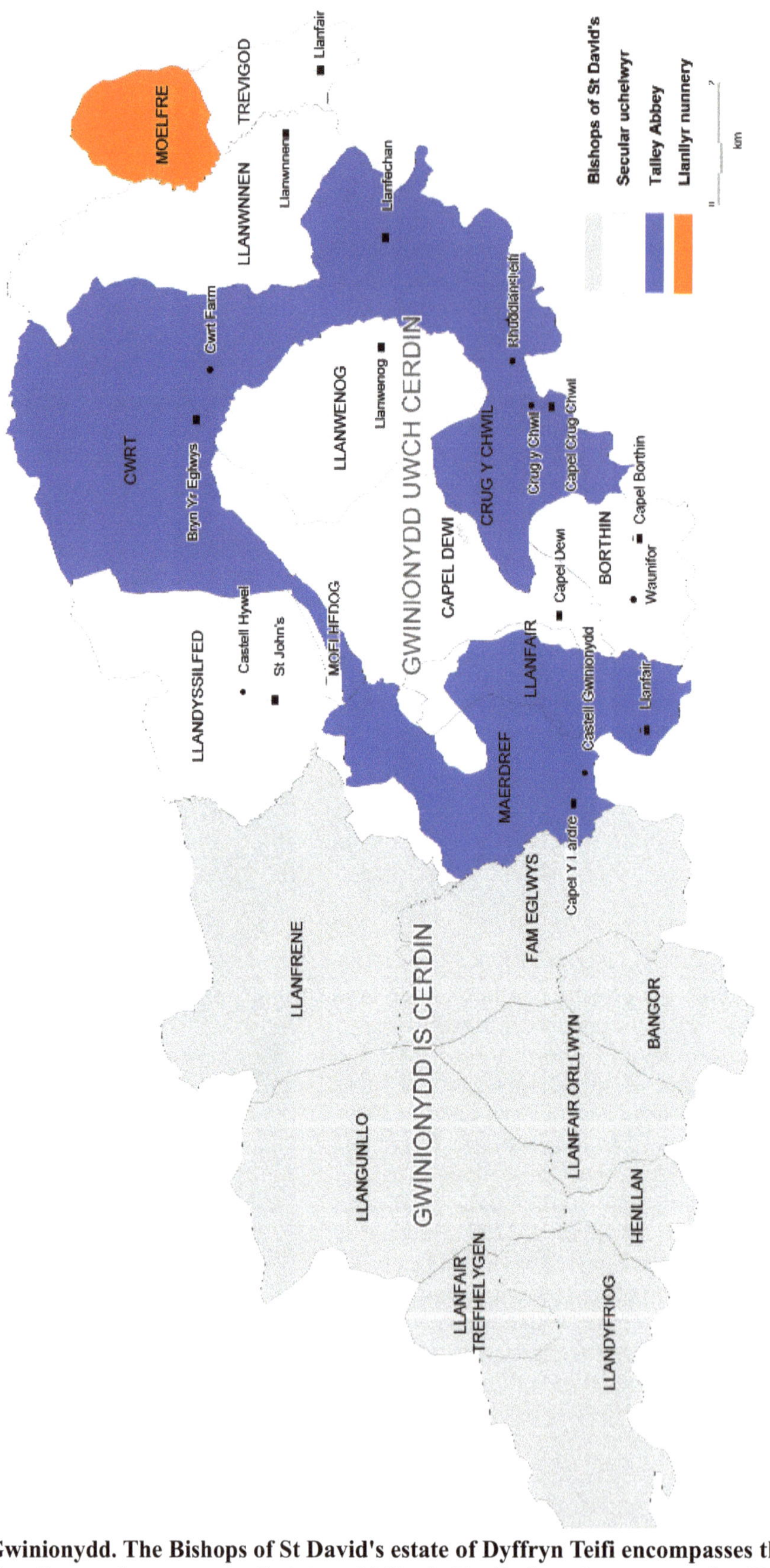

Figure 41. 12th century Gwinionydd. The Bishops of St David's estate of Dyffryn Teifi encompasses the whole of Gwinionydd Is Cerdin. The elite secular estates in Gwinionydd Uwch Cerdin have been granted to Talley Abbey by Lord Rhys (blue), Moelfre (orange) went to Llanllyr, and some trefi stayed in the ownership of the uchelwyr; Llandysulfed became the caput of the Lloyd family descended from Cadifor Ap Dinawal. The importance of royal control over the southern slopes of the central Teifi is evident. The former royal estate stretched between Llanfechan and Maerdref completely controlling the east-west routeways. The cwmwd was administered from the maer's caput at maerdref complex and its demesne core was strung along the lower slopes of Llanfair and Maerdref. The early medieval royal llys and maerdref complex was centred around Rhuddlan Teifi in the east.

occurs as a place name appearing only in the *Black Book of St. David's* as Dedewyth in 14th century Glamorgan (Richards, 2007). The nature of Llandysul's chapelries has led to speculation that the region may have been a focus for pilgrimage in the early medieval period (Neil Ludlow pers. comm.) and the eastern spine of the Castell Hywel estate is a straight holloway that runs north-south for over seven miles connecting the Llandysul area with the early churches at Henfynwy and Llandysiliogogo on the coast. This gwestfa included the trefi of Llandysulfed and Capel Dewi, both major components of the post-medieval Castell Hywel estate.

4. Gwestfa Arborthen & Gwern[ ]bran. The small but important tref of Borthin or 'place of the gate' would have controlled access to the only known medieval bridge crossing the Teifi between Borthin and Llanfihangel-Ar-Arth and where the County Gate hotel still stands (Lloyd, 1935, 316-7). Interestingly at Aberffraw a *Gwely Porthorion*, 'gatekeepers gwely', was recorded as having responsibility for the upkeep of the gate and wall of the court buildings (Jones, 1972b: 333). Medieval activity may have been the antecedent to Waunifor that developed into the principal gentry estate of the Bowen family between the 16th and 19th century (Jones, 2004: 272).

To summarise, Gwinionydd contains four gwestfau units spanning 13 former trefi. Only Gwestfa Arborthen remains as a single tref unit. Elsewhere at Gwestfa Bedwyt, Gwestfa Aber Grannell and Gwestfa Fawr, the gwestfa is comprised of groups of various numbers of trefi. Only the name of the rent survives but it is still based upon the framework of the trefi within it. As part of Rhys's restructuring, and in order to ease collection and administration, the gwestfa would have been collected from the secular caput of each holding. Gwestfa Fawr was coextensive with the Dyffryn Teifi Estate of the Bishops of St David's and the individual gwestfa payments of each vill or tref were still evident in 1326 but the payment would have been due as a lump sum and collected centrally.

The areas not paying gwestfa were the monastic estates, which would have been exempt from gwestfa as at Moelfre and Moelhedog. But as former royal bond estates and administrative centres under the maer or reeve as at Llanfair, Maerdref, Llanwenog, Cwrt, Rhuddlan and Crug y Chwil, these trefi would have been exempt from gwestfa in any case. Whilst Rhys was generous in granting such rich and significant estates to the monastic houses, it must be remembered that he would not have lost any gwestfa revenue from these grants and this may have been a consideration when deciding which holdings to apportion.

Discussion

The previous chapter was able to reconstruct regional ownership patterns based on the cymydau framework and it proposed that these reflected early patterns of ownership based on complex collections of smaller territorial units.

This chapter has identified those smaller units based on the framework of the maenor and the tref as outlined within the Law codes. Maenorau at Manor Teifi, Manor Forion and Manor Rhuddlan have been identified but the way in which the latter may have related to other maenorau within the cwmwd has been largely obscured by the later gwestfau arrangements put in place by Rhys.

It has emerged that chapelries, smaller parishes and other parish divisions can be used to reconstruct trefi. Each tref was served by a church or chapel with pre-conquest origins suggesting a self-contained provision that predates the parish system. The important 'mother' churches, however, were situated along the valley floor with Merthyr Geler at Llangeler, St. David's at Bangor Teifi, St Tysul's at Llandysul and St Gwenog's at Llanwenog serving busy river crossings and vallerouteways. The important lower valley trefi were smaller at between 1-2,000 acres in size and preserved in the parishes of Llandyfriog, Llanfair Treflygen, Henllan, Llanfair Orllwyn, Bangor and Llanwnnen and the chapelries of Fam Eglwys, Maerdref, Llanfair, Capel Dewi, Borthin, Crug y Whil, Llanwenog, Llanfechan, Trefigod and Moelfre. The upland trefi to the north were larger at around 3-4,000 acres as at Llangunllo, Llanfrene, Llandysulfed and Cwrt and the identification of early tyddynod holdings in chapter six will demonstrate how these upland trefi were more sparsely settled above the 200 metre line but still retained complex tenurial and territorial systems.

The relationship between Maerdref and neighbouring Rhuddlan Teifi has emerged as crucial to the understanding of the political development of the central Teifi valley in the medieval period. The proximity of Castell Gwinionydd, Pencoedfoel and a former maerdref had led to the suggestion of a former royal llys and maerdref in the vicinity. The early history of Rhuddlan Teifi, however, is significant and must be regarded as the location of a high status early medieval site: the royal llys of Gwinionydd (see fig. 41 above).

In fact, maerdrefi of non-royal origin are known from elsewhere where the royal version known from the Laws provided an exemplar that was employed by uchelwyr managing smaller lordship centres, many of who were of royal descent in any case. The neighbouring secular estate of Castell Hywel was administered from Gwarallt y Fardre for example. The Bishop of Bangor maintained a bond settlement at Treffoss on Anglesey which was sometimes known as maerdref notwithstanding the nearby royal maerdref at Llanfaes in the same cwmwd (Longley pers. comm.). It is likely that these maerdrefi would have operated along similar lines to royal maerdrefi with all the landed estate functions but none of the 'governmental' ones. Castell Gwinionydd represented the bond settlement of the royal administrator, the cwmwd maer or rhaglaw. It is worth stressing therefore the different types of maerdref:

1   A maerdref belonging to the rhaglaw or 'maer'

who managed the cwmwd under royal patronage, for example at Maerdref centred on Castell Gwinionydd.

2   A maerdref belonging to the maer y biswail who specifically managed the royal demesne, the classic llys and maerdref complex, of which there would have been one inside each cwmwd, as at Rhuddlan Teifi.

3   A maerdref of the 'private' estate of a local lord, at Gwarallt y Faerdre centred at Castell Hywel.

Therefore we must no longer identify former royal estates simply using the presence of maerdrefi to do so. The llys at Rhuddlan developed different foci in the pre-12th century period, losing its royal political status and had gained a reputation for being fertile and productive (Brewer, 1873: 152). It is likely that the farm at Crug y Whil had emerged at this time as the focus of agriculture within the estate which had collectively become known as Maenor Crug y Whil and echoed the former status of the holding as a royal maenor.

SIX: THE FARMSCAPE

Introduction

This chapter studies the evidence for 12th century settlement patterns at the scale of individual and community, endeavouring to identify the tyddyn meaning farm-holding or farmstead containing ty from 'house'. Developing the notion emphasised in the previous chapter that the 12th century landscape was highly organised, complex and populated by sedentary, freeholding communities, the landscape of today's dispersed farmscape will also be analysed for fragments of the rhandir or shareland. It will develop a methodology whereby these early tyddynod can be identified using a set of morphological characteristics and equated to today's dispersed farmscape. This analysis has also highlighted some interesting agricultural and land use practice, highlighting differences between areas farmed as monastic granges and those not. The theme stressed throughout this chapter is one of community and identity expressed through place.

Place and identity have always been closely linked within the Welsh community. Here, people are place. *Where are*

1987, 2002 and 2004) and Lloyd (1989) for example have been helpful in understanding the landscape at its smallest scale - that of the individual, the family, the community. The impression, however, that these histories have created is one of community rooted in a landscape of great time depth, but which, if any, of the physical elements within our present farmscape have medieval antecedents?

Often invisible from the historical record, the individual, family and community nevertheless lie at the core of territory and settlement. Today it is the dispersed landscape of farms and villages that underpins this arrangement but what of the medieval? The individual, family and community were also the basis for the tenurial practice known as the gwely meaning 'bed' or resting place (occasionally *lectus* in the documentary record), and identified those who occupied the tyddyn. The gwely is sometimes conceived as becoming visible at the moment when a tribal, pastoral community makes the leap to sedentary practice. But the gwely survived in Ceredigion into the middle of a thoroughly sedentary 14th century so a more sophisticated system can be envisaged, one of territory not simply tenure. Jones (1996b: 167) explains the gwely as a tenurial system based on partible inheritance and as the name of the territory that it entailed, a homestead or tyddyn, open field arable and common meadow and pasture.

In pursuing the gwely it has become apparent that it is also possible to recognise agency within the landscape. Individuals can be identified and the relationships with the landscape structures that characterise their lives can be studied and, historically, there has been a particular emphasis on this critical relationship between

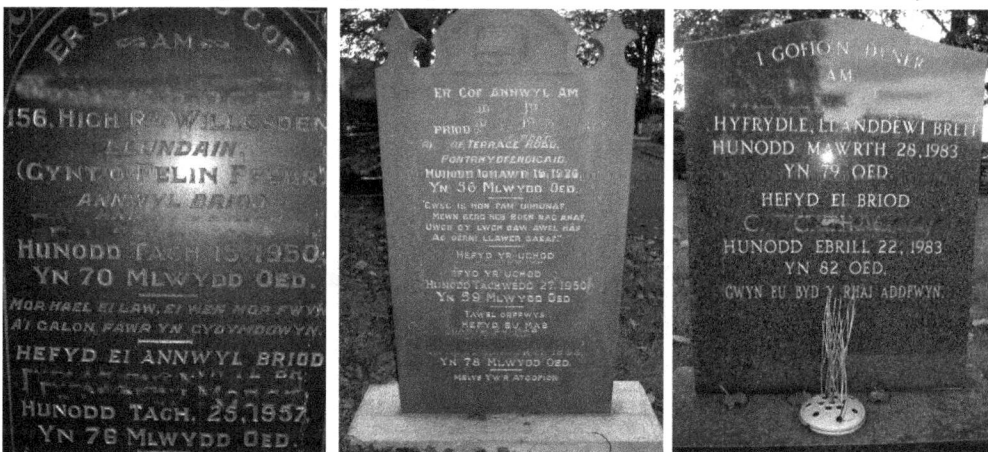

Figure 42. Place and identity. Gravestones from Strata Florida graveyard where the emphasis is on where you are from. The graves of Thomas,(centre) and Mary (right) reinforce the point by also providing full postal addresses and David (left) gives both his London address and his former local address.

you from? is still the first information demanded of strangers. *Sy'ch perthyn* asks not just who you are 'related' to but also where do you 'belong' to. This knowledge is useful if we are to reconstruct a landscape that explains the minutiae of everyday life, the individual, the family, the community. This is perhaps typical of many rural communities comprising dispersed farmsteads and small hamlets. Although the demographic and economic changes of the post-war years have resulted in the fragmentation of farms many of the families still living on the 'family farm' are both careful and proud to be able to trace their lineage at least as far back as the 16th and 17th centuries and sometimes, although without documentary evidence, into the medieval period. Genealogies and family histories provided by Baker Jones (1999), Francis Jones (1960,

people and place in Wales. This understanding underpins settlement at its most intimate scale and allows the identification of the individual occupying the tyddyn by virtue of gwely tenure as part of an extended kin network.

The way in which the occupants of the gwelyau related to others within their community will also allow the identification of the rhandir or shareland, a settlement pattern repeated across the study area and allows valuable observations about the nature of settlement and agriculture. I will first examine some 14th century evidence for the (unusually late) survival of the gwely in the Teifi valley which comes from a detailed survey of the Dyffryn Teifi estates of the Bishops of St David's (Willis-Bund, 1902). This has allowed the identification of named individuals and their families occupying freehold gwelyau, a stage in the development of the present farmscape. Evidence supplied by 16th century surveys for the Manor of Gwinionydd Is Cerdin shows the individual farmstead paying a gwestfa or cheefe rent to the Lord of the Manor. The farmsteads have been located and mapped which has allowed the development of a methodology that will be used to identify potentially early farmsteads in the adjoining region of Llandysul Uwch Cerdin. Field survey and remote sensing at Moelhedog farm, and excavation at Llanfair has pushed the chronology of these holdings back into medieval period, and in some cases to the 12th century. Thus a firm link between the tyddynod of a 12th century landscape and today's farmscape will be demonstrated. The characteristics of these early holdings and evidence regarding their agricultural practices has also allowed a new settlement model to be developed. Behind this landscape reconstruction is the realisation that this is the study of a landscape of deep antiquity and the origins of our farmscape lie in the gwelyau. That it is not just the collective memory and community that is ancient but, actually, today's landscape is too.

Dyffryn Teifi

A survey of rentals for the Bishops of St David's estates contained within the *Black Book of St David's* of 1326 (Willis-Bund, 1902) provides the earliest detailed information for forms of tenure and settlement in this region. The Pembrokeshire and Carmarthenshire portion records very little gwely tenure as this ancient form of tenure had been steadily replaced outside Ceredigion. All of the Ceredigion estates, however, were still at this time based upon the gwely as the unit of assessment providing a rare and unusually detailed glimpse of this smallest unit of institution. Each 'vill' (or tref) records a number of gwelyau ('*lecti*') named for their owners and coheirs and these were assessed for cash payments with occasional labour services to the Bishop as Lord.

A group of eight 'jurors' (presumably representatives of eight kin groups) in Llandygwydd collectively paid 13s 4d annually for the assize of stone and wooden buildings (Willis-Bund, 1902: 229). This represented the gwestfa payment rendered on what the survey termed the lectus or gwely groups. This gwestfa payment was payable only by freeholders. The rentals due from the Lord's demesne were made separately and presumably rendered on bond tenants (ibid: 230-231). The gwestfa payment characterised almost all of the Dyffryn Teifi returns; Lodrepedran contained two gwelyau or lecti paying 6s 8d each Michaelmas, Henllan one gwely also paying 6s 8d and Bangor contained four gwelyau each paying 5s (ibid: 211-215). Lodrepedran remains unidentified and is not named in later documents although Willis-Bund (ibid: map facing cover) places it at Lampeter over 15 miles to the east. Although Lodrepedran is not named in any later documents, 'Llanbedr' is listed as exempt from tithes in the *Episcopal Register of St David's* in 1512 (Isaacson, 1917: 801) but the suit obliging the tenants to do suit at the lord's mill in Adpar and Llandygwydd suggests a closer location, perhaps within the small parish of Llanfair Orllwyn situated between Henllan and Bangor.

The Law texts describe the members of the gwely as the descendants of a common great-grandfather to a distance of four generations and it was always mentioned in relation to the partible rights of freehold over the gwely members' land in direct contrast to bond tenants that were allotted land from the lord's demesne (Jenkins, 1986: 277). Jones Pierce (1959b: 276-277) suggests that the nature of some of the labour services due from the Dyffryn Teifi occupants is an indication of a former bond status, only achieving freehold gwely status later through some unknown mechanism. If we accept this it would be difficult to assume continuity for ancient traditional freehold tenurial practice based on a 14th century snapshot. But there is little evidence for Pierce's assumption and, in fact, the gwelyau members (labour services notwithstanding) and their payments are listed as freemen or liberi, separate from those occupying the demesne bond land at Llandygwydd (Willis-Bund, 1902: 229-231). It is clear then that the *gwelygordd* (family or members of the gwely) as free holders were solely responsible for the payment of the gwestfa. Although the payments are not specifically named as gwestfa, the regular amounts make it is clear that is exactly what is being paid. Jones Pierce (1959b: 272) claimed that harrowing, reaping and carrying for example were never rendered upon freemen although as he himself notes, light agricultural services were required of freeholders at Trefilan and Lampeter and are comparative to the reaping and carrying of corn required at Llandygwydd, Lodrepedran, Bangor and Henllan.

The vill of Bangor can be related to the small parish of Bangor Teifi (Fig. 43 below) which contained four gwelyau. Three of these are named thus: the holders of Gwely Enewris are named as Llywelyn the chaplain, Gruffudd ap Ieuan and their co-owners, paying 5s at Michaelmas. Gwely Oyron Redewyth was held by Yweryth verch Gronw, Ieuan ap Richard, Res ap Gruffydd and their co-owners, also paying 5s. Oryon Cuelyn's holders are named as Gruffydd ap Res, Ieuan ap Adaf and their co-owners, again paying 5s at Michaelmas. They all paid a cow for commorth every 3rd year at the 'calends of May' and all rendered services to the lord at Adpar. Oryon or 'wyrion' is 'descendants' or 'grandchildren of' but at this period there is little evidence that the gwely name actually changed with each new generation and must be regarded as a way of eponymously describing a distant founder. This process reflects the gradual adoption of a fixed family or surname, perhaps as a result of the increasing adoption of documentary records as part of an increasingly bureaucratic and detached administration. Despite the detail offered by the Bangor Teifi survey we cannot trace any of the occupants or their families beyond the 14th century. It was late into the 15th and 16th century when the adoption of fixed surnames started to become more common making it difficult to locate the medieval gwely's physical remnants within the landscape.

Under *cyfran* inheritance, each sibling would have been eligible to shares in the property. Some of these shares emerge into the documentary record as extremely complex arrangements. Parcels, messuages, tenements and fractions thereof could be owned in neighbouring trefi. Gwely land was inalienable outside the family hinting at an element of compulsion sometimes described as being 'tied to the land' (Jones Pierce, 1959b: 274). Different, however, from the ties that controlled the lord's bond this element of inalienability was part of a long-held customary practice that essentially protected the inheritance of the extended family. The named owners would represent family heads; the eldest (usually) male heir whilst the co-owners, mentioned but unnamed, in the Black Book Survey, representing other family members, possibly siblings. If all family members were due an equal claim, Jones Pierce's observation of excessive fragmentation would be likely, but there is little evidence for the physical fragmentation of estates and it is likely that a form of ultimogeniture inheritance was practised. This meant that the youngest son would inherit the family household, allowing parents and other members of the family to remain in the primary holding whilst older siblings were able to provide for themselves within the rest of the estate. Thirsk (1966: 145) outlines the practice in English gavelkind and also the form of inheritance that developed in the middle 14th century known as Borough English where holdings passed to the youngest son as a way of easing pressure for land.

Each named heir within a gwely would represent a household that comprised a family household along with a certain amount of land. The named heir as head of that household would farm that land and his family would live at the house, his offspring would inherit that holding in equal shares with the youngest staying at the family home, literally 'keeping hearth' to provide for the rest of the family. The siblings or unnamed coheirs are problematic and remain essentially 'homeless' under this scheme and herein lies the fundamental difficulty in relating gwely as tenure to the physical landscape. In practice, however, people were not actually making use of one-fifteenth part of a house. Fleming (1998: 56-57) describes a comparable situation in the German Tyrol. When the holdings had become divisible at the thresholds of viability, the householder supplemented their income by trade or craft, by working outside the village or by marriage into another family. The community ended up with a core of land-owners represented by all the family groups with a fringe of labourers and trades people, some with common rights, some leaving to work outside. This, Fleming suggests, may be the reasoning behind the practice of sons from better-off families going into one of the professions; military, law, teaching, medicine or church.

When records first begin to appear in the 13th and 14th centuries they reveal a complex system of division and co-ownership. In attempting to explain the fragmentary nature

of this system Jones Pierce sees the zenith of a short-lived system that failed as division increased beyond the point of viability. He (1951: 257) attributes the origins of the gwelyau within the township of Twrcelyn on Anglesey, for example, to two or three individuals founding 'new' territory between them between c.1150 and 1170, apparently as part of a process whereby tribal nomadism gives way to sedentism. Thirsk (1966: 145) likewise highlighted the 'problems' with partible inheritance where she explained that population rise in the 13th century created pressure for land leading to ever more division with smaller and smaller holdings. However, she also identified the same problems occurring in the Tudor period demonstrating at the very least a certain longevity to the system. Where partible rights of common land have survived into the 20th century in parts of the Yorkshire Dales, for example, both the complexity and persistence of a system rooted in medieval land management is clear. The 'cattle-gate' (referring literally to a gated entrance onto the common) described the amount of grazing animals an individual could keep on the common and the subdivision of these rights led to complex allotments of portions of tenancies. In 1704, Michael Peacock of Angram was the tenant of two and a fortieth part of a house and several parcels of ground; one fortieth of a cattle-gate is recorded elsewhere, and in one instance there were 124 cattle-gates shared between 35 owners, some with only 1, 23 or 3 and one with 2/5 + 9/30, 8 3/5 + 1/03 + 1/40 + 1/8 (Fleming, 1998: 56). In practice, partible inheritance seems to have been a remarkably stable regime not leading to the fragmentation of holdings but serving to tie the family together and, in some instances, behaving with more stability than primogeniture.

The way in which gwely tenure can be linked to the physical landscape can be seen in a Crown rental for Anglesey in 1549 which details all the occupants of the various townships. The gwely occupants are named but alongside a physical, topographical description of the landholding. For example within Gwely Dolfyn ap Karwed:

"Thomas Lloyd dros dir mab y goys yn y *cay hen yn llystulas*   21 d
        William Gruffudd dros dir David ap Tudor ddu *yslaw llanerchymedd wrth yr avon*   7 d
        Thomas Lloyd dros dir Ierwerth ap Tudur yn *llanwenllwyvo o'r tu gogledd y'r capel*   7 d"
                (Jones Pierce, 1941a: 98, my emphases)

This serves to illustrate the gradual movement from the identification of a place with the personal name of its owner, as in gwely custom, to the modern form of topographically descriptive place name.

Whilst it is difficult to identify the eponymous gwelyau with the later, topographical farm names in areas where this kind of rental is not available some observations can still be made about the Bangor Teifi gwelyau. The small motte at Castell Pistog overlooks the narrow Teifi valley and St David's church within its early enclosure is a short distance away with its Rectory and glebe land which may locate Gwely Enewris accommodating the chaplain, Llywelyn amongst others. Meyrick (1810) describes Blaendyffryn hall on the northern slopes as the 'only house of consequence in the parish' and it was home to Rhys David Morris as early as 1712 (Jones, 2004: 23-24). The estate also appears on a 16th century survey but no earlier information exists. The current farmscape is essentially the same as that of the tithe with all of the present farmsteads represented. How far do they represent the landholdings expressed in the 1326 gwelyau survey? If we calculate that the seven tenants (in the three gwelyau) plus an estimated three or four tenants (in the fourth unnamed gwely) occupied a total of ten tyddynod this is comparable to the ten primary farmsteads identified in figure 43. Is it possible to make any further links between the complex tenures of named individuals and families in the medieval period and the modern farmscape?

The Post Medieval Evidence

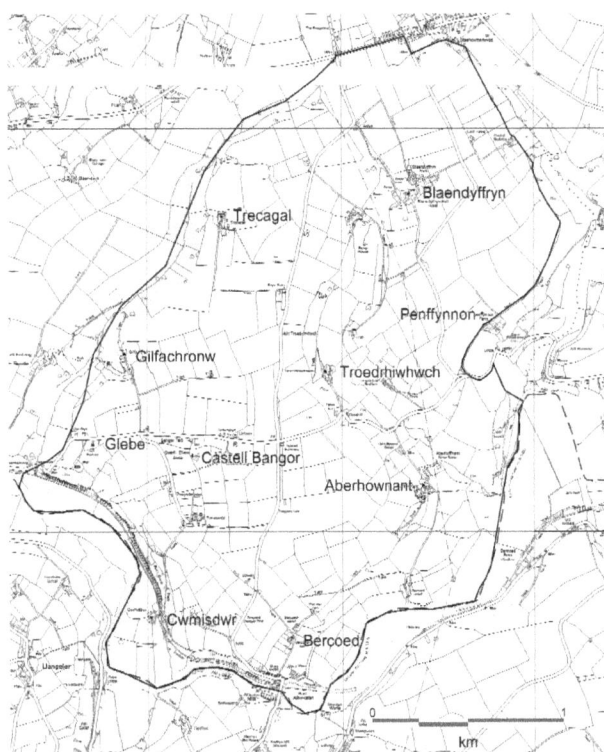

Figure 43. The ten primary farmsteads of Bangor Teifi - location of the ten 14th century gwelyau holdings. Crown Copyright/database right 2008. An Ordnance Survey supplied service

The gwelyau tenancy with its gwestfa payment survived late in Ceredigion as the 14th century Black Book survey demonstrates. A Crown survey of Gwestfa Llandissil within the 'Manor' of Gwinionydd Is Cerdin conducted in 1564 (Table 4) by Howel John Lloyd (Richards, 1964a) indicates that its tenants were still making the gwestfa payment, a practice that continued into the late 17th century (Richards, 1960a) This record differs from that of the Anglesey rental above in that place names are mostly topographically descriptive:

Gwestva Llandyssil   facta per Howel John Lloyd 1564

	£	s	d
Tir y gilvach wen vchaf		2	
Tir y gilfach wen yssaf	6	0	0
Tir kymanvoydwy			12
Tir ystlys merwydd			4
Tir parck llandyssyl			3
Tir llandyssyl			15
Tir lloyn tyssyll		13	0
Tir dol ganved		2	0
Tir aber kerdin	2	9	0
Tir pant hoylwen			20
Tir melindre wion			20
Tir arall melindre wion		4	0
Tir pen y pompren (alias keven y llyest)			8
Tir gwern gadwgan			8
Tir ystlys pant y moch		6	0
Tir pant y moch			7
Tir Cwm y gaist			16
Tir Rhiw ffenyd `			16
Tir y heol hir			4
Tir Cwm yl		3	11
Tir pant y Rhedyney		3	0
Tir glan nythan		20	0
Tir ystlys pant y veillionen		2	8
Tir pant yskythan			20
Tir gwar allt y maerdy	5	8	0
Tir blaen nythan a phant Wilkin		5	8
Tir Cwm meredyth			4
Tir Rhiw lygg			8
Tir Cwm llin vechan			12
Tir fforest Gerdin		6	8
Tir y wern			4
Tir llether hyar		5	0
Tir Cwm hyar			12
Tir y gryg dyon		10	0
Tir argod y brain			16
Tir y goitre			12
Tir pant y krychydd			8
Tir y pant glas			16
Tir y henduy			12
Tir blaen kerdin vawr		18	0
Tir y gilvach Redynog		6	0
Tir y dinas			8
Tir yr ardd hen		4	0
Tir nant y cunstabyl		2	0
Tir llether eithinog		2	2
Tir y tuckwr teg			13
Tir kegynan		3	0
Tir gwarallt annerch			2
Tir bryn y kwtta			12
Tir y gelli vraith			20
Tir y vron vedw			6
Tir agelin lynod			10
Tir yr esgeir wen		2	0

	col1	col2
Tir dyffryn llynod		10
Tir y ffos helig a blaen y ffos helig	4	0
Tir kilvach dafydd		11
Tir blaen Cwm fforest	16	0
Tir blaen cribor	8	
Tir ystlys y darren		8
Tir glan Rhyd yr-ee		8
Tir lloyn oydoes		8
Tir aber nant y kribor	16	0
Tir y glaslwyn		14
Tir cwm y dyllest		12
Tir melindre glettwr		6
Tir y ffynnoney hirion	2	0
Tir Ieuan ap Rhys ap Meredyth Goch		2
Tir gwarallt Keveil		12
Tir dyffryn Keveil		16
Tir y logyn		12
Tir trer groes ar gerdin	12	0

It is has been surprisingly easy to locate the majority of these and in most cases the place name has survived unchanged, correlating with a modern farmstead as identified below (and these are mapped alongside other early gentry holdings in figure 60 below):

Name of Holding	Location	easting	northing
Tir y gilfach wen vchaf	Gilfachwen Uchaf (major dwelling)	240890	24063
Tir y gilfach wen yssaf	Glfachwen Isaf (farm)	240370	240740
Tir kymanvoydwy	Cwmmeudwy (farm)	240340	241540
Tir ystlys merwydd	Cwmerwydd (farm)	239860	242250
Tir dol ganved	Dolganfed (farm)	241960	241190
Tir aber kerdin	Aber Cerdin Mills	242050	241490
Tir pant hoylwen	Pant Olwen (farm)	241340	242050
Tir melindre wion	Felin Pant Olwen (mill)	241350	242660
Tir parck llandyssyll	in the vicinity of Pant Olwen?	241350	242230
Tir lloyn tyssyll		241160	242400
Tir ystlys pant y moch	Pantmoch (farm)	243408	245892
Tir Cwm y gaist	Cwmgeist (farm)	240730	243920
Tir Rhiw ffenyd	Troedrhiwffenyd (farm)	240910	242550
Tir Cwm yl	Cmw-ul (farm)	240240	243050
Tir pant y Rhedyney	Pant-y-rhedynen (farm)	239800	243430
Tir glan nythan	Blaenythan (farm)	239260	244360
Tir ystlys pant y veillionen	Pantfeillionen (farm)	239690	243770
Tir pant yskythan	Pantscythan (farm)	239100	243800
Tir Rhiw lygg	Rhiwlug (farm)	240270	244800
Tir gwar allt y maerdy	Gwaralltyfaerdre (farm)	249120	243890
Tir fforest Gerdin	Forest Cerdin (farm)	239510	245310
Tir llethr hyar	Cwmhyar (farm)	238925	245409
Tir Cwm hyar	Allt Cwmhyar	238830	245700
Tir y goytre	Goytre (farm)	238230	246990
Tir blaen kerdin vawr	Blaen-Cerdin Fawr	238630	248960
Tir y dinas	Dinas Cerdin (farm)	238610	246780
Tir nant y cunstabyl	Nantycwnstabl (farm)	239140	248270
Tir llether eithiniog		238900	246870
Tir kegynan	Ceginan (farm)	239370	246390
Tir gwarallt annrch	Cwm-anerch (farm)	239850	246230
Tir y gelli vraith	Gelli-Fraith (farm)	239970	245300
Tir dyffryn llynod	Dyffryn Llynod (farm)	240560	245520
Tir ffoss helig a blaen y ffos helig	Ffoshelyg (farm)	240960	245890
Tir kilvach dafydd	Gilfachdafydd (farm)	240520	246690
Tir blaen Cwm fforest	Lancwm (farm)	240820	246850
Tir blaen Cribor	Cribor Fawr (farm)	241701	247449
Tir ystlys y darren	Darren Fawr (farm)	241250	248700
Tir glan Rhyd yr-ee	Glan-rhyd-y-dre (farm)	242500	248650
Tir aber nant y kribor	Cribor Fach (farm)	241220	247510
Tir y glaslwyn	Glaslwyn (farm)	242100	246970
Tir cwm y dyllest	Cwmdyllest (farm)	242170	246820
Tir melindre glettwr	Felin Clettwr (farm)	242710	246810
Tir gwarallt Keveil	Gyfeile (farm)	241760	245260
Tir dyffryn Keveil	Cwm-gyfeile (farm)	241634	245030
Tir y logyn	Login (farm)	240950	244630
Tir trer groes ar gerdin	Tregroes (village)	240730	244740
Tir llwyn oydoes	Gwarllwyneidos (farm)	241734	247990
Tir pen y pompren (alias keven y lluest)		0	0
Tir gwern gadwgan		0	0
Tir blaen nythan a phant wilkin		0	0
Tir cwm meredyth		0	0
Tir cwm llin vechan		0	0
Tir y wern		0	0
Tir y gryg duon		0	0
Tir argod y brain		0	0
Tir pant y krychydd		0	0
Tir y pant glas		0	0
Tir yr henduy		0	0
Tir gilvach Redynog		0	0
Tir yr ardd hen		0	0
Tir y tuckwr teg		0	0
Tir bryn y kwtta		0	0
Tir y vron vedw		0	0
Tir agelin lynod		0	0
Tir yr esgeir wen		0	0
Tir lloyn oydoes		0	0
Tir Llandyssyll	in the vicinity of Llandysul? (village)	241890	240690
Tir Ieuan ap Rhys ap Meredyth goch		0	0
Tir blaen dyffryn koll	Dyffryn (farm)	237380	242520
Tir y berth loyd		0	0
Tir Meredyth ychan		0	0
Tir nant y bwch	Cwmbwch (farm)	235760	247320
Tir dol wrgan		0	0
Tir howell ap Jenkyn		0	0
Tir aber y ddoyddwr		236790	243331
Tir bwlche y ddwyfed		0	0
Tir allt y keviley		0	0
Tir y ffynnon wen	Llwynffynnon (farm)	237410	244710
Tir gwar yr allt vawr		0	0
Tir dol mab lloyd		0	0
Tir baili gruffuth goch	Penbeili-mawr (farm)	236380	243650
Tir doley kwerchir	Dolau Cwerchyr (farm)	236960	243560
Tir yr allt gam		0	0
Tir llain y kerrig llwydon		0	0
Tir y pant mawr		236860	244070
Tir y velin Felin Gernos (mill)		236610	244120
Tir pen allt kwerchyr	Towerhill Farm? (farm)	237330	243960
Tir y wern dduy		0	0
Tir y pant bach	Pant bach (farm)	236720	244260
Tir klyn lynog	Glynhynod	237140	245350
Tir aber pant y sais	Pant Sais (farm)	237120	245870
Tir blaen pant y sais	(land above) Pant Sais	237560	246170
Tir y Rhyd goch	Rhyd Goch (farm)	236720	246180
Tir llain dafydd ap rhys dafyd	Gwern Dafydd (farm)	235520	247350
Tir y gilvach		0	0
Tir y geirnos isaf	Cwmgernos (farm)	236400	245090
Tir Ichaf y holl ap Rhys ap gw	Gernos estate? (major dwelling)	236380	245140
Tir blaen y geirnos	Gernos estate? (major dwelling)	236710	246400
Tir oddyar Rhiwr geirnos	Gernos estate? (major dwelling)	236910	245650

Name	Identification	Easting	Northing
Tir pen allt gokyn	Pengallt (farm)	235990	243050
Tir noyadd holl decka		0	0
Tir bronwyth	Bronwydd (major dwelling)	235400	243280
Tir koed y Rew	Coedfryn (farm)	235840	243500
Tir pant iago	Pant (farm)	236210	243930
Tir blaen nant y llan	Blaen-llan (farm)	235470	244390
Tir nant y popty	Nantypobty (farm)	235060	245020
Tir ystlys nant y popty	(land in the vicinity of) Nantypobty	234550	244680
Tir blaen nant gwylen	Nnatgwylan (farm)	234920	245700
Tir hawen Hawen (Place name)		234560	246810
Tir maen lloyd		0	0
Tir fynnon gruffith goch	Blaenffynon? (farm)	239360	242530
Tir blaen machno	Blaenmachnog (farm)	239010	242240
Tir y gilvach whith ar berthyn	Gilfach-chwith (farm)	238660	242720
Tir dol Ivor	Dolifor (farm)	238350	242380
Tir y ddol gay	(in the vicinity of) Dolifor?	0	0
Tir llwyn y gwair	(in the vicinity of) Dolifor?	0	0
Tir fynnon Rydderch		0	0
Tir blaen Hiago	Blaeniago (farm)	238810	243200
Tir y glwysmor		0	0
Tir y berllan		0	0
Tir aber allt y glwysmor		0	0
Tir pirian Pryan (farm)		237920	242130
Tir fynnon gruffith a chaer gwrgene		0	0
Tir nant y garan	Nant y garan (motte)	237040	242090
Tir y bryn gwyn	Bryngwyn	237710	243390
Tir lleiney llether y bystach	Llain (farm)	236920	241290
Tir pwll y korner		0	0
Tir gwern filli		0	0
Tir y pant glas		0	0
Tir y felin Dol Felin (mill)		235930	242000
Tir Llywelyn ap Rhys ap ierwerth		0	0
Llain John Thomas ap harry yn y Rhyd galed	Glyn Caled (farm)	236390	241140
dol aber nant hiago	Aber Nantiago (place name)	236400	240720
Tir y heol hir		0	0
Tir gweyn Rygan		0	0
Tir parke korrws	Parc (farm)	235850	241110
Tir y parke gwyn		0	0
Tir troed y Rhiw		0	0
Tir korrws Felin	Cwrrws (place name)	234750	241860
Tir allt yr Eryr		0	0
Tir pen y Rhiw		0	0
Tir y gilvach		0	0
tir perth y wrach		0	0
Tir kilfach dafydd		0	0
Tir allt Dyfriog		0	0
Tir y vagwyr hen		0	0
Tir bron ayrwen	Bron-orwen (farm)	234200	242530
Tir lloyn Cadwr	Llwyncadfor (farm)	234000	242700
Tir y wern dew	Wern-fach (farm)	233980	242070
Tir treflygen	in the vicinity of Llanfair? (place name)	234390	244320
Tir pant y gwenith	Pantygwenith (farm)	233590	243290
Tir arall y pant y gwenith	in the vicinity of Pantygwenith	0	0
Tir blaen gwenlath	Blaengwenllan (farm)	233730	243840
Tir llanvair dreve lygen	Ffynnon Fair (farm)	234430	244600
Tir pant dafydd	Pantdafydd (farm)	234790	243650
Tir y Noyadd	Neuadd Fawr (major dwelling)	253630	248000
Tir perth y whith		0	0
Tir Erw angharad		0	0
Tir y pistill gwyn		0	0
Tir y llech loyd		0	0
Tir baili llywelyn ap gruffith		0	0
Tir aber grannell	Abergranell (farm)	253770	246430
Tir fynnon vair	Ffynnon-Fair (farm)	254230	246640
Tir y gors		0	0
Tir yr allt vawr	Allt Fawr (farm)	254340	247490
Tir hyw Lewys		0	0
Tir pen y Lan las		0	0
Tir Kryg Kynvilog		0	0
Tir letty adda		0	0
Tir Rhys ap lewys		0	0
Tir Cwm bydyr		0	0
Tir pen y lan		0	0
Tir y vron vedw	Fronfedw (farm)	248520	257300
Tir nant y gwynvaen	Nantygwynfryn (farm)	248900	256560
Tir y piwlwyd		0	0
Tir y gors Rydd		0	0
Tir hendre vorran	Hendre Forant (farm)	249100	258230
Tir holl ap Ieuan lloyd		0	0
Tir dafydd ap gruffith ap philip		0	0
Tir Rhyd y beirdd	Rhyd y Beirdd (place name)	249020	256400
Tir pentre yr velin		0	0
Tir llettyr coch		0	0
Tir llettyr whith		0	0
Tir kil y llwch	Cil-Llwch(farm)	247420	256580
Tir y Drybedd		0	0
Tir bailir gwenyn		0	0
Tir llettyr krydd		0	0
Tir merch Jenkyn ap Rhys ap Dafydd		0	0
Tir gruffith ap morgan		0	0
Tir llettyr llwan		0	0
Tir havotty Rhys Dafydd lloyd		0	0
Tir ynys veilir	Ynys-felen (farm)	249600	254530
Tir y banal		0	0
Tir y cwm towill	Cwmtywyll (aka Gwynfryn) (farm)	249730	255590

Out of the 197 entries in the rental it has been possible to locate 110 of those using the OS 1st edition map and tithe schedules. Eighty-six holdings remain unidentified and a smaller number of those (23) were eponymous illustrating the trend towards the gradual replacement of family and individual names with topographical place names. Tir Ieuan ap Rhys ap Meredyth goch, the 'land of Ieuan son of Rhys son of Meredith the Red', Tir cwm meredyth the 'land of the valley of Meredith' and Tir gwern gadwgan, the 'land of Cadogan's marsh', for example do not survive in modern place names and remain unidentified.

Only very occasionally has a place name changed completely from the original 16th century source. Tir blaen Cwm fforest is the Blaen Cwm Fforest of the tithe of 1841 and by 1891 the holding had become Blaen-cwm and is known today simply as Lancwm. The 'forest' element is relatively unusual within Ceredigion and indicates the introduction of a suite of management practices known only from outside those areas identified as grants to monastic houses.

Another section of the 1564 survey lists properties for the adjoining parishes of Llangunllo, Llanfair Orllwyn, Llandyfriog, Trevigod and Dihewyd. These are listed in a similar way, as place names and amounts payable, but it is unclear whether the payment in this case would represent a gwestfa or a different form of rental. Under customary practice, only the occupants of the gwelyau as freeholders would be liable for the gwestfa payment. It is significant, however, that some of these place names are also eponyms, perhaps hinting at gwelyau holdings and, again, it is these specific holdings that have been difficult to trace: Tir y

Berth loyd 'Lloyd', Tir Meredyth ychan 'Meredith', Tir Howell ap Jenkyn 'Howell son of Jenkin', Tir dol mab lloyd 'meadow of the sons of Lloyd', Tir fynnon Rydderch 'Rhydderch', Tir fynnon gruffith a chaer gwrgene 'Griffith', Tir Llywelyn ap Rhys ap ierwerth 'Rhys son of Iorwerth, Llain John Thomas ap harry yn y Rhyd galed 'John Thomas son of Harry', Tir Erw angharad 'Angharad's acre', Tir baili Llywelyn ap gruffith 'Llywelyn son of Griffith, Tir hyw lewys 'Hugh Lewis', Tir Rhys ap lewys 'Rhys son of Lewis', Tir holl ap Ieuan Lloyd 'all the land of Ieuan Lloyd', Tir Dafydd ap gruffith ap Philip 'David son of Griffith son of Philip' and Tir merch Jenkyn ap Rhys ap Dafydd lloyd 'land of the daughters of Jenkin son of Rhys son of David Lloyd.

Where the eponym is rarely accompanied by topographical information however, this has provided a useful clue to the location of the holding. Francis Jones (2004: 230-231) visited Pen-beili-mawr in Llangynllo parish, to the northwest of Llandysul (fig. 44).

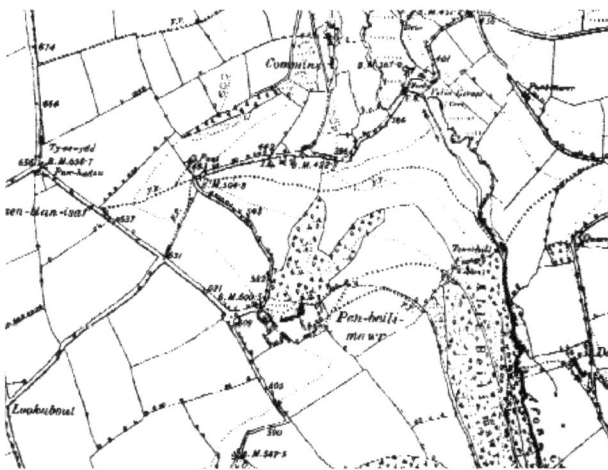

Figure 44. Pen-beili-mawr, formerly Tir baili gruffuth goch, a remnant of the gwely system. Crown Copyright/database right 2008. An Ordnance Survey supplied service.

Noting a Jacobean staircase he was also able to identify an early occupant in Morgan Howell whose will was proved in 1646. A later document of 1725 refers to the holding as Pen y Bayley Coch thus allowing the identification of it as the Tir baili gruffuth goch listed in the 1564 Crown rental. This is a rare example of the entire process whereby a personal name, gruffuth, is eventually dropped entirely from the place name, in this instance sometime between 1564 and 1646. This is representative of the gradual replacement of the eponymous gwelyau holding with one referred to by a place name that refers to morphology and topography, perhaps as a result of the complex ownership and marriage settlements of Morgan Howell.

Although the gwely was deeply associated with kin and lineage, by the middle ages it reflected a sophisticated form of freehold tenure deeply embedded within the physical landscape. There is little evidence to suggest that it was a failed move on the behalf of tribal communities to settle

down permanently and, in fact, the gwely in Ceredigion survives the turbulent conquest process intact into the 14th century where it was used by the otherwise Normanising St David's church. Rentals and place-name evidence of the 16th and 17th century illustrate the occasional retention of personal names and we can see here and elsewhere in Anglesey, for example, the gradual incorporation of topographical information that has proved useful in the location of former gwelyau tenancy as at Tir baili gruffuth goch. This phase represents one where eponyms that described an ancient lineage have gradually been lost over time and survive only in fragments. This was a gradual process reflecting the move away from land held by custom and right to land held as property that could be transferred by contract.

Gwely was an inalienable holding. One was tied to the land and family but with the process of time, failure of lineage, marriage, alienation, death, mortgage and sale, a new owner could expect to rename or favour a toponym over a family name that they might have few personal links with. This appears to have been a very, very slow process in a landscape deeply influenced by family and community social practice so that we can expect the surviving eponyms to be very ancient, challenging Jones Pierce's notion that the gwely was a new institution that failed because of the necessity of fragmentation every generation.

Llanfair

That freehold gwelyau tenants paid the gwestfa rental from the 14th to the 16th and17th centuries demonstrates a remarkably stable and long lived institution. The character of the tyddynod holdings is hinted at Bangor Teifi but evidence from archaeological excavation at the modest gentry estate of Llanfair just east of Llandysul allows us to push this chronology back into the 13th century.

A modest Georgian-fronted plas typical of the central Teifi valley, virtually nothing is known of the early history of the Llanfair estate. Rhys Thomas lived at Llanfair in 1709 and his father Thomas ap David (he was a younger son of David ap Rhys ap David Llewellyn Lloyd of Castell Hywel) is described as of Llanfairperthycyndyn and his will was proved in 1731. The status of these gentry families was at its apogee in the 18th century and one of Rhys's daughters married the respectable Harry Evans of Court Manorforion (Jones, 2004: 163) They had no sons but another daughter married into Ffos Esgob 'Bishop's dyke', a farm marking the northern edge of neighbouring Maerdref and she was also of the Castell Hywel family. Their eldest son succeeded to Ffos Esgob but he had no issue when he died in 1758 and therefore Rhys Thomas, who was his second son inherited. In 1752 Rhys Thomas's son, Thomas married Mary Evans, daughter of Cwrt farm in Llanwenog and it was his son David who inherited Llanfair. In 1758 Plas Llanfair, was worth £8, a modest estate the same value as neighbouring Fardre Fawr worth £14 with the larger Lloyd family estates of Alltyrodyn worth £15 and Castell Hywel at £20. The Thomases were one of the emerging lower gentry familiar to the Tivyside region and by marrying into important local families were able to consolidate their status. The Thomases did not prosper much longer at Llanfair however, and although David Thomas was High Sheriff in 1874 the estate was sold after his death in 1882. In 1908, the estate only comprised 120 acres and it eventually came into the possession of the Lewes family of Llysnewydd and Llanerchaeron.

Figure 45. Looking north along the Teifi Valley at Llanfair. The gentry house to the far right is shadowed behind by Pencoedfoel hillfort and behind the photographer looms Craig Gwrtheryn on the other side of the river. The park landscape conceals a buried medieval landscape.

Still privately owned today by the descendants of the Leweses, a home farm operates adjacent to the mansion which is modelled around a square courtyard with arch-headed windows and stone voussoirs in the vernacular 'polite' style probably dating to the 19th century, a style seen at neighbouring farms. The house was substantially remodelled and extended in the late 18th century to provide a new south-facing façade and again in the early 19th century to supply a library and chapel to the east wing. A late 18th century date can probably be ascribed to the landscaping of the meadows below the house in order to form a modest parkland. Levelling and clearance created a gently undulating, 'naturalised' landscape which has not totally obscured some earthwork features. Routine aerial survey in the dry summer of 1984 by Dyfed Archaeological Trust identified a sub-circular earthwork some 100 meters in diameter (fig. 46 below). This feature was subsequently recorded in the HER as an Iron Age or Roman defended enclosure. However, following the evidence for medieval activity at Llanfair a programme of archaeological excavation was proposed and is outlined below.

The earthwork is elevated 1-2 metres above the floodplain, is sitting on the edge of a former river terrace and the river dynamic seems to suggest the possibility that the earthwork site would have actually sat on the edge of a river bank (M. Bates pers. comm.). The area between the earthwork site and the river is characterised by a lower terrace and a younger, lower terrace towards the outside of a bend appears to the south-east. Devensian gravels and coarse cobbles were encountered at the lowest within the enclosure at a depth of 1 metre and outside the enclosure at a depth of 1.5 metres and the probability is that these were laid down

Figure 46. Aerial survey at Llanfair (looking south) shows the circular earthwork on the Teifi valley floor. Reproduced by kind permission, Dyfed Archaeological Trust.

prior to the Iron Age. Grits, silts and clays deposited in top of this were clearly waterborne and provide a depositional sequence up to 40 cm deep. The upper deposits are disturbed and there is evidence for former land surface with soils formation. This context produced Neolithic flint debitage including some worked and prepared pieces. Glacial terracing higher up the valley sides provides a narrow level on which the estate buildings and road sits (fig. 47).

and truncated by the present road is a series of former braided routeways and tracks. To the rear of the house and parallel to this road runs a very deeply scored holloway that runs for a distance of several hundred metres. This feature is some 6-7 metres wide at the bottom and some 2-3 metres deep between steep earth-banked sides. The trackway appears to have gone out of use sometime after the late 19th century as the 1st edition OS shows it running through an open field that is presently planted with softwood timber-

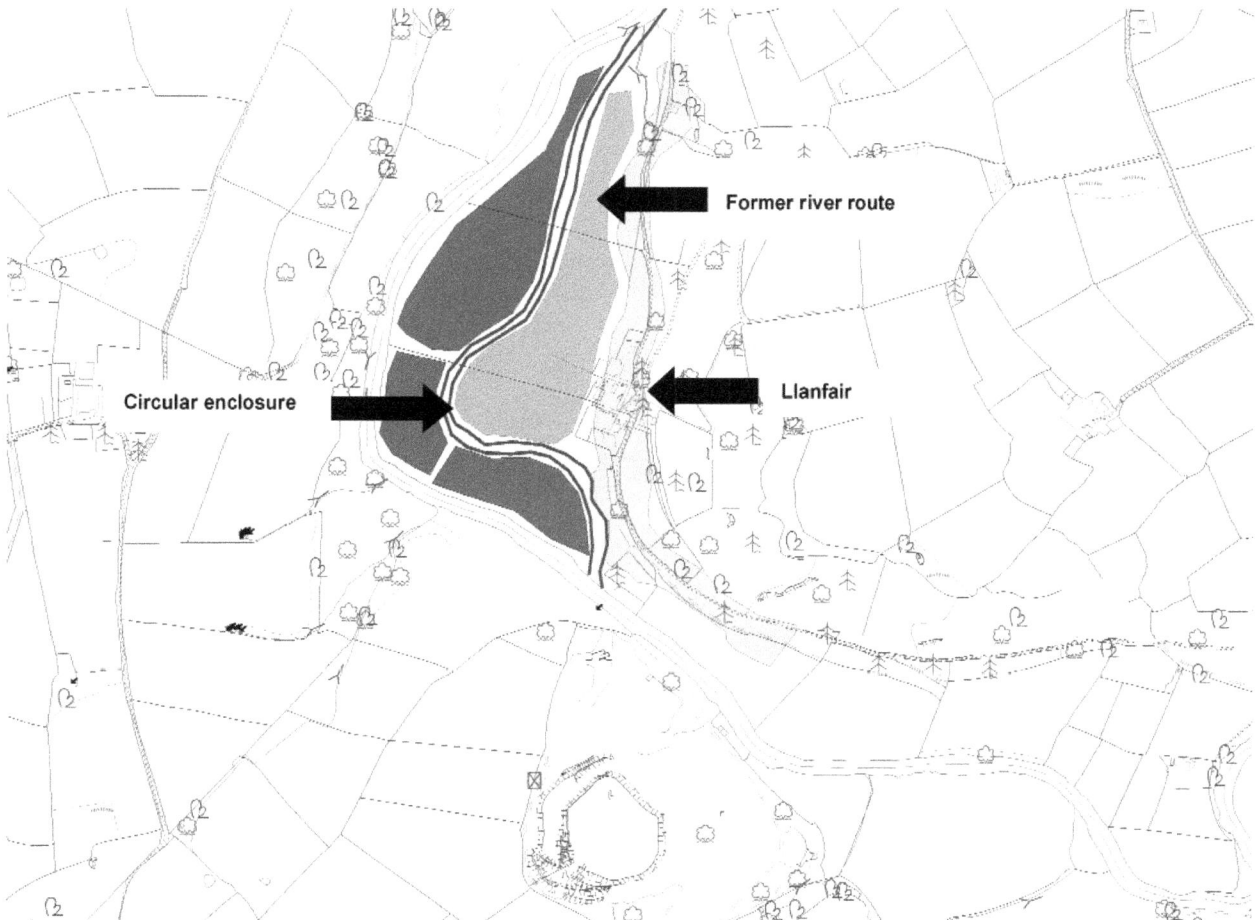

Figure 47. Llanfair river terraces mapped from topographical survey and the proposed former route of Teifi with the circular enclosure sited on edge of western river bank. Crown Copyright database right 2008. An Ordnance Survey supplied service.

The land is currently farmed organically comprising improved pasture for the most part. The estate is registered for the Agri-environment scheme, *Tir Gofal* that incentivises conservation and sympathetic farming techniques. As part of an agreement with the landowner, the earthwork field has been removed from the arable regime in order to minimise disturbance to the archaeology. The earthwork field has been ploughed only very occasionally; during the 1940s and again in the 1970s but the surrounding fields to the north and south are cultivated regularly to provide stock fodder. As a parkland reserved for leisure since the late 18th century any archaeological deposits will have suffered minimal disturbance, the benefits of which were demonstrated at Llanerchaeron where the remains of extensive medieval settlement underlies the parkland there. The valley here is narrow and wooded but would have formed the main access east-west,

crops. This part of the valley is characterised by very steep, boulder strewn slopes yet the area around the house and trackway have been cleared and these would have provided a good source of building stone. The road indicated on the tithe map is also substantially different to the modern route towards the east when it gets to Dolfor Mill and Dolwilym and these are now merely tracksways.

Where the holloway meets the present parallel road, ruined building remains are present and are anecdotally thought to be the site of a former lodge or gatehouse. There is, however, no evidence of enclosures or garden features, there are no buildings marked here on any of the earlier maps and the rubble remains contain modern debris; bricks, roof slate, late ceramic ridge tiles, concrete and asbestos sheeting. It seems likely that this handy lay-by may have been used as a tip where building rubble has been dumped.

Despite a field visit by the archaeological curator of the Tir Gofal scheme the woodland and farmland have not been surveyed and an extensive range of earthworks and built features within the woodland indicate water management systems and leats and deserve further investigation which lies beyond the scope of this thesis.

Geophysics

Figure 48 displays the geophysical survey results which essentially confirm the circular nature of the earthwork feature. In addition, the feature exhibits evidence of highly complex phasing showing both negative and positive features. The site is of a highly complex nature with many phases of banks and ditches cutting and recutting each other but essentially creating the circular enclosure. The enclosure also seems to be overlain by a series of linear anomalies. It is compelling for example to speculate that tvvvvhe two dark parallel features to the centre may represent the remains of a building aligned east-west (the two end walls are not visible possibly because their alignment coincides with the direction of survey making detection difficult). The central southern area appears to show disturbance with a strong slanted linear feature and the two roughly parallel lines running across the bottom of the figure also seem to have been truncated in this area. The pale faint line slanting across the south eastern corner represents the remains of the former orchard enclosure. Figure 49 (next page) presents the simplified interpretation of a circular site enclosed by a bank representing several phases of rebuilding on slightly different alignments. An

outer ditch can be seen to the west. A series of linear features may represent trackways but the nature of the signal tends towards interpretation of negative features perhaps the ditch of a large outer enclosure with possible further structures outside this.

Other point anomalies depict strongly bi-polar readings that normally indicate ferrous or other metallic objects. Often these represent modern 'noise' such as nails or coins but some of the larger features may represent dumps of material or even a concentration of slag or smelting waste. There are some very dark patches on the survey that are not bipolar in nature and probably represent areas of localized burning or dumps of burned or fired material.

Excavation

The geophysical survey was highly successful, clarifying the nature of the visible earthworks but also demonstrating the surprisingly complex nature of the archaeology. Also, many of the features depicted are not in fact visible on the ground, having been totally truncated and levelled by subsequent activity on the site. The likelihood that the chapel of St Mary's stood here and serviced the needs of the chapel of ease of Llanfair remains high. The opportunity to supplement the meagre archaeological record for rural west Wales, and to address the nature of the medieval chapel and its relationship to its clients and landscape led to the proposal of excavation in order to:

• Confirm the presence of archaeological deposits.

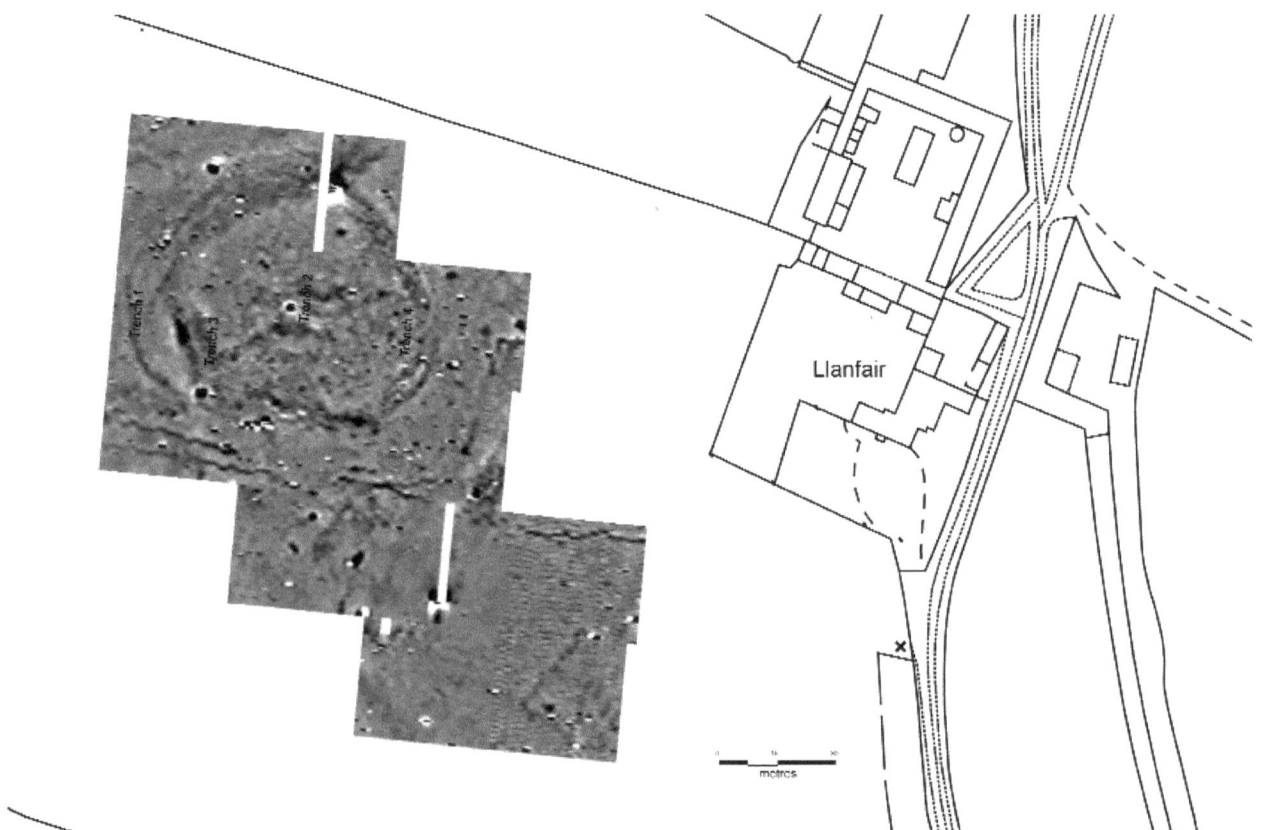

Figure 48. Llanfair geophysical survey (values clipped to + 6 nT.). Crown Copyright database right 2008. An Ordnance Survey supplied service.

- Determine the nature, extent and condition of any deposits.
- To establish the nature and extent of any medieval activity on the site

it was completely devoid of finds so that it is probable the stony fill represented a single event. Contrastingly the deep top and sub-soil contained both worked and unworked flint, a small amount of field lime, charcoal, iron, coal and

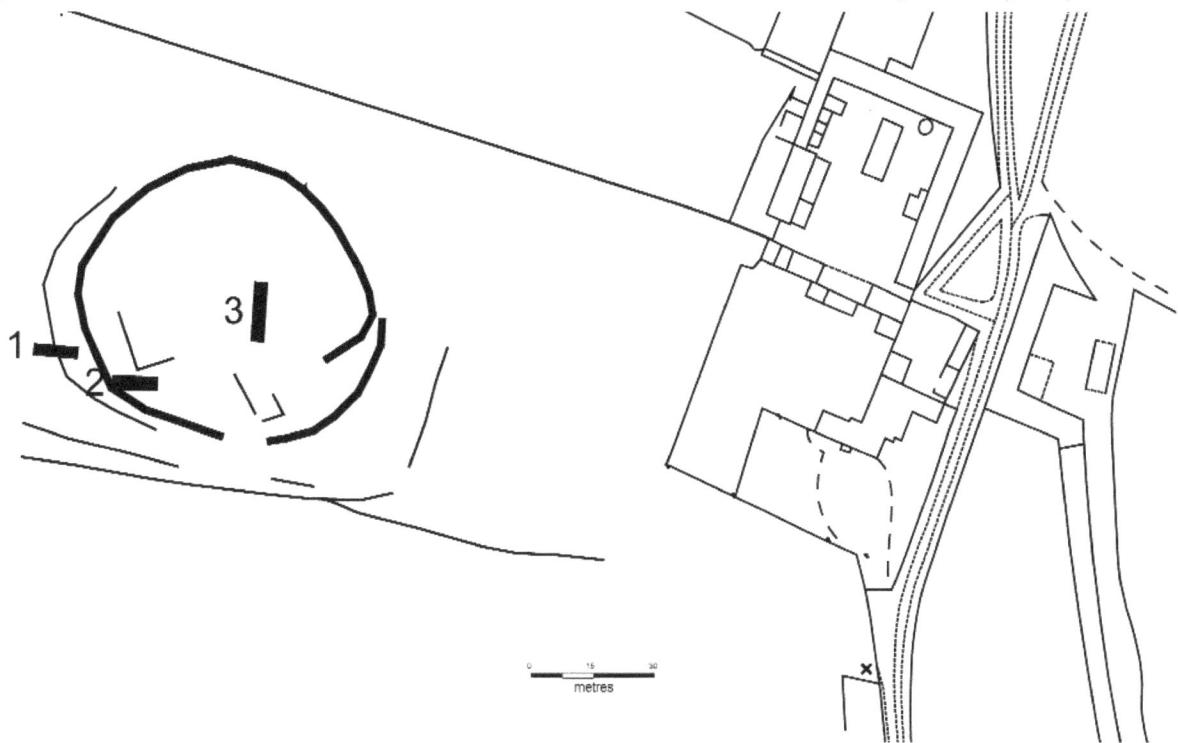

Figure 49. Interpretation of geophysics survey showing positions of trenches. Crown Copyright database right 2008. An Ordnance Survey supplied service.

In all, three trenches were excavated by the University of Wales, Lampeter's Department of Archaeology under the direction of the author. Medieval material was recovered in considerable quantities but in very fragmentary state and a summary of the finds can be seen in table 6. Very little post-medieval material was found attesting to the limited invasive agricultural and domestic activity on these meadows since the medieval period. This follows a similar trend at Llanerchaeron where the emparkment of the valley floor surrounding the mansion had 'sealed' the medieval landscape beneath and with subsequently very little invasive activity.

A trench (number 1, fig. 50) 4.5 x 1 metres was opened across the outer 'ditch' feature. This particular section of the feature was chosen because the geophysical survey indicated a crisp outline indicating that the feature was well preserved at this point and was away from the 'noisier' interior of the enclosure. The evidence suggests a palisade trench (see fig. 51) possibly predating much of the main medieval activity and may even be prehistoric considering the considerable Iron Age activity on the surrounding hilltops.

The ditch is 1 metre deep with steep, almost vertical sides and a flat-bottomed, 'U' shaped profile. The ditch appeared to have been hand-dug and open for only a short length of time before backfilling. The sides were loose showing no signs of compaction there was no indication of silting and

clinker, a late clay pipe stem and both medieval and post-medieval ceramics. Therefore no dating evidence was found for the trench. The ditch whilst deep is relatively narrow at less than 1 metre wide, which would hardly constitute an effective barrier.

The geophysical survey also indicated the absence of a corresponding bank suggesting immediate backfilling,

Figure 50. Trench 1 showing a palisade trench.

perhaps a palisade trench but with acid soils precluding the possibility of any timber survival. A gravely layer containing both medieval and post medieval ceramics sealed this activity which did not contain any dating evidence although the palisade trench appears to be truncated by subsequent activity and in the light of evidence

Table 6. Llanfair finds summary.

Trench	Context	Date	medieval pot	Cooking pot	Saintonge	post-med pot	Roof Tile	clay pipe	roof nails	Iron	O/metal	Lime	Flint debris	Struck flint	Bone	Tooth	Glass	O/Fired	Plaster	Slag	coal/clinker	modern	misc
1	1	6.12.4	1			10			3					2				2	2	1			
1	1	7.12.4							1									2	2				
1	2	8.12.4	4					1															
1	3	8.12.4	3																				
2	28		6	1			1		9			1	1		1			2					
2	28	26.5.5	7				1		3			4	1		1			13	3				
2	29	19.4.5	2				73		2			4	2					3	4				
2	29	28.5.5					6																
2	29	26.5.5	2															2					
2	10	29.1.5								1							1	7		1	4	2	
2	10	28.1.5	44	2		1	11		7			1			2			2	1	1	4	1	
2	10	17.5.5	5			1	3		5									1					
2	28				1	2			1			4						9			3		
2	27	18.5.5	98											1									
2	27	17.5.5	26								3					1							
2	27	18.5.5	10		1	6			13	3		10		2		1		12	1		2		
2	27	20.5.5	24			1	21		5									5	3				
2	27	5.4.5	31							4	1	1						2					
2	27	7.4.5	9				5			3		2	1	1		1		3					
2	27	2.6.5	2	3								2											
2	28	28.5.5										10			8	2			1				
2	28	31.5.5	1									4	1		4								
2	36	28.5.5	23	14	1		1		13			10	2	2	1			15	1	1			
2	32	3.6.5	9									3	3										
2	28	30.5.5	1			1			1			1				1		2	1				
2	35	28.5.5																					
2	36	2.6.5		11						1		8	1			5		3			1		
2	36	30.5.5	5	1						1		2			1			4			1		
2	44	2.6.5	1						7		2	35			9	1		6	4		1		
2	44	3.6.5							2			78			1			3					
2	44	4.6.5		2						3		18						2					
2	44	2.6.5	6				1							3	3								
2	44	3.6.5					1																
2	40	2.6.5								3		2							3				
2	40	3.6.5		1						2									8				
2	45	2.6.5		10						1													
2	38	6.6.5												2									
2	38	4.6.5											1										
2	50	6.6.5																					
2	43	2.6.5																					
2	37	28.5.5		1							1					1							
2	49	6.6.5	1							3		4	1	1				2					
2	42	3.6.5		1					1				1							3			
2	48	5.6.5																		3			
2	48	4.6.5																					
2	48	3.6.5											2	2									
3	24	20.5.5		1		2	2		1	1								2			1		
3	12	2.2.5	10			2															2		
3	25	5.4.5																					
3	12	18.2.5	1			1																	

Table 6. Llanfair finds summary.

96

Trench	Context	Date	Ceramic medi	Cooking pot	Saintonge	post-med cera	Roof Tile	clay pipe	roof nails	Iron	C/metal	Lime	Flint debris	Struck flint	Bone	Tooth	Glass	O/Fired	Plaster/f	Slag	coal/clinker	modern	misc
3	17	30.3.5		1																			
3	15	2.3.5																					spindle whorl
3	16	2.3.5	1																				
3	14	2.2.5					1													1			
3	19	30.3.5												3									
3	19	31.3.5												3									
3	19	1.4.5												2									
3	24	4.4.5												2									
3	22	31.3.5												1									
3	21	5.4.5												4									
3	19	18.5.5											1					5					
3	11	6.3.5							2			3		1									
4	30	23.5.5	3			3				1				1			2			1		1	
4	30	24.5.5				1								1									
4	30	25.5.5	8	1			3		2	2		1						1			1		
4	30	26.5.5	31				4			1		3	7				1				8		
4	31	28.5.5	4				2					1					1				6	1	
4	31	30.5.5	4									1		1				1				1	
4	31	31.5.5	12				1			3				1									
4	31	1.6.5	5															1			1		
4	32	28.5.5	23				1			2	1			3			1			2	2		
4	32	1.6.5	6				1																
4	51	6.6.5	4	9		1								2	2								
4	53	6.6.5	1										1										
totals			434	57	5	30	139	1	77	35	8	208	28	39	34	12	7	110	31	13	37	6	

below must predate the late 13th century.

A second trench (fig. 52) measuring 5 x 1.5 metres was opened across the outer edge of the enclosure in order to test the nature of the enclosure wall or bank. A low earth bank was constructed on the edge of the enclosure, as the result of the upcast of ashallow, narrow ditch to the interior. The result would be a very low earth bank with a timber fence or palisade running along its interior (see fig. 51 below). Ceramic evidence derived from this sequence date the cutting of the palisade trench to the late 13th century, and I am grateful to both Dee Williams and Neil Ludlow for their ceramic identifications. The lower levels of this trench comprise Devensian gravels overlying which are silty deposits from which we found a large concentration of struck flint tools and flakes. Although small, these have been tentatively dated to the Neolithic period based on type (Eleanor Breen pers. comm.). The source for this flint would probably have been coastal some 22 miles downstream (John Davies pers. comm.). The whole was again sealed by rubble clearance of the type present in trench 3 below. Rubble stone, some flags and medieval ceramics were joined by a spindle whorl, seemingly carved from a ceramic ridge or floor tile. A third trench (figure 53 below) was opened on the highest central point of the enclosure to investigate the possible structure. A long narrow trench some 2 metres wide was opened over part of this feature at a right angle to the east-west trend and this was subsequently extended to 18 metres. The deposits here were very shallow and had clearly been affected by the minimal ploughing regime. Comprising building rubble with high amounts of small, rectangular roof slatesthere was also a considerable quantity of locally-derived glazed ceramic ridge tiles. This deposit also included iron nails, some charcoal and glazed and unglazed locally derived domestic ceramics including some cooking-pot types.

To north end of the excavated trench a linear feature c. 80 cm wide cut into natural deposits were filled with this rubble clearance and represents a robbed-out foundation trench (fig. 54 below, page 249). To the southern, and less disturbed, end of the excavation, the rubble lay over an occupation floor of large rough paving flags and produced evidence of cooking pot, charcoal, clay/lime mortar and a small amount of sheep, bird, pig and cattle bone, characteristic of a domestic assemblage (Ros Coard pers. comm.). The recovery of small sherds of Saintonge-ware confirms this activity associated with this structure to medieval period, somewhere between the late 13th to early 14th century. The large amounts of locally derived ceramics date more loosely to the same period (Dee Williams pers. comm.). The findings at Llanfair as elsewhere at Llanerchaeron for example are beginning to challenge these assumptions. We can begin to challenge notions held for example by Butler and Redknap where 'elite' ceramic imports of the 12th to 15th century are only found at Anglo-Norman controlled sites.

The Welsh-built fortification (c. 1221) at Castell y Bere was

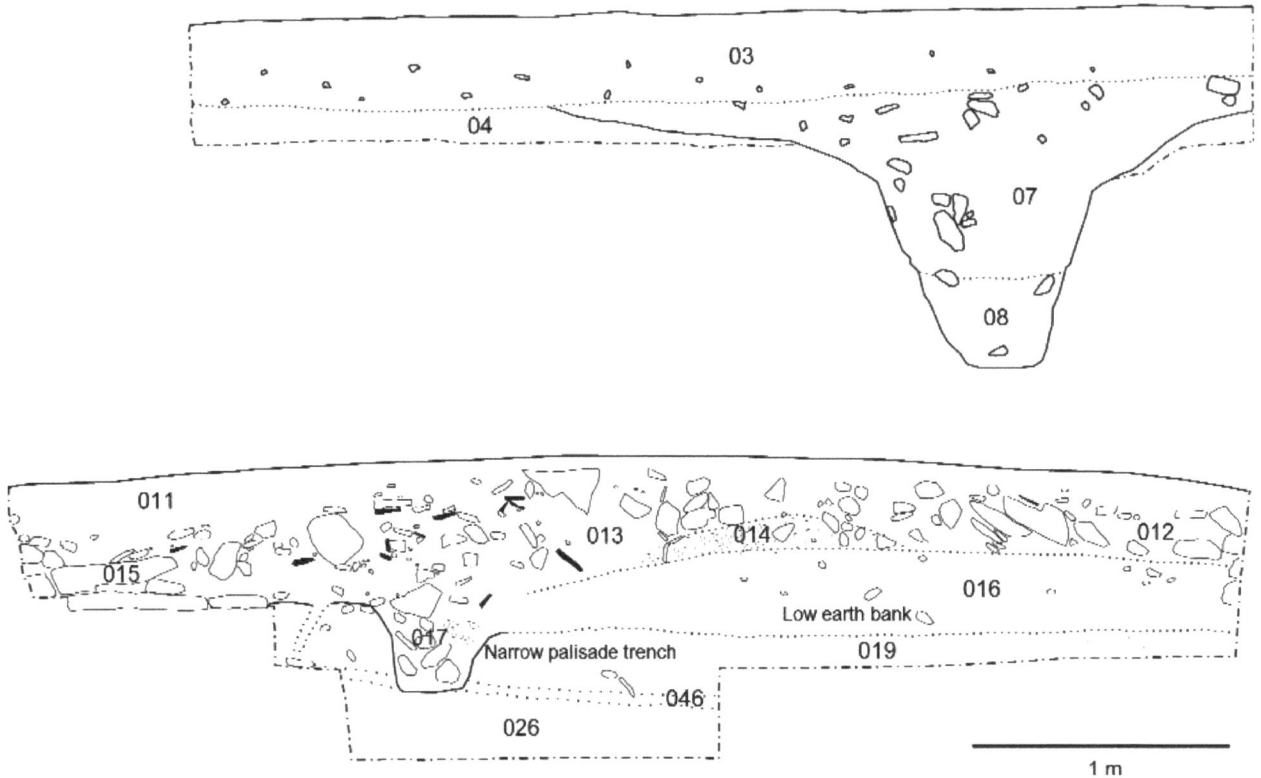

Figure 51. Trench 1, south-facing section across outer palisade ditch. Drawn by R. J. Bale and J. Bezant.
Bottom: Trench 2, north facing section across enclosure bank and shallow ditch. Drawn by J Bezant.

only occupied by Anglo-Norman forces for a short period between 1284-1295 and yet despite 'stratigraphic uncertainty', Butler (1974: 78) closely dates a French Saintonge jug to this ten year period because the foreign administration of the castle. Redknap (2004) attributes the distribution of imported French ceramics to coastal sites which were more easily controlled by the English but this needs to be treated cautiously, reflecting a bias in

Figure 52. Trench 2. Shallow palisade cut inside enclosure bank.

excavation not distribution. There is also lime mortar present in some quantity and where this survives soil conditions have been altered to allow the preservation of bone and tooth, mainly sheep and cattle. There is no glass, lead, iron or any other metallic objects present although a significant quantity of roofing nails were

recovered. The paved occupation layer was not excavated at this time, as it was unlikely that the strategy of long narrow trenches would be able to make sense of any structural plan that we might encounter.

The archaeological deposits represent the systematic demolition and clearance of a building that exhibits at least some domestic types of activity associated with cooking for example. This building was of significant status having a tiled roof with ceramic ridge tiles, iron nails and lime mortar. It seems that the site was probably deliberately dismantled over a relatively short period of time before being levelled and cleared. Some smaller timbers appear to have been burnt in-situ on a bonfire and all of the roof and window furniture and larger and dressed stone having been removed leaving rubble core and broken roofing roof slates. A robber trench contained a 'stack' of roof slates that perhaps were meant to be reclaimed later. There were no glass or metallic objects aside from roof nails present and all the ceramics recovered are highly abraded and fragmentary. Someone had gone over this site with a keen eye and everything of use has been removed. Excavation at Llanfair has yielded information vital to the narrative of medieval rural Wales that challenges the view that circular earthwork sites that must be Iron Age.

When we consult the databases of known medieval sites we see only the obvious castles and churches. This has reinforced a false impression that there is very little or no medieval archaeology in these areas. Even ring-work sites are only now being recognised as such despite the illuminating work in the 1960s by Alcock (1963) at Dinas Powys. Our understanding of medieval settlements in this region is poor and is usually confined to the study of 'visible' elite, fortified sites.

Figure 53. Trench 3, looking north across rubble spread (left) and robber trench with slate and stone fill.

This excavation has demonstrated the extensive survival of the remains of Llanfair church built by the Premonstratensians after they acquired the estate by grant of Rhys ap Gruffudd in the late 12th century. This comprises the only known chapel site of the seven chapelries that comprise Llandysul parish. The excavation strategy of narrow evaluation trenches greatly facilitated an efficient and informative approach but did not allow excavation beyond the latest deposits at 13th century. To fully understand the origins of the site, open area excavation would be appropriate but would need a much larger scale operation. Nevertheless, 'Kynbyt Issald' suggests that an enclosure already stood on the meadow below the woodland and this may be the palisade trench (trench 1) that had been truncated by the main phase of activity. It is impossible to speculate on the nature of this former enclosure based on the results of the excavation but it is likely to have been an earlier chapel site serving the tref and other early church sites favour this valley floor location along the Teifi. The Mary dedication may have replaced a former dedication as is also possible at Capel Mair, Manorforion. The church would have attracted domestic activity, evidenced by the bone assemblages and cooking pot and was perhaps of the form seen at Llanerchaeron where a collection of ancillary buildings were loosely grouped to the east of St Non's church (Evans, 2003). With very few parallels it is difficult to assign status to a building of this type based on material assemblages but the building excavated was stone-built with locally derived slate roof and ceramic ridge tiles. Dating to the late 13th century, it is rather earlier than the structure at Llanerchaeron where a coin was found dating to the 14th century and where the principle building was of clom and cruck construction with thatched roof (ibid.). At this early date, a rural church building of slate under stone in infers a high level of investment in construction beyond that seen

elsewhere. Church inspections by the Archdeacon of Carmarthen during 1710 lamented the ruinous fabric of the churches of northern Carmarthenshire reporting the need to repair thatch, rebuild walls and bury uncovered bones (Griffiths, 1974a). The building appears to have been dismantled systematically after the late 13th century, perhaps as a result of domination by the church at Llandysul nearby. Although it will become apparent that monastic management had complicated the pre-12th century landscape it is evident that the extent of Kynbyt Issald survived in the later Maerdref grange and that the siting of the church may have reflected existing settlement.

Using the approach familiar to landscape archaeologists based upon rentals, maps and other historical documents alongside topographic and morphological assessment it has been possible to predict with accuracy the location of the medieval archaeology here at Llanfair. These techniques, when combined with excavation have confirmed the scale and status of the Llanfair estate during the late 12th to 13th centuries when Ceredigion and other Welshries were undergoing such dramatic upheavals. This methodology is to be especially recommended for other rural farmland perhaps particularly those farmed under the Tir Gofal scheme where the archaeological record is presently underestimated. Ceredigion has suffered long enough from the apparent 'gap' between the highly visible Iron Age enclosures and the 18th century polite gentry estate. The discovery of medieval archaeology at Llanfair demonstrates the suitability of this approach especially when supported by the research community and facilities of research departments. This level of logistical support means excavation is monitored at the highest level whilst at an economical cost. We must question the validity of preservation in-situ as the basic tenet of archaeological practice in a rural landscape that is looking to utilise limited regimes such as Historic Landscape Characterisation as a way of informing management practice.

Moelhedog

Apart from Rhys's grant of Llanfair and Maerdref, a couple of smaller holdings on the coast near Penbryn, some extensive estates south of the Teifi at Gwyddgrug and Brechfa, a small holding just north of Llanfair and Rhydowen was granted again, described by a perambulation. The reconstruction of this holding has revealed that the estate has remained intact, preserving a tyddynod for holding over 800 years. The text of the grant runs thus:

"De terra eciam de Molhehedauc sicut hiis terminus continetur: Ab Hescluyn artabetur usque Cribin;

99

Figure 54. Trench 3 west facing section. Drawn by J. Bezant, C. Wakeham, D. Sables, S. Chadjas and A. Lawrence.

ab inde yr Carn; et ab inde fossat ducente usque Cruc; et a Cruc usque Carn super montem; ab inde usque Carn arall iuxta Moyle Hedauc; ab inde ad lapidem album stantem in valle; ab inde usque Blayn Cathil; ab inde valle ducente usque Carn; et a Carn usque Blayn Camnant; Camnant in longitudine sui usque Caletur; et Caletur usque Heslunen The land also of Moel Hedog, as by these bounds encompassed: It is defined from Islwyn unto Cribin; thence to the Cairn; thence by a ditch leading to the Crug; and from the Crug unto a Cairn upon the hill; thence unto another Cairn by Moel Hedog; thence to the white stone standing in the valley; thence to the source of the Cathal stream; thence by the valley leading to a Cairn, and from that Cairn to the source of the Camnant; along this stream unto Clettwr stream: and from Clettwr to Islwyn"

(Evans, 1878: 66-67)

•   Coflein and Carn databases (Historic Environment Record held by RCAHMW).

The text of the perambulation lists a variety of locales and topographical elements that appear to identify an area ranging from the Clettwr valley floor onto the upland around Moelhedog before returning back to the valley floor. The first location is at *Hescluyn* or Islwyn. Llwyn; 'grove' or 'shrub', is a common place name and is encountered on the valley floor nearby at Capel Llwynrhydowen, Llwyn Marlas and Llwynglas. Is - 'below' or 'beneath', also directs us to the area of level meadow lying below the steep hillslopes, adjacent to the Afon Clettwr.

The next direction given states: unto cribin where cribyn is a small cottage or tyddyn. The present hamlet of Pontsian lies just to the north and is predominantly a late 19th

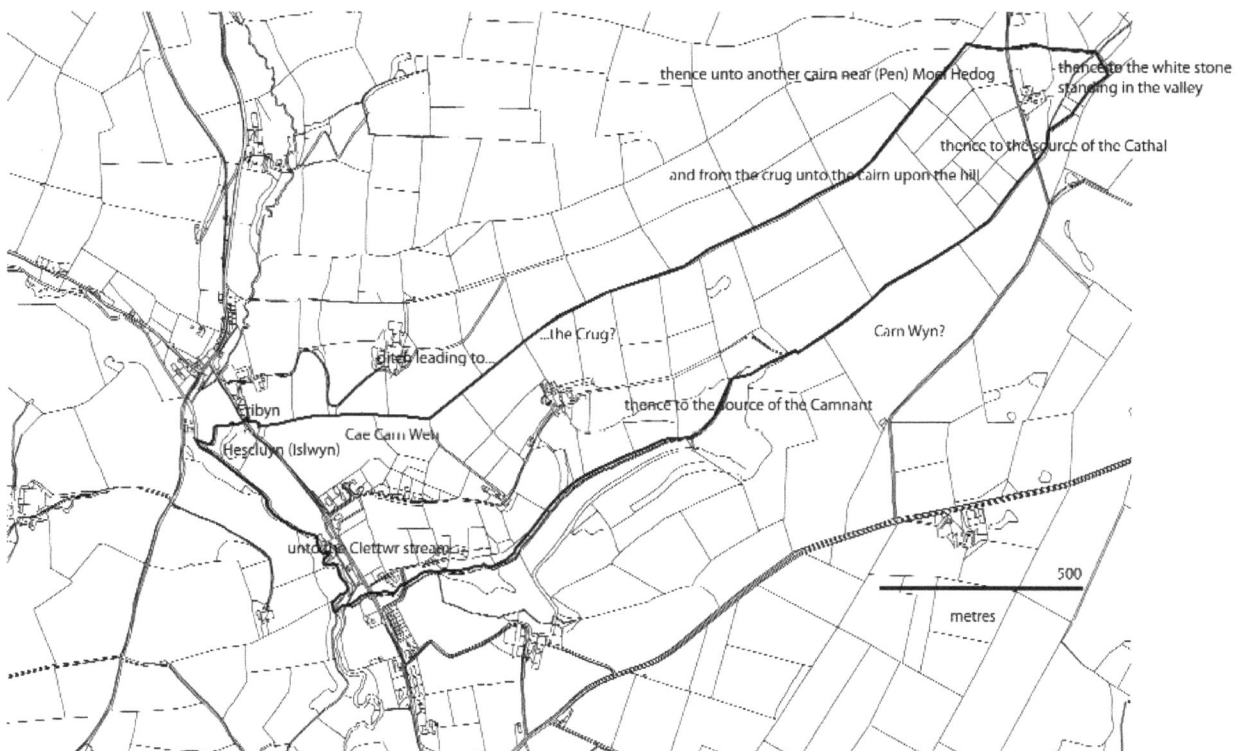

Figure 55. Moelhedog. The 12th century boundary mapped using the perambulation matches the 19th century chapelry boundary. Crown Copyright/database right 2008. An Ordnance Survey supplied service.

This has allowed the mapping of this boundary onto Ordnance Survey base maps via GIS to allow interpretation (fig. 55). Field survey as a method of ground-truthing this boundary was used alongside the following historical sources in order to identify the specific topographical features named in the grant:

-     1331 Inspeximus (Evans, 1878)
-     19th century chapelry boundaries (Evans, 1960)
-     Ordnance Survey 1st edition map 1891, Landline digital 1:10,000 2005 and 1:25000 raster 2005.
-     Llandysul parish tithe map and Schedule 1841
-     Castell Hywel estate map c. mid 18th century (James, 2001)
-     Wmffre's place names of Ceredigion (2005)

century 'ribbon' development focussed on the former woollen factory at Y Ffatri in the centre of the village. However, the school, telephone exchange and village hall lie adjacent to a small curvilinear enclosure at SN 43954605, clearly predating the current B4459 road that truncates it. This enclosure boundary also forms the terminus of a lengthy linear bank (fig. 56 below) that runs up and over the hill forming the separation between Heol Feinog and Moelhedog farms and represents the boundary described in the rest of the perambulation. This boundary is unremarkable but for its length and sinuous nature, up to c. 2 metres wide but modestly low, roughly faced in stone in only a few places and hedged with mixed deciduous and gorse for much of its length.

The next five locations describe a cairn, ditch, crug, cairn and another cairn near (Pen) Moelhedog. Cairns proliferate in this upland area but many have undoubtedly been lost to ploughing and robbing. Only one of the five named features remains identifiable today as a raised stony heap northwest of the farm at the edge of the plateau on which the farmstead sits. An estate schedule dating to 1885 describes names this field as Cae Garnwen - 'enclosure of the white cairn'. None of the other cairns or crugiau survive above ground and are likely to have provided the stony material with which many of the field boundaries have been faced. The LiDAR data (fig. 57) is of sufficient resolution to note a faint linear feature running parallel partway along the boundary and this may represent traces of a ditch running to the crug. This eroded ditch and bank runs uphill until crossed by another substantial field boundary that is part of

Figure 56. Left, The fertile slopes below Moelhedog. Centre, the 12th century boundary between Moelhedog and Heol Feinog marked by a wide earth bank. Right, an unrecorded levelled cairn at the junction of field boundaries and trackways on the upland above Moelhedog.

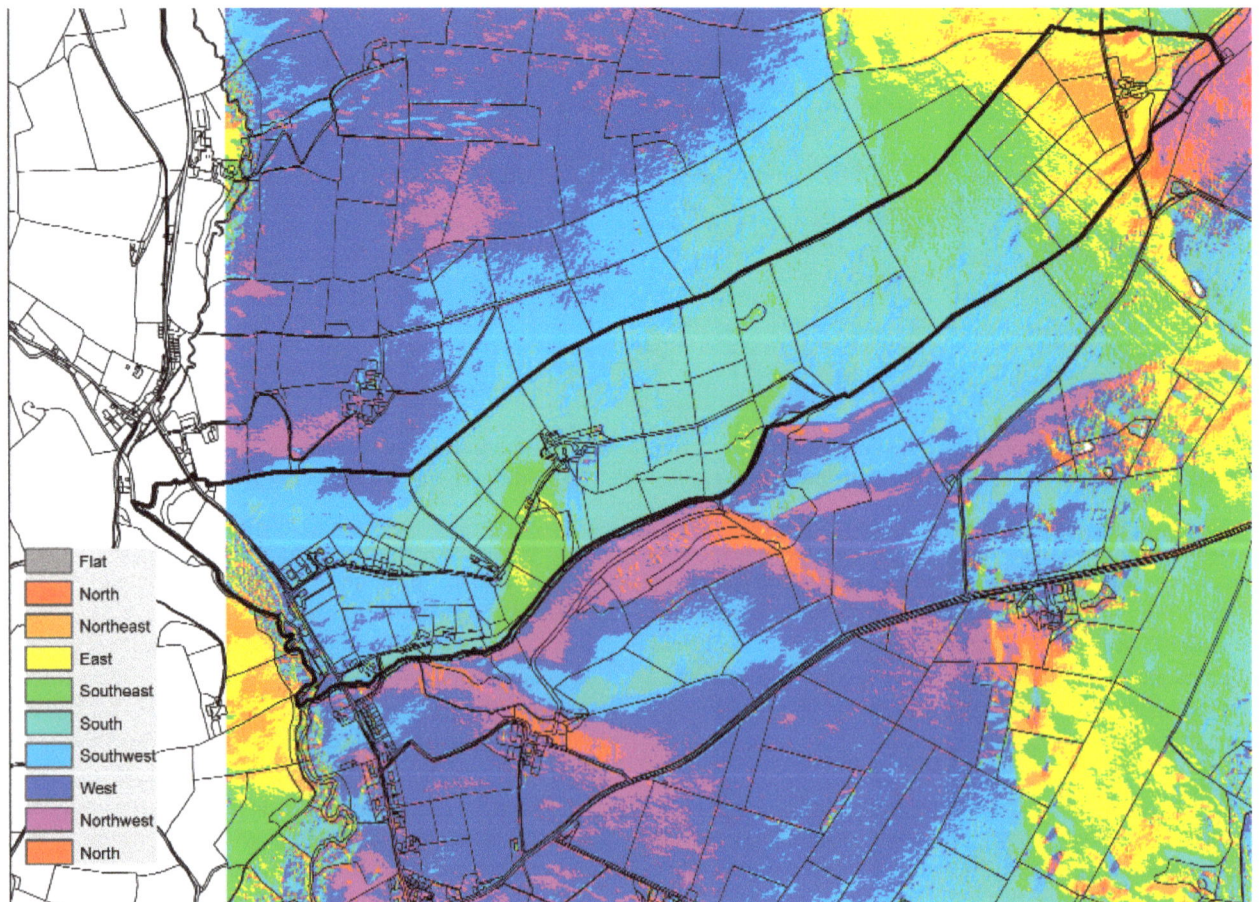

Figure 57. Lidar survey at Moelhedog. Aspect analysis; the light blue colour indicates south facing slopes (dark blue is north) and defines the extent of the 12th century farm. Crown Copyright/database right 2008. An Ordnance Survey supplied service.

an early enclosure. The 'cairn near (Pen) Moel Hedog' is also lost but takes us further upslope to the vicinity of the summit at around 300 metres. The next location refers to a 'white stone standing in the valley' which again is lost but must refer to somewhere at the head of the Cledlyn valley on the eastern side of the upland slope. The source of the Cathal, 'Blaen Cathil' is apparent by a boggy, wetland area and lending its name to the nearby 19th century smallholding of Blaencathal. The boundary continues along the course of this stream 'leading to a cairn' which has been identified by Evans (1878: 67, n.1) as Carn Wyn, ¼ of a mile south of Blaencathal. The HER locates Carn Wyn (PRN 5637) adjacent to the road at SN 45604628 but this is no longer visible and its exact location remains unknown. The source of the Camnant is only 500 metres distant and

centuries are similarly constructed making dating without documentary evidence difficult, and they are often topped with either ash, beech or blackthorn and these are seldom mixed. The faint evidence for a lyncheted enclosure surrounding Moelhedog containing possible former building platforms and ridge and furrow is supported only by the contrast between the mixed deciduous and gorse hedgerows here and the low, thorny banks of 18th century enclosure (fig. 58 below). Ancient boundaries and trackways have remained in use for over 800 years and rebuilding, renovation and robbing have removed much of their character so as to make it a difficult exercise in the field. Buildings are vernacular and late, a date stone at Moelhedog gives us 1709 for the rebuilding or extension of a modest farmhouse.

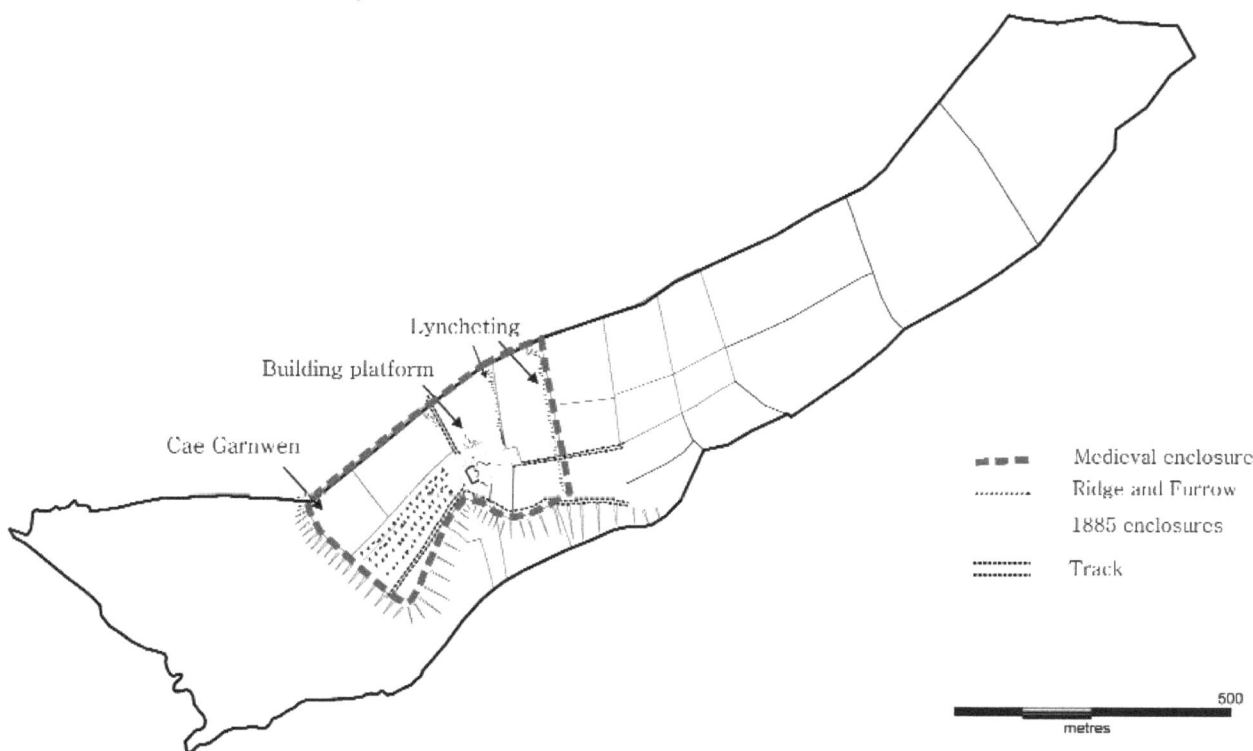

Figure 58. Field survey has identified an ancient farm enclosure around Moelhedog. Within this enclosure are faint earthwork traces of building platforms, ridge and furrow, an eroded cairn and lyncheting. A later patchwork of small, rectangular fields represents enclosure onto the upland as it was in 1885 - the largest fields to the north east were still known as 'open ground' at this time.

the stream leads us back to the valley and its confluence with the Clettwr and thence to Islwyn.

The reconstruction of the external boundaries of the 12th century Moelhedog estate is significant. The opaque nature of the present Moelhedog landscape is one that is typical of the gentle, settled agricultural Teifi valley. There are few surprises here - it is a familiar landscape of dispersed, but heavily improved, farmstead and is devoid of any of the usual clues to antiquity. There are few earthworks. Field boundaries are earthen banks, sometimes faced with rubble stone, sometimes in rough, slanted courses, herringbone pattern or simply random patching.

The smaller, regular enclosures of the 18th and 19th

Although the reconstruction of Moelhedog gives us a rare and important illustration of a 12th century holding its significance lies its relationship with neighbouring farmsteads of similar morphology. Figure 59 illustrates the Castell Hywel estate holdings in 1795 and the linear nature of the farmsteads on the eastern bank of the Clettwr have the appearance of an arranged landscape which lead to speculation on their antiquity by Dodgshon (1994: 358). Each holding shares a river frontage and runs up and over the upland with the spine formed by an ancient north-south routeway and would have formed part of the pre-12th century Castell Hywel estate.

The Lloyd family of Castell Hywel was to become one of the most important families in post Medieval Wales. In

1545, Dafydd ap Llwyd of Castell Hywel was M.P. for Cardiganshire (Baker-Jones, 1999: 9), an office in the hands of only a few families until between 1700 and 1750 the squires of Alltyrodyn, Blaendyffryn, Bronwydd, Cilgwyn, Dolau Clettwr, Llanfechan, Llysnewydd, Mountain Hall, Penybeili, Penyrallt, Fardre fach and Waunifor had all been sheriffs. Lordship of the neighbouring cwmwd of Is Coed Uwch Hirwen was claimed by the Lloyd branch of the family of Coedmore during the 17th century. Lloyds from the Castell Hywel pedigree also married into the families of Gilfachwen, Gwernmacwydd, Blaendyffryn, Alltyrodyn, Llanllyr, Ffos y Bleiddiad and Waun Ifor and many other minor gentry families. The family trace their ancestry far back into the middle ages where the core estate was part of a grant made to Cadifor ap Dinawal by Lord Rhys in the late 12th century, one of the few surviving records of a grant by Rhys to a secular owner. The motte and bailey here was superseded by a hall, now a much altered modest gentry home. The tyddyn or farmstead apparently stood within an enclosure, fossilised within the remnants of lyncheted field boundaries and this and other characteristics forms the basis of a new methodology whereby early farmsteads can be identified where archaeological or historical information does not exist.

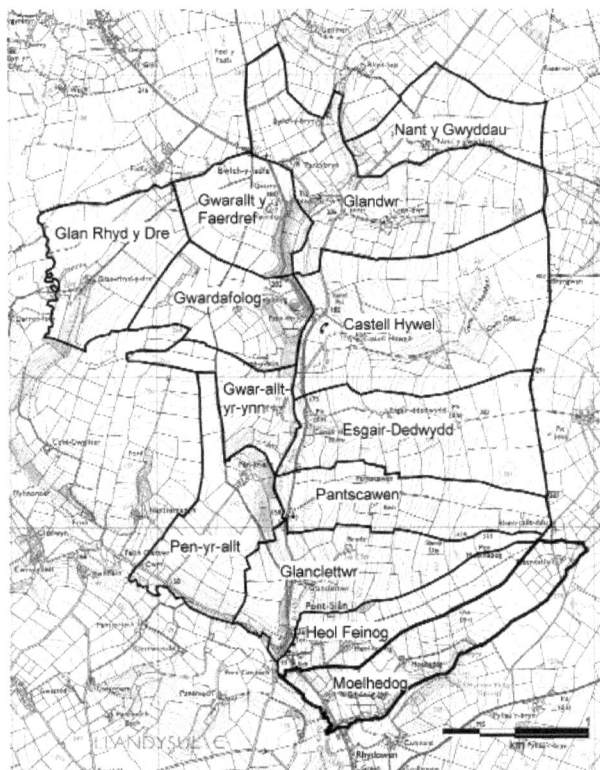

Figure 59. Castell Hywel Estate plus Heol Feinog and Moelhedog. Crown Copyright/database right 2008. An Ordnance Survey supplied service.

Morphology

Drawing on genealogical information alongside the rare, well-documented examples such as Moelhedog plus the results of excavation and survey at Llanfair it has been possible to develop a methodology by which early farms can be identified in Gwinionydd. The majority of the farm holdings in this area house families that have records that predate the late 18th century and many have earlier records. The Golden Grove Book relates the Lloyd family of Castell Hywel to a branch of the family at Gilfachwen Isaf for example, and it was Jenkin ap Rees ap David ap Howel Vychan ap Rhys Foel ap Rhys ap Rhydderch ap Cadifor ap Dinawal who built a house at Castell Hywel around the early 14th century (Green, 1910: 16). Likewise the families of Blaen Cerdin, Bronwydd, Cilgwyn, Cwmmeudwy, Dinas Cerdin Dyffryn Llynod, Faerdref, Ffos Esgob, Alltyrodyn and Pantstreimon were able to record an ancestry back to the 15th century and earlier. Francis Jones (1987: 89) relates how he went to school with one of the Gwernmacwydd Lloyds that had been resident on the same farm since at least the 16th century. A database has been created that locates these early holdings as described by Francis Jones (2004) and this has been combined with table 5 above that has located the properties recorded in the 1564 Crown rental.

The two datasets have been plotted to Ordnance Survey map bases via GIS (figure 60) in order to form a study group for comparison and analysis. It has become apparent that the holdings share a number of features in common:

• All of the properties are either farms or land-owning estates.

• They are all situated below the 200 metre contour line - a transitional zone to unenclosed upland in this region.

• They are all situated near to streams or along river valleys but seldom on the valley floor. holdings also share a number of morphological characteristics.

Troedrhiwffenyd sits within a parcel of small, irregular fields and gives access via a number of routeways onto the common grazing above. Pantheulwen also appears in the 1564 rental and sits within a striking subcircular enclosure as does Coed y Foel and Pant y Creuddyn (fig. 61).These serve as examples to highlight a number of characteristics shared by all of the farms:

• They sit on a network of trackways and routeways that are independent of modern main roads.

• They sit amidst a pattern of smaller, irregular fields.

• The farm buildings are often encircled by an enclosure.

All the holdings within the study group exhibit two or more of these features and those without these attributes can be dismissed as modern. For example, Tynewydd at Croeslan is situated directly adjacent to the main road. The out-

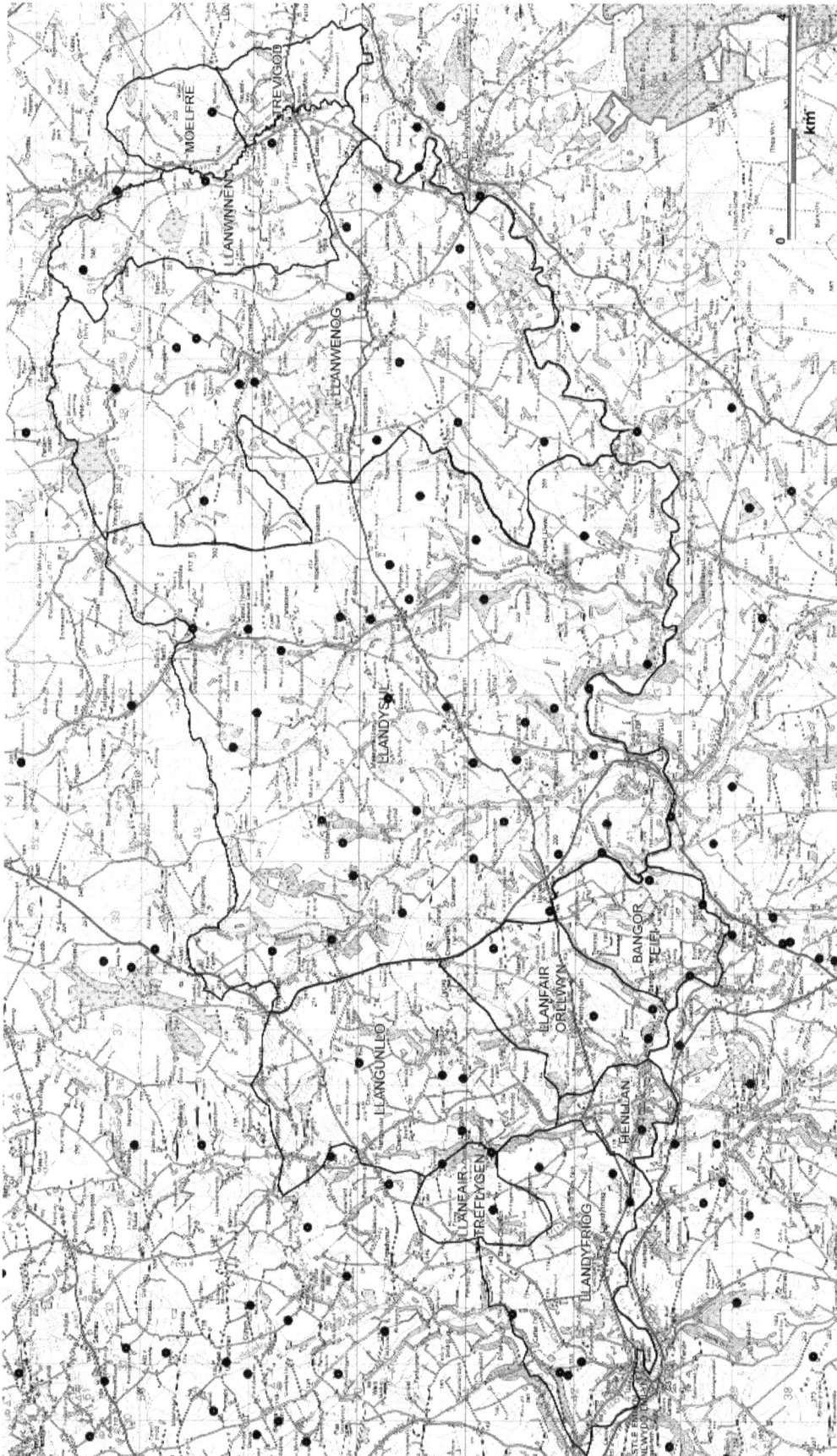

Figure 60. Gwinionydd and its parishes showing the location of early holdings information supplied by 16th century survey evidence for Gwinionydd Is Cerdin (to the east of Llandysul) and other genealogical and documentary information. All are farms or landed estates that lie below the 200 metre contour line, are on or near a water course and are situated in valley slopes away from level floodplain and upland plateau. Crown Copyright/database right 2008. An Ordnance Survey supplied service.

buildings are rectangular and modern and it sits within a regular pattern of large, squarish fields, a pattern echoed with the adjacent modern farm of Bronant. Neither of these

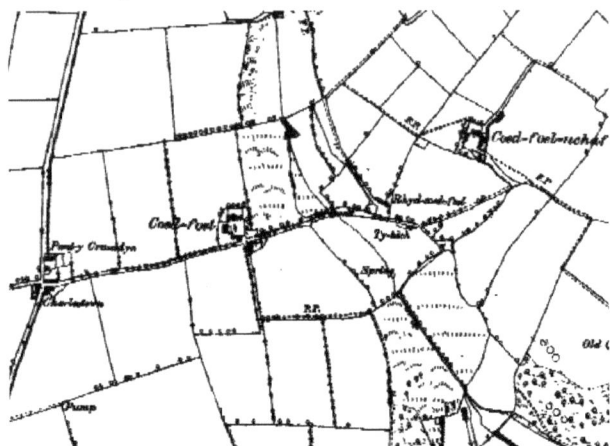

Figure 61. Farm enclosures at Coed-Foel and possible enclosure remains at Pant y Creuddyn (just north of Llandysul). © Crown Copyright and Landmark Information Group Limited 2008. All rights reserved. 1891.

two holdings appears on the 16th century rental and are of 19th or even 20th century derivation, sat within late enclosed land with access to a modern road. This useful model has allowed me to propose early farmsteads for areas where we do not have medieval or Crown surveys and on the basis of morphology and situation alone. This methodology has allowed the identification and mapping of potentially early farms in an area where we do not have early documentary evidence, for Llandysul Uwch Gwinionydd (the chapelries of Llandysulfed, Capel Dewi, Maerdref, Borthin and Llanfair) in order to produce figure 62 (below).

This chapter has analysed the evidence for medieval gwelyau holdings and proposed that the ten families occupying Bangor Teifi by gwely tenure and paying gwestfa in the 14th century are the same ten farmsteads still extant within Bangor Teifi parish today. A rental from Anglesey shows that gwely was still in use there in the 16th century and the family names were beginning to be accompanied by topographic descriptions of the properties they held. This kind of evidence is absent from Ceredigion but it serves to emphasise the move away from the identification of the homestead with a larger kin group. This creates a challenge to the identification of gwely holdings within the study area. But the majority of farms listed as paying gwestfa (and therefore freeholders of gwely tenancy) in 16th century Gwinionydd Is Cerdin are still present in today's landscape with the same name and demosntrates that this landscape has remained substantially unchanged since then. Moelhedog and the linear arrangement of the Castell Hywel estate farmsteads have the appearance of a planned landscape which is surprisingly modern looking in character but has been dated to the 12th century at least. These sophisticated tenurial and settlement systems were evidently part of a dispersed, but thoroughly settled farmscape.

Complex patterns of lordship deploying different strategies and motives have not obscured the basic frameworks of settlement in the medieval Teifi valley. The castle and church were previously the only recognisably medieval landscape element but we can add the farmscape to this; the landscape of people. Utilising the information above it has been possible to develop a methodology that enables identification of likely medieval holdings in areas where documentary evidence is scarce, based on a set of distributional and morphological characteristics.

Agriculture

Emerging from the historical record alongside tenure and render are clues to the types of land use and settlement practised by the tenants of the tyddynod which supplies useful information landscape development over time. At a regional scale it will emerge that practices within 19th century Ceredigion differed substantially from Carmarthenshire to the south and there is evidence to suggest that this reflected medieval practice. The more fertile gentle landscapes of Carmarthenshire remained predominantly uncultivated whilst the larger consolidated estates along the Tywi valley developed more organised forms of cattle production. In contrast, the steeper, wetter Ceredigion landscape to the north was given to mixed arable production perhaps as a result of the smaller, self-contained estates of the freeholders.

The extent to which the scant historical evidence from these areas can be used to recreate landholding and the settled landscape has been, until now unsuccessful, "a subject not easy to grasp" (Morgan, 2005: 82). Where Norman influence was strong, isolated examples of the manorial system were in place. Below the Teifi at Cilgerran for example, regular burgage plots were laid out along the street adjacent to the castle. This system was imitated in the 12th and 13th centuries by the Bishops of St David's in the Welshry of Adpar at the centre fo their Dyffryn Teifi estate. Despite this, those areas with the Teifi as their northern boundaries were always somehow more 'Welsh' than the rest of Pembrokeshire and the historian and genealogist, George Owen was able to observe during the late 16th century, "that you shall find in one parish a pathway parting the Welsh and English" (Charles, 1973: 40). Owen (ibid: 178) describes the Welsh inhabitants of Cilgerran parish having a special affinity with Cardigan, across the Teifi, regularly visiting the fairs there and using the specific terms for weights and measures of this market town. Landholding within these manorial areas was cultivated within open, unenclosed fields where land was held communally in strips or shares with uncultivated waste and common grazing beyond. Here the assignment of strips was rotated on annual basis. The seasonal movement of livestock is less visible here in the south of the county. Evidence for transhumance of the kind described by Sayce (1956 and 1957) is almost entirely absent from the study area but

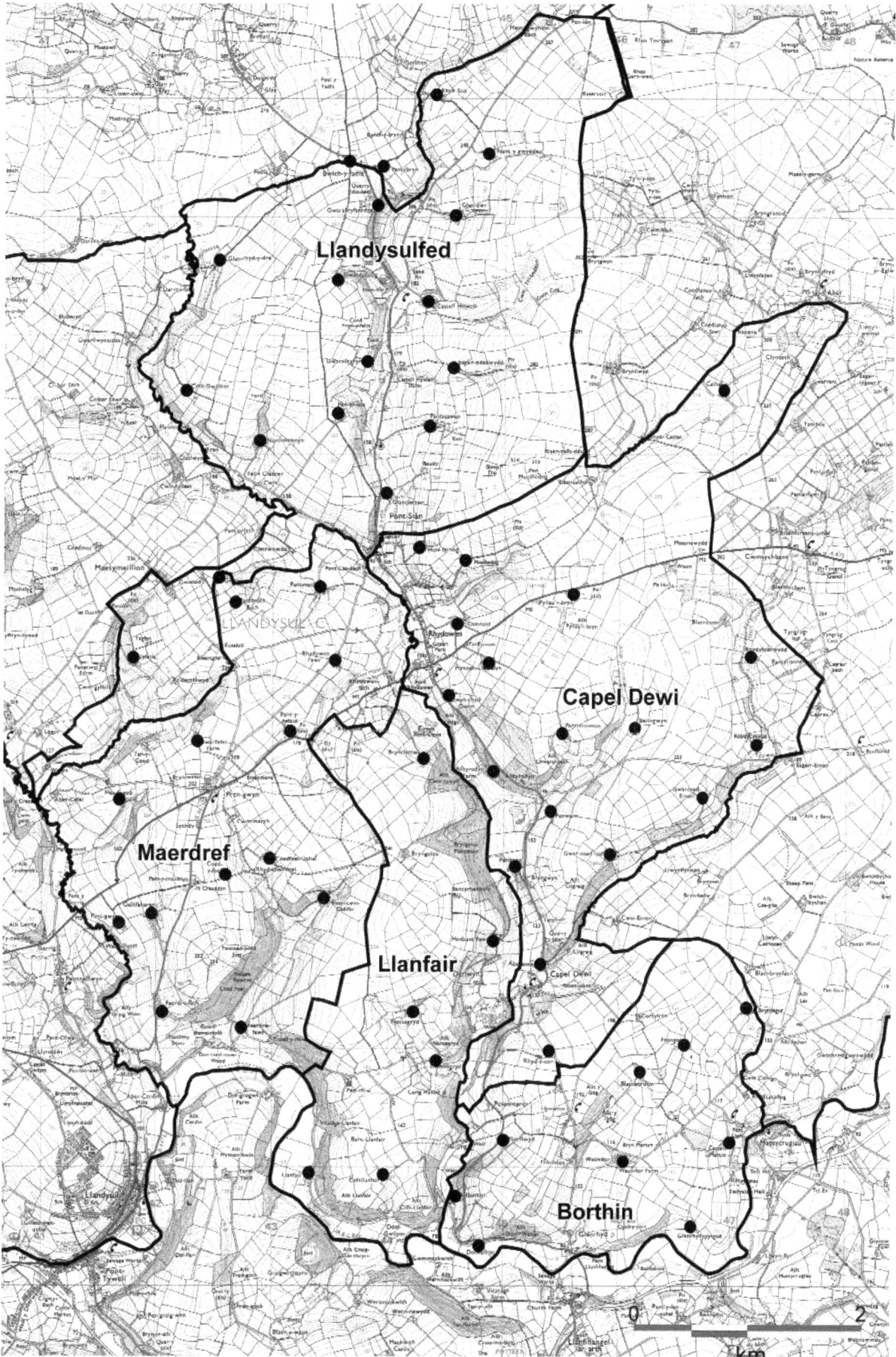

Figure 62. Early holdings in the trefi of Maerdref, Llanfair, Borthin, Llandysulfed and Capel Dewi identified using specific distributional and morphological characteristics. Crown Copyright/database right 2008. An Ordnance Survey supplied service.

implied in the upland Cambrians to the north where *hafod*, 'summer dairy', place names are more common.

The invaluable Soil Utilisation Survey Of Britain conducted by Dudley Stamp in the immediate pre World War II years captured an essentially pre-industrialised landscape. This has fossilised early land-use practices that relied on traditional, pre-mechanised landscape farming methods.

Some startling trends appear: the middle Teifi valley and its catchment area is quite distinct from the surrounding landscape. It is peppered by many small arable fields, scattered amongst permanent pasture and this perhaps directly reflects a 'self-sufficiency' on a localised scale amongst the prolific minor gentry holdings. This trend spans both the Ceredigion and Carmarthenshire sides of the Teifi valley including its hinterlands but is most marked in the middle Teifi valley area. This area is 'cupped' to south-east by the Mynydd Llanllwni range and to the east by the smaller Moelfre uplands. These 'gentle' upland areas summit between 3-400 m and are predominantly given to heath, moorland, commons and rough pasture. Along the Teifi, wooded areas are confined mainly to the immediate demesnes of gentry estates especially at Highmead, Bronwydd and Falcondale and also at smaller estates such as Alltyrodyn and Llanfair. The contrast with the wide Tywi valley to the south in Carmarthenshire is evident. The broad fertile valley is dominated by meadowland and permanent grass and is characteristic of this traditionally dairy-oriented heartland. This is reflected in the estate and farm structure where larger, more contiguous estates developed in the post medieval period. Centres at Golden Grove, Dinefwr and Middleton had convenient access both to the large trading port at Carmarthen and an increasingly populous and industrialised south Wales.

Arable production in southern Ceredigion seems more purposeful and intensive in this region under the influence of larger gentry estates at Llangynllo, Llandygwydd and Troedyraur and it is significant that this area is also contiguous with the Dyffryn Teifi estate since the early medieval period. To the east of the Llandysul is a more even scattering of smaller arable plots spreading upstream along the Teifi as far as Lampeter and stretching northwards to the Aeron valley. This pattern of small, scattered arable fields is broken only, but not completely, by the intervening plateau surrounding Gors Goch. The valley floor of the middle Teifi begins to narrow at this point but is still utilised for arable whereas further upstream, the wider Ystrad at Lampeter is almost entirely meadow. This trend is also mirrored in parts of the upper Aeron valley. Predominantly arable is shown at Talsarn and Trefilan whilst the ystrad around the former Cistercian nunnery at Llanllyr is given to meadow but with some rough pasture on this poorly drained wetland. A denser concentration of arable around the central Aeron depicts the Ciliau-Ty Glyn-Llanerchaeron 'zone' of estates which have medieval origins. Unsurprisingly this inclination for arable also runs

along the fertile coastal plain. At Llansantffraid, remarkably well-preserved strip fields or lleiniau still remained in separate ownership into the 19th century and was recorded by the tithe survey. Strip fields are also apparent in some upland lleiniau in the tiny parish of Bangor Teifi just to the west of Llandysul. Both Llansantffraid and Bangor Teifi were part of the estates of the Bishops of St David's and strip fields seem to reflect agrarian practice common to these areas.

Where we might expect arable production on the easily-worked, fertile valley floors and lower slopes there is none. Arable cultivation in this pre-War period is confined to the uplands, it peaks and summits as at Bryn Golau near Alltyrodyn, Gwar-Dafolog, Rhos Ymryson and Pen Moel Hedog which are are all in the vicinity of Castell Hywel and typical examples. Although enclosure was generally late in this region (James, 2001), by the middle of the 20th century we can see an essentially modern field system in place.

It is clear that geology and topography of the area has created an environment favourable to certain agricultural regimes. Temperate, Atlantic systems and the fertile glacial and lacustrine deposits make for superior cultivation, but the often steep terrain has been unable to sustain an arable tradition beyond the arrival of modern farming methods. The steep, narrow and hilly terrain has been parcelled into tiny enclosures – the patchwork fields evocative of the area, but how did the contrast between the arable of the Teifi and the pastures of the Tywi develop in areas of similar terrain, soil composition and climate?

A rental of 1560 (Jones, 1939: 83) describes the medieval custom of 'duty oats', "every freeholder in the manors of Iskoed (Iscoed) and Guymonethe (Gwinionydd) are to render:

> "for every tenement held, 1 bushel of oats, containing 4 ryndles or syvethes, each syvethe being ¾ yard broad and 5 inches deep, and each such syvethe to be filled and heaped with oats and pressed down by hand, according to the custom and usage of the next manor adjoining, called the Baron of Koedmore's Lordship"

Despite the detailed methods for measuring the quantity of oats to be paid, this was merely a descriptive device. Most renders had been commuted to a fiscal payment by at least the 13th and 14th centuries, but the retention of traditional render types with their names and descriptions preserves the connection that these types of rent had to land and tenure. Some of the tenants claimed some exemption from this render, paying only one bushel regardless of how many parcels of land they held and the value of 4 years-worth of rent had been calculated to be 20s (ibid.).

A later rental for Gwinionydd Is Cerdin in 1651 (Richards, 1960a) describes the 'custom of oats' still being rendered but in purely fiscal terms:

"The tenants within ye seuerall parishes of Llandyssall, Ikerdin, Llangynllo, Llanvayer orllwin, Llandevryog and Llanvayer trefflygen, must pay yearely towards ye Costome of Oates called Crech March ye some of some sixteen pence apiece."

The residents of Dehewid, Killie, Llannigcharon and Trevigod outside the Teifi valley were also included separately and were charged slightly less at 14d per annum, perhaps because the land was not so good and so yielded slightly less.

The senior officer of the cwmwd, the *rhaglaw*, described by English recorders as *ballivus* or *bedellus* was charged with the collection of renders due to the lord (Griffiths, 1974b: 59). As the Lord's representative within the cwmwd, Welsh custom provided him with freehold land, plus an income of food and stabling for his horse as part of his circuit or cylch. This had already been commuted to 2s per day prior to the conquest although even as late as the 16th century, traditional weights and measures were used as the basis to calculate the amount due. By 1298, Genau'r Glyn, Gwinionydd Uwch Cerdin and Mefenydd also recorded returns made by the rhaglaw or bailiff, the *rhingyll* or bedellus under him and a newly created officer called the *prepositus* or reeve (ibid: 60). The three officers each received different allowances for their own lands and differing amercements or *camlyriau* imposed by cwmwd courts.

During the 1280 royal assessment of the rents and customs of Carmarthenshire and Cardiganshire, the amalgamation and commutation of all customary rents (not already commuted) apart from the gwestfa, into a single payment which became known as the 'rent of extent' or stent (Griffiths, 1974b: 61). This may have been the reasoning behind the creation of the new prepositus in order to collect the 'new' rent, the rhingyll was charged with collection of the gwestfa, a rent due only by the freemen of the cwmwd (Dodgshon, 1994: 350). It is clear that English administrators were striving to regularise alien and complex forms of render. To this end, Carmarthen Castle held a number of reference books and manuals on estate and fiscal management including Ralph de Hengham's *Summa* (Griffiths, 1974b: 61).

Nevertheless Ceredigion retained a strong element of continuity in administration which serves partly to explain the late survival of the gwestfa in Ceredigion which was linked to the office of *cais* or sergeant, known from Welsh areas of the southern Principality from the 11th century at least (Rees, 1924: 103). Each unit of assessed land contributed 1d per day for the maintenance of the sergeant but the office disappeared after 1280 and the rent was incorporated into the new 'stent'. The *ceisiad* survived slightly later in Cantref Mawr in Carmarthenshire where it was recorded after Edward's acquisition in 1287-8 that each (unfree) cwmwd rendered a *portura*. This became

standardised at £5 6s 8d for each of the four cymydau of Caeo, Catheiniog, Mallen and Manordeilo, eventually being subsumed into the general commorth available to the bailiff (Griffiths, 1974b: 64). A payment called *porthiant cais* was also paid by "certain persons" in 1302 and "all the tenants" of cwmwd Emlyn in the Carmarthenshire Teifi valley as late as 1328 (Evans, 1922: 99)

Traditional forms of rents in the Principality had been based upon the *cylch* meaning 'to circulate' or 'circuit' hinting at these territorially-based rents similar to, or even rendered upon the gwestfa, and cylch eventually came to translate in modern Welsh as 'district'. Outside areas still rendering gwestfa payments we see the commorth known as commorth Calan Mai (Calends of May) traditionally rendered at the beginning of May in alternate or 3rd or 4th years (Rees, 1924: 229). Values based on the tribute of cattle were originally fixed at 6s 8d prior to the 14th century and paid in Brecon, Builth, Narberth, Amgoed and Pwlliniog. Cattle were fundamental not only to diet but to power structures and social relationships in many early societies and is reminiscent of the Irish hero tale, Táin Bó Cuailnge, '*The Cattle raid of Cooley*' (Gribben, 1990). They were the basic surplus product of these societies and became units for measurement.

Some areas still paid in kind; cattle were slaughtered and others sent to English manors (Rees, 1932: 231, n. 1) as part of a long-established droving tradition. In 1555 the traditional pasturage of cattle on the wastes of Glyncothi and Pennant forests still operated (Jones, 1939: 103). This form of rent, named cow or *vaccae* units, was mainly rendered in the Welshries outside Ceredigion though its assessment was based upon territorial units like the gwestfa payment. Manor Iscoed, was divided into ten cow-units and others are known from Vacca *Ithole* (Idole) in Llandyfaelog parish; Vacca *Kellymarch*, de *Treflymsy* and de *Kelthetege*; Cil-y-march, Treflymsi, and Gelli-deg, in Llandyfaelog parish (Rees, 1932: 230). Cows were also rendered at Kidwelly, Penryn and Achddu, all within Carmarthenshire (Llawhaden for example had a sheep-rent, presumably grazing on the salt marsh foreshore). Also recorded was the *parva commorth*, described as 'money with these cows' (Lloyd, 1935: 228-229).

Although the commorth Calan Mai was rendered on lands outside those where the gwestfa survived, it was rendered on the Cardiganshire holdings of the Bishops of St David's at Morfa Bychan and Dyffryn Teifi. Tenants of Lodrepedran near Adpar carried material for the 'five buildings' including the hall, Lord's room, kitchen, stable and grange from the forest of Adpar to Llandygwydd. Others at Henllan, Gruffydd ap Walter, Iorwerth ap Gruffydd, Gruffydd Lloyd and their co-owners were to pay commorth Calan Mai every 3rd year. The occupants of Bangor also rendered services at Lodrepedran and paid the commorth of four cows at Calan Mai every 3rd year (Willis-Bund, 1902: 215). Indeed, the mild, fertile pastures in this region share some similarities with the cattle heartlands of the Tywi valley but on a much smaller scale. Ceredigion saw arable as an important part of a mixed economy contained in smaller, self-sufficient estate units that enabled the payment of oat rent. Production in Carmarthenshire was more specialised and predisposed to cattle production and dairying on an organised, wider, more coherent scale.

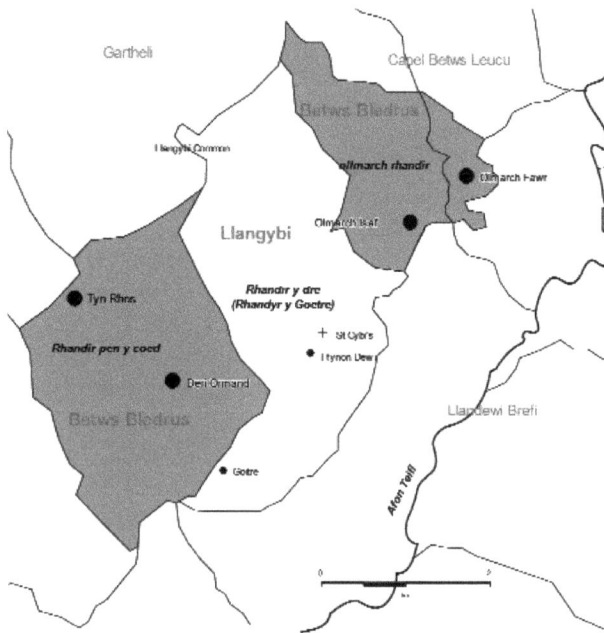

Figure 63. The three rhandir of Betws Bledrus; Rhandir pen y coed, Rhandir y dre and Ollmarch rhandir. Together these comprised the bond tref of Betws Bledrus with the common grazing at Llangybi common. Llangybi became detached and became a parish in its own right.

Both northern Carmarthenshire and Ceredigion can be considered as Welshries; areas under English rule but conquered late and retaining many customs and traditions administered on a local level by local officials, often holding ancient administrative positions. Two different renders, the oat rent or cylch march and the commorth Calan Mai seem to have survived differentially in Ceredigion and Carmarthenshire/Cantref Mawr respectively. This difference is partly reflected in estate and lordship developments in the two areas; the many small, self-sufficient gentry estates of the Tivyside and the larger 'Anglicised' estates that line the Tywi valley in Carmarthenshire. These estate structures also dictated the course of landscape developments into the modern period so that we see these different land-use patterns etched into the 19th and 20th century landscape. The gentle fertile grasslands of Carmarthenshire and Pembrokeshire are still farmed mainly for beef and dairy. London had long been a fashionable target for the genteel of Carmarthenshire but this was built on a long tradition of travel with droving and the Welsh dairies that emerged in the 19th century London. In the same way that the fertile lowlands of Anglesey are regarded as the granary of Wales (cf. Thomas, 1962: 1), so Carmarthenshire might be regarded as its dairy.

Grazing and arable cultivation in shares was known as rhandir and this system left considerable physical evidence in the landscape as a clue to medieval agricultural practice. In the late 13th century William de Knoville was granted four rhandiroedd making him lord of Gwestfa Llyswen. Gronow ap Tudor held one third of Gwestfa Cellan hinting at the subdivision of the tref into the rhandir unit. The Master of the Hospitallers held half a rhandir in the cwmwd of Creuddyn and Cadwgan ap Gruffydd was granted one-sixteenth share of a rhandir (Rees, 1932: 35, n. 1 and 202). Lhuyd's (1909-11: 68 and 87) late 17th century Parochialia records the division of the small parish of Bettws Bledrus into three rhandiroedd called *rhandir pen y coed*, *rhandir y dre* and *rhandir ollmarch* (fig. 63). This information is significant in two ways. Firstly we can see that the groups of rhandiroedd comprising trefi are the unit that the gwestfa was rendered on in Ceredigion. Secondly, that the groups of three rhandiroedd indicate bond status. Jones Pierce (1967: 357-380) described the communal nature of the rhandir with farmsteads or tyddyn creating a girdle pattern of settlement around the shared lands and in an examination of the evidence for Anglesey, the free township of Llysdulas contained seven gwelygordd arranged as loose clusters of tyddynod known locally as rhandiroedd scattered amongst small quilleted strip fields (Jones Pierce, 1951:9). Elsewhere, rhandir became synonymous with hamlet or amlwd as seen at Rhuddlan (Jones Pierce, 1959a: 332). At Bettws Bledrus, Rhandir pen y coed relates to Pencoed, one of two units of land in Bettws Bledrus granted to Strata Florida in 1198 by Maelgwyn ap Rhys, the other unit was a holding named Rhossan centred at Ty'n Rhos to the north (Pryce, 2005: 183). During the 18th century the antecedent to the Deri Ormand estate was known as Tyrpen y Coed Isan representing Pencoed (Jones, 2004: 87). Rhandir Ollmarch can be located at the nearby Ollmarch estate which now forms part of a detached portion of the Bettws Bledrus parish. Rhandir y dre was also known as Rhandyr y Goetre and this is retained in the name of a farm at Llangybi. Llangybi had formerly constituted a prebendary of the collegiate church of Llanddewibrefi to the south east across the valley. The parish of Llangybi together with Bettws Bledrus later formed the Lordship of Bettws Bleddwrs, the property of Captain Powell, of Nant Eos (Meyrick, 1810 and Morgan, 2001: 119). Collectively then the two portions of Bettws Bledrus and the portion of Llangybi comprised the original tref unit which contained three rhandiroedd, the rhandir y dre providing the reserved pasture for the other two at Llangybi Common, scene of later turbulence during 19th century enclosures.

Rhandir is a relatively uncommon place name in Ceredigion but where it does survive it corresponds with areas of remnant strip fields. The name rhandir survives at Alltyblacca near Llanwenog (SN 52484625) and Blaencelyn near Llwyndafydd (SN 3533 5453) where there are small rectangular coaxially aligned field systems and relict strips. At Rhos Haminiog (SN 54116469) just to the north of the Aeron valley, an extensive area of rhos or moorland comprises upland open grazing with relict strips and late enclosure (fig. 64). A rhandir at Brongest (SN 32344493), to the north of Newcastle Emlyn also sits amidst relict strips and nearby is Llainarthen where llain ('strip') occurs as a place name.

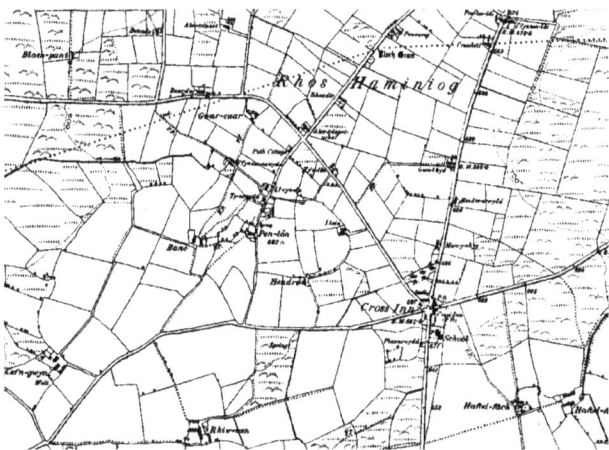

Figure 64. Rhandir Haminiog (Anhuniog commote). An upland area of relict strips (1st ed. OS, 1891). © Crown Copyright and Landmark Information Group Limited 2008. All rights reserved. 1891.

Periodic ploughing of the upland mynydd in blocks or strips of arable was common. Jones (1972b: 341) describes the cultivation of *terra montana* for extended periods and *Tir mynythe* produced corn, rye and oats along with peat for burning in 16th century north Pembrokeshire (Howells, 1955: 325). Cultivation by both free and bond tenants occurred on the *terra Montana* over c. 300 ft within the Lordship of Denbigh and strip fields some 800 ft long have been recorded at an altitude above 650 ft in Caernarfonshire (Jones, 1972b: 351 and 371). At Blaen-Cil-Lech (SN 3297 4323), a small hamlet to the north of Llandyfriog, a farm called Mynydd Bach stands adjacent to Plough farm. A small 19th century hamlet called Pentrellwyn approximately one mile north of Llandysul contains a house called Rhandir that apparently survives from an adjacent field name. It stands downslope from Troedrhiwffenyd which is an ancient farmstead supplying access to the formerly open moorland above and where strip remnants survive. Figure 65 shows the area of mynydd above Troedrhiwffenyd where grazing and arable cultivated in strips coexisted. Troedrhiwffenyd appears in the will of Eleanor Thomas dated to 1684 (Jones, 2004: 261) and appears as Tir Rhiw ffenyd in the 1564 survey where it was valued at 16s. (Richards, 1964a). Jones (2004: 261) notes the form Troed-rhiw-ffyned in 1831 and 1841 and links this to 'penyd' or penance giving 'Foot of the hill of Penance'. Troed translates as foot but in this context could refer to a footpath or trackway. Wmffre (2004: 246) suggests the name contains ffunud meaning 'manner' or 'form' but is unconvincing about why. However, the 1st edition Ordnance Survey map (1891) gives the farm its correct spelling as Troed-rhiw-fynydd containing the element mynydd. The mynydd was encircled by ancient holdings in a girdle pattern of the type described by Jones Pierce (1959a: 332) where he suggests that this model is characteristic of the dispersed 'Highland Zone' in Wales.

The 'Rhandir' at Pentrellwyn is joined by another rhandir on the western edge of the mynydd at Horeb and Troedrhiwffenyd is joined by other early farmsteads at Cwmmeudwy, Cwm Merwydd and Panthaulwen. These encircle the mynydd and all sit on the spring line at, or just below, the 200m contour or on streams and on good communication routes. The enclosure earthwork site of Castell Gwilym (Iron Age or early medieval in date) sits on the eastern edge of the mynydd commanding the view over the Teifi valley and is adjacent to a recently excavated multi-period prehistoric enclosure. The individual's share in the open upland eventually became physically manifest as individual strips, remnants of which survive and are still recorded as having different owners into the 19th century. There was very little common land left in Llandysul parish by the 19th century but identification of former mynydd with strip remnants can allow the identification of former rhandir with its girdle of early farms

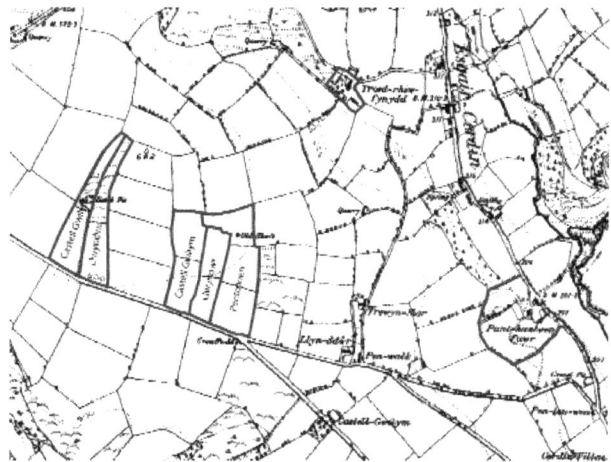

Figure 65. Troedrhiwfynyd and Pantheulwen Fawr (1st ed. OS, 1891). Note the upland 'mynydd' to the east with relict medieval strips, still apportioned in 1841. © Crown Copyright and Landmark Information Group Limited 2008. All rights reserved. 1891.

Open field agriculture with strips and ridge and furrow is not generally associated with the dispersed rural Welsh landscape and where it is more common in the Englishries of the south and east it is seen as a Norman practice, often going hand in hand with nucleated, planned settlement. Davies (1957: 86) suggests that although the practice spread westwards from the Midlands with Anglo-Norman occupation, communal fields were probably already cultivated by 'tribal' units and that it is only the surviving pattern and nomenclature that is Norman. The open field strips at Llanynys in Denbighshire, described as quillets by Glanville Jones (1964) are taken from 19th century tithe survey but, using 15th and 16th century rentals that describe shares in a patrimony, he was able to make a link with early Welsh tenures. The complex arrangements of the rhandir from my study area has allowed the identification of individual tyddynod, also with early origins and demonstrates the use of complex landscape management practices.

Occupants under different types of tenure used the landscape in the same way however, and, by the 13th century at least, court officials, uchelwyr and even bondmen held land by hereditary tenure (Jones, 1976: 11). Tir cyfrif or reckoned land was held by bondsmen and individual holdings in the form of strips and communal grazing were distributed annually by the reeve. The difference between bond and free needs unpacking. The simple and contrasting types of tenure are over-simplistic and in any case, evolved and changed constantly. The law texts refer to aillt, taog or bileyn (villein) but all have been interpreted simply as 'bond'. Likewise the breyr, gwas or uchelwyr are all used interchangeably to mean free-notable, the early land-owning gentry (Owen, 1841). For Anglesey, Jones Pierce (1951: 253). splits the inhabitants into broadly free and bond but does so for convenience, speculating that the bondsmen were reduced to servitude at some point in the distant past perhaps by the immigrant dynasty of Cunedda and correspondingly, the free might represent the lineage of this successful ingress.

The 12th century grant of Maerdref to Tally includes "all the common, mills and waste" and the mills at Rhydowen formed the most valuable asset in an area where arable production was vital in the payment of the oat rent. By the 19th century, virtually no common land had survived within Llandysul parish and that very small portion was confined to Gwinionydd Is Cerdin in the north west of the parish. It is in this half of the cwmwd that there is substantial evidence for the remnants of *lleiniau* or strips that characterise the enclosure of an individual's share of common grazing on the mynydd. The lleiniau at Bangor Teifi are still visible as hedged strips and indicate the former upland common grazing exploited by the occupants of the gwelyau (fig. 66).

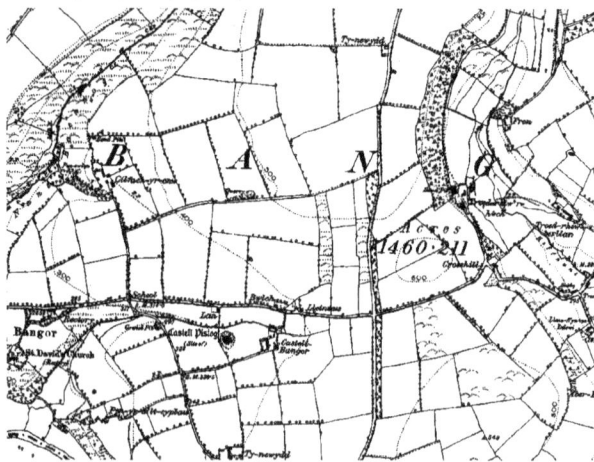

Figure 66. Enclosed strips at Bangor Teifi (1st ed. OS, 1891). Note the Lleiniau place name (centre). © Crown Copyright and Landmark Information Group Limited 2008. All rights reserved. 1891.

Other remnant strip systems can be observed in the lower Teifi valley area at Capel Iwan, Llandyfriog, Alltyblacca, Rhos Haminiog, Brongest, Llainarthen, Pentrellwyn and Llandysul and, with the exception of the well-known slangs of the Bishop's of St David's estate at Llansantffraid, it appears to be a much more common feature of medieval agriculture in this part of Wales than previously realised. The village of Llan-non provided the focus of the parish of Llansantffraid which fronts the low coastal plain on the west, rising to over 250 metres in the east and provided a range of agricultural resources and practices. The nucleation around the early medieval church of St Non's has early origins and Thomas (1959) speculated that the majority of inhabitants would have been subject to tir cyfrif tenure where the strips were allocated equal in equal portions within the small nucleated bond settlement. He proposed that the estate was the former holding of an uchelwyr and whilst not royal as such would nevertheless have been managed as a demesne modelled on the llys-maerdref system. This should not mislead however, the communal farming of land in strips was also practiced by freeholders as demonstrated at Bangor Teifi whose occupants were gwely tenants.

Common to parts of south Wales, strips were farmed as open field agriculture and are identified as a direct English introduction associated with post-conquest management practices (Davies, 1957). Earlier forms of strip agriculture or quillets are known however. Strips held by *tir cyfrif* tenure became fossilised in the later *gerddi* or 'gardens' surrounding Llanynys church substantially challenging the post-conquest nature of these forms of farming (Jones, 1964). The strips evident in Ceredigion probably have more in common with this form of early bond or reckoned tenure and remnants of these seem especially prevalent in the Dyffryn Teifi estate areas.

There is also evidence for the survival of another specific form of management in these areas, notably forest. Tir coed or woodland was significant enough to merit intricate valuations and apportionments in the Law texts (Linnard, 2000: 21). *Coed cadw* is described as that part of woodland kept aside for pannaging but forest in the modern sense of the word is translated as *coedwig* but is a term absent from the early texts.

The concept of royal hunting was highly developed within the law texts, the falconer was a member of the royal household and a lord would have been free to hunt anywhere within his kingdom. But although the texts describe *fforest y brenin* 'king's forest', the term was a Norman one and appears to be without a direct Welsh equivalent and outside the Marcher regions and Englishries there were no English royal forests (Jack Langton pers. comm.). Falconry in Wales had been a specifically Norman import and it is significant that this practice is also absent from the comparable Irish texts, the *Crith Gablach* (Jenkins, 2000: 257). The fforest y brenin then was a borrowed term and may have been inserted into later redactions of the Laws, perhaps by Rhys ap Gruffudd as the author of the Blegywryd (cf. Owen, 1841). Because "forests and forest lordship were symbols of supreme privilege" (Langton & Jones, 2005) it may have been another of Rhys's innovative practices.

Forest as a place name does survive in certain areas, however, and predominantly in areas that were formerly part of the St David's estates. In Llandysul parish the farms of Blaencwm and Blaen Ythan fell within the Forest of Cerdin north west of Llandysul. Other forests occur at Llanbedr, 'Lampeter' Forest, Llanfair Clydogau Forest adjoining Llanddewibrefi, Llangybi Forest also adjoining Llanddewibrefi and Nantcwnlle. Llysnewydd Forest adjoined Ystrad Meurig, Fforest *Yr Rescob* or the Bishop's Forest was in Llanddewibrefi parish and was also known as the 'Four Forests of Tremynts' and Tythin Forest in Llandyfriog parish may have been part of the extensive Forest of Adpar (Langton & Jones, 2005). The lordship of these areas by the powerful Bishops was secular in nature and they were administered like any private estate. The establishment of the 40 acre forest above the town of Adpar may have predated the confirmation of the town as a borough during the 13th century and the survival of both the early quillet systems and the later forest only within specific areas reflects the specific management practices of the Bishop landlords.

Despite the presence of forest, there is no evidence in this area for the specific suite of laws and management practice that is well-attested from its English counterparts. A permanent hunting reserve it would have had defined boundaries and, although not necessarily wooded, were protected by laws against the felling and assart of trees which provided cover for game, timber, fuel and pannaging and were greatly prized. During the mid 15th century, the celebrated poet Lewis Glyn Cothi wrote of the valuable wooded forest of Glyncothi in northern Carmarthenshire that had been established by Edward I in the late 13th century (Linnard, 2000: 39):

There is further evidence to suggest an association between coed and forest. The Aeron valley represented the northernmost sphere of influence of St David's prior to the 12th century, bordered on the north by the ancient clas-lands of Llanbadarn. The parish of Nantcwnlle on the northern banks of the Aeron is dominated by farms and holdings with 'coed' place names indicating the presence of a valuable woodland resource. Nantcwnlle forest occupied the south-facing slopes of the upper Aeron valley and by the post medieval period occupied around 200 acres (Wmffre, 2004: 656). The adjacent holdings of Coedmawr and Pencoed uchaf existed during the 12th century and were original holdings of Llanllyr before appropriation by Strata Florida. The extensive tracts of Llanddewibrefi forest lay south of this on the southern bank of the Teifi indicating that this part of the upper Aeron valley would have provided valuable woodland resources of all types including hunting, pannaging, grazing, timber and underwood for craft and construction industries.

The Llanerchaeron estate in the lower Aeron valley also contains elements relating to earlier woodland management. The subject of a dendrochronological study in 2002, Bale (2005) was able to demonstrate the sophisticated plantation of wooded slopes with oak crops in order to supply high grade timber also as part of a bark stripping industry that flourished into the 18th to early 20th century. The practice of bark stripping to supply the tanning industry is known from 13th century Tintern Abbey where the monks purchased the bark from felled timber at Wentwood for use in the monastic tannery (Linnard, 2000: 44). *Wig Wen* Farm 'fair forest', stands above the Aeron valley floor and nearby is the early thatched cottage of Wig-wen. The still-wooded slopes here are named Allt Wig Wen and *Wig Ddu* 'black forest' which gives its name also to an abandoned estate farm and on the slopes above, the larger farm of *Cefn Wig* 'forest ridge'. The name wig is relatively uncommon within Ceredigion but it survives as an echo of Lampeter forest in *Heol y Wig* 'forest road' and the coastal parish of *Ferwig* 'large forest' ais seen as early as the 16th century with Ty Lodwig in the former Bishop's forest of Nantcwnlle. Elsewhere in Wales, wig is also consistently associated with former woodland; Lower Wig is known from woodlands in Newtown with Melin y Wig in Coed Clocaenog forest in Flintshire (Richards, 2007). As late as 1996, the Forestry Commission had an area of woodland simply known as Wig for sale at Allt Wig Wen and the name may be seen as an alternative to forest in areas where this description does not survive providing a useful indicator of former wooded forest. The income generated by such woodland would have been considerable but perhaps just as important were the political considerations of power and authority that would have accompanied the status of, not just woodland, but forest in the medieval period.

Forest does not occur as a place name within any of Ceredigion's monastic-held granges; likewise remnant strips only occur within parts of the Rhuddlan Teifi grange where the rhandir place name also survives. This represents a marked difference between the agricultural practice of monastic estates but to what extent monastic management techniques might have preserved or obscured earlier practices is unknown. Evidence for a highly specialised Cistercian grange system is beginning to emerge as a result of the Strata Florida Landscape Project (David Austin pers. comm.). Farms circling the demesne core represent different types of agricultural production; *Dol Ebolion* signifies 'meadow of the foals' and *Dol Beudy*, 'meadow of the cow barn' for example. Donkin (1962: 43) discussed cattle production by Cistercian houses during the 13th and 14th centuries noting that it made an increasing contribution alongside sheep production and in 1291, the temporalities of Whitland Abbey were four times greater in cattle than in sheep.

A group of early tyddynod within the grange of Maerdref (fig. 67) are also named for specifically different forms of livestock production suggesting organised, specialised management *Pant y Defaid*, 'hollow of the sheep', *Cwm March* 'valley of the stallion', Blaen*cefel* from *ceffyl* or 'horse' and *Pantmoch*, 'hollow of the pigs'. *Gellifaharen* or 'grove of the ram' or 'wether' is still evident in the 16th century Dissolution survey as *Kelthy Vaharren* and *Pant y Creuddyn* derives from a piggery or stronghold implying some sort of enclosure.

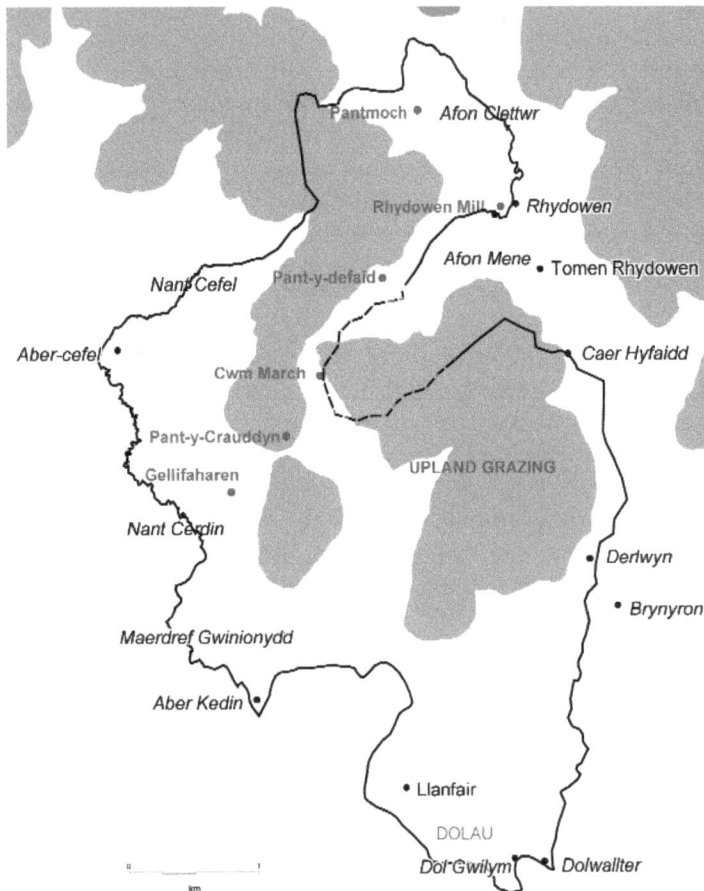

Figure 67. The specialist farm centres of Maerdref grange with Llanfair providing mynydd and dolau.

The neighbouring tref of Llanfair had slightly different resources which were exploited differently and complement the grange's agricultural provision providing extensive upland grazing on the unenclosed mynydd north of the Teifi. The meadow or Dolau do not merely describe the topographical characteristics of a particular type of enclosed field but the specific function that was required of it; providing lush grass and hay. Access to this resource was absent from Maerdref where the valley floor was narrow and the valley sides steep but the fertile meadows of neighbouring Llanfair provided this resource along with access to good fishing. A prized resource, the settlement activity here was restricted to the important early church at Llanfair, other domestic settlement would have been well away from the valuable floodplain. This was not simply to escape flooding but to preserve the valuable hay-lands. The Teifi here is deeply gorged and not prone to flooding in any case and the river dynamics have suggested that the chapel would have stood on the edge of a river bank as in numerous other cases, not least a mile away at Llandysul.

Discussion

This chapter has expanded on the issues identified in the previous chapter that established the survival of trefi units and the gwestfa system rendered on them into the late medieval period. Investigations by Jones Pierce of the gwely tenure in north Wales had mistakenly supposed a late origin, a deliberate introduction that eventually failed due to excessive fragmentation. But it has become apparent that the communal sharing of land provided the basis for the rhandir into the modern period. The information supplied by the 12th century grants of Llanfair, Maerdref and Moelhedog have allowed the reconstruction of their boundaries revealing that they have remained intact for over 800 years. The complexity of the apparently planned Castell Hywel estate with Moelhedog has allowed the identification of other early farms which have been implied through 16th century gwestfa payments. The deep antiquity of this landscape has always been alluded to by the families and communities that occupy them through the study of pedigree and lineage and the genealogical information supplied by Francis Jones has allowed the mapping of these early farms. The morphological and distributional characteristics have provided a model by which it has been possible to propose early farms for areas outside those with documentary information as in Gwinionydd Uwch Cych demonstrating that the dispersed farmscape is one with a medieval antecedent.

This chapter has also emphasised the influence on the landscape of families who have traditionally associated lineage and status with place. It has established that these farmsteads represent the tyddynod occupied by the families of gwely tenure and the evidence from Bangor Teifi suggests that these were present in the 14th century at least. Some of the farms mentioned in a 16th century rental reflect settlement characteristics that reflect early forms of land use and tenure, for example the rhandir represent by the girdle of farmsteads surrounding the former mynydd at Llandysul, Troedrhiwfynyd and Pantheulwen and at Llangeler, Hendre, Mountain Hall, Hen Gae and Pen yr Allt. The inability to identify those 16th century farms named eponymously demonstrates the gradual move towards topographically descriptive names. Excavation at Llanfair plus the longevity of the Moelhedog estate has emphasised the longevity of the landscape structure that has changed little since the 12th century. Aspect analysis has allowed the identification of Moelhedog as a prime, south facing holding, indictating the generosity of Rhys's gift. The location of the territorial framework of the tref and the tyddynod and specific management regimes such as the remnant strips of rhandir has allowed the following settlement model to be produced (fig. 68). It has become apparent that the fertile valley floors were prized locations providing the meadowland or dolau cropped for hay, grazed in order to manure and perhaps planted with winter root crops on a seasonal basis. Settlement on the ystrad is specifically restricted to early churches which favoured this location in the Teifi valley. Secular settlement occurred at or around these locations as a result of nucleation attracted to churches and castles sites as at Newcastle Emlyn, but does not occur elsewhere on the ystrad. Fourteenth-century settlement at Llanerchaeron for example occurs around the early church of St Non's but may be specifically associated with the trading mechanisms established at the nearby nunnery of Llanllyr. Likewise, Llanfair may have early antecedents but the main phase of activity and likely associated settlement is associated with the farming of the grange by Talley Abbey, the main farms, Fardre Fawr and Fach being located on convenient level slopes above the valley floor.

retention of native practice is also seen however in the early tenurial practice of tir cyfrif at the bond settlement of Llansantffraid. A contrasting tenure, like that of the gwely, generated similar land use techniques and this can be seen in the enclosed strips of Bangor Teifi and Llandysul. Thus the lordship of Rhys has demonstrated a range of traditional and novel management and administrative techniques. In contrast the monastic granges at Strata Florida, Manorforion and Maerdref appear to have masked native practice with the introduction of new specialised farming techniques, that is, with specific farms producing specific products, but the former status of the granted lands must be emphasised and it is possible that specialisms may reflect other pre-conquest forms of specialism within the maenorau unit.

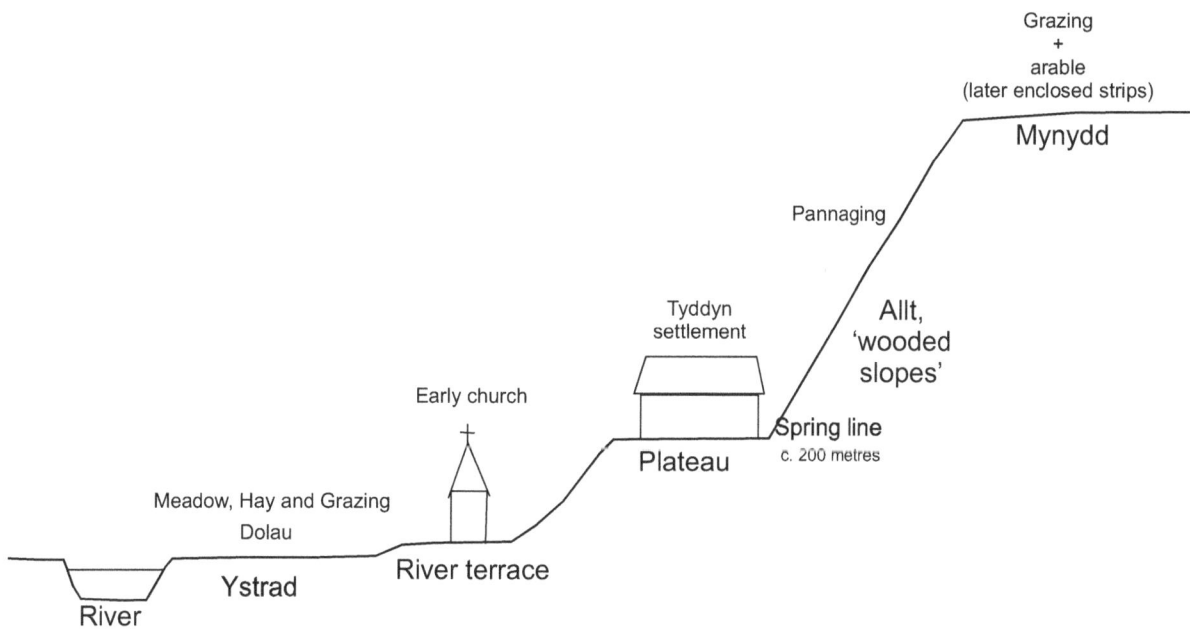

Figure 68. Medieval settlement model southern Ceredigion.

The settlement model shows the early church, occasionally attracting domestic settlement as at Llangeler, Llandysul, Llanerchaeron and Llanfair. The ystrad was valuable meadow land and settlement here was restricted to the valley edges and raised terrace and plateau. The farmsteads and tyddynod for example are situated on convenient plateaux, generally served by the spring line but always away from the valley floor and always below the 200 metre contour. The allt or wooded slopes provide woodland resources such as grazing and pannaging and the upland mynydd is farmed in common, either by allocation under bond tenure or via rhandir of the freeholders, these strips become enclosed.

Despite these the underlying principles of the settlement model some differences in land use remain in different areas. The presence of forest outside monastic-held areas highlights the novel forms of land management adopted within the estates of the Bishops of St David's. The

SEVEN: CONCLUSION

The principal outcome of this research is that we no longer have only dots on maps. I have been able to prove a territorial framework for those places we suspected were medieval but have been unable to demosntrate until now. I have also been able to reconstruct the political geography of 12th century Ceredigion and have demonstrated that it is possible, using a range of sources, to identify some of the early maenorau structures, including the royal maenor and llys at Rhuddlan Teifi. This allowed me to analyse the relationship with neighbouring estates of high status and I determined that Rhuddlan was eventually eclipsed for the new administrative functions undertaken at nearby Castell Gwinionydd near Llandysul. I have also been able to define and identify the territorial units of the maenor, tref, gwestfa and rhandir, some of which are preserved in the chapelry, hamlet and small parish. These institutions are incredibly long lived and are characterised by certain forms of tenure and render, occasionally preserved in documentary sources ranging from the gwestfau survey of 1303, the 14th century Dyffryn Teifi survey and even into the 16th and 17th century returns made in Gwinionydd Is Cerdin.

The consideration of the historic, topographic, and excavated evidence from within the study area has opened up a range of possibilities and connections for the way in which the landscape 'behaved' during the reign of Lord Rhys in the late 12th century. Jones Pierce (1959b: 274) had been puzzled by the absence of tir cyfrif tenure associated with bond communities in Ceredigion but by Rhys had granted all the former royal estates to monastic institutions whose new practice obscured ancient tenure. This concluding chapter provides an assessment of how the study met the objectives set out in the introduction. Some of the themes that have emerged as a result will be identified and explained and a number of implications for future research will be outlined.

Aims Met:

The aims of this research were two fold: The first was to reconstruct settlement and territorial structures during the 12th to 13th centuries for an area of west Wales in the central Teifi valley, and the second was to assess the degree of survival and continuity or otherwise of these structures. This area was chosen primarily because it presented a number of interesting place name survivals such as Maerdref, a church of obvious importance at Llandysul and a remarkable concentration of modest, 'yeoman' status families occupying the local farmsteads. It has proved possible to establish a medieval antecedence for these elements, and in some cases it has hinted at pre-conquest origins. Although a focus for early royal and political activity, the emphasis throughout has been on a familiar and unremarkable farming community and the results generated have demonstrated that rural communities can be confident in their assumptions about longevity. Far from being a far-flung corner of Europe, away from the political developments affecting the rest of northern Europe, medieval Deheubarth was subject, under Rhys, to some of the most advanced and politically mature activities of the period.

Using the territorial units outlined in the Law codes it has been possible to define the cwmwd-maenor-tref as the basic system of pre-conquest administration in this region of Wales. Despite the differences between the north and south Wales redactions. these units retain their basic relationships based on the exploitation of renders such as gwestfa and dofraeth according to status and tenure. Glanville Jones had established the efficacy of an approach that combined history and landscape and his multiple estate model has emerged somewhat intact as a way of landscape explanation. Long-established patterns of lordship and custom were thrown into turmoil due to the military activity of the 11th and early 12th century and this partly helped to obscure the maenorau system. But the cwmwd clearly emerged intact into the late 12th century as regional mechanism for administration and was used as the basis of Rhys's comprehensive overhaul of renders and management. This reorganisation meant that although it has been difficult to identify the constituent maenorau of Gwinionydd, the former royal maenor at Rhuddlan had been fossilised by Rhys's grant to Talley Abbey. Rhys had purposely chosen not to resurrect the ancient royal systems, instead he took specific elements of an already existing framework in order to more efficiently exploit the gwestfa to finance his government. This probably accounts for the apparently stronger survival of the maenor in the Englishries of southern Carmarthenshire for example, where a foreign administration adopted the main elements of an already sophisticated landscape, using new terms and jargon but essentially leaving the unfamiliar frameworks unchanged.

Despite Rhys's re-shuffle, it has been possible to recreate the territorial and settlement frameworks for Ceredigion's medieval landscape. The trefi units that were used to assess the gwestfa are fossilised either as small parishes or as subdivisions of larger parishes: the hamlet or chapelry. Land-use in the form of share land or rhandir is readily identifiable through the mynydd or common upland grazing areas which was enclosed late, preserving relict strips. Former strips are sometimes even preserved in portions of the parish boundary as at Dihewyd, and even within someof the upland areas designated accessible by the Countryside Rights of Way Act in Tregaron. The rhandir was a well attested form of land use and settlement known from the Laws and it is characterised by the tyddynod or homesteads girdling these sharelands. These farms are still extant and are still the dominant element within the landscape.

The data collected for this study demonstrates that a rich and diverse landscape of complexity accompanied Rhys's rule during the 12th century and that it had ancient antecedents. The central Teifi valley was centred around a royal llys and maerdref complex at Rhuddlan Teifi. This was a rich and fertile estate but also politically significant, controlling access east-west along the river valley, but also the medieval river crossings at Borthin and Llanfihangel-ar-arth. It was valuable enough to be prized as a possession originally of Talley Abbey who, even after being the subject of an appeal to Rome were dispossessed of their holdings.

As a result of this research a number of wider themes have emerged that serve to summarise the findings here and to highlight the direction of possible future research directions.

Theme 1: Fusion not Fission

Landscape complexity did not commence with the advent of documentary history and I have provided a challenge to the common historiography that pre-conquest Wales was a somehow simple, immature landscape (eg. Gresham, 1987; Jones Pierce, 1959a; Jones, 1998a; Jones, 1998b; Jones, 1998c and Jones, 1999). The paradigm whereby an essentially tribal system was governed by a peripatetic lordship must be pushed much further back in time in the light of the evidence produced here. That the early kingdoms of pre-conquest Wales were increasingly subdivided must also be questioned. The emphasis instead must focus on the periodic splitting of larger territorial structures like the cwmwd along the boundaries of their smaller constituent elements, the tref. This preserved an early landscape framework and the periodic political and governmental changes had little effect on the ground. Indeed it was the fusion of these small community units that created larger administrative units, not the other way round. This can be described, in effect, as a modular landscape, a series of early and indivisible community units that can be attached to other units in a series of different ways. Thus the parish of Llandysul was created around the rich church in the later medieval period by taking trefi elements from two different lordships: the royal estates 'above' the Cerdin and the Dyffryn Teifi estate below it, but preserving the basic units themselves.

The former royal maenor at Rhuddlan was divided into at least four trefi and these comprised rhandiroedd elements. Further excavation and survey targeted on the possible llys enclosures at Broncwrt may provide valuable dating evidence of an obviously important secular site that may involve the devlopment of an early medieval llys into a monastic grange centre. The emphasis here must be on the clarification of this sequence through dating, which whilst problematic on these well-drained glacial deposits in an area of acidic high-rainfall, has nevertheless proved fruitful at Llanfair where test-pitting and narrow evaluation trenches were used to good effect. If this is a llys site it will only be the second ever excavated after Llys Rhosyr in north Wales which dated to the 14th century (Johnstone, 1999). Rhuddlan therefore has the potential to address the holy grail of Welsh archaeology; pre-12th century secular settlement.

Theme 2: Agency and Lordship

Rhys had granted vast swathes of Ceredigion to new monastic houses for a variety of reasons; as a way of forming a neutral buffer from Gwynedd in the north and Norman in the south but also as a way of removing the estates from their military potential, especially his warring sons. Also though, spiritual gain was provided for by way of a link to the former Welsh clas church by recycling their ancient estate lands and staffing the houses with Welsh, representatives. These estates were often former royal, bond estates that meant that Rhys inherited the right to dispose of them as he saw fit and, perhaps more significantly, this ensured no loss of revenue, these former estates being exempt from the payment of gwestfa for example. The reconstruction of these grants geographically serves to highlight an unprecedented level of information about Rhys's actions and possible motives but also serves to emphasise the agency of the individual response of the community. The obligations and responsibilities of the lord, to maintain the security and boundaries of the cwmwd and its subunits, to provide administration and management of trade centres, government, agricultural regime and mills etcetera, were much more onerous than those imposed upon the individual tenant or freeholder. The labour dues and renders supplied by such individuals were conceived of as rights not expectations. The 16th century evidence from Rhydowen mill demonstrates this point where tenants were continually recorded as removing their suit from the mill which was seen as their resource to be continually renegotiated and used under their own terms and provided for by the lord. In a similar way, the gwely tenure was not a tie to the soil but an inalienable right to a share, in a physical holding but also a right to membership of that community. These ties were strengthened and transformed into the late medieval period and beyond where the emergence of new gentry saw renewed emphasis on consolidation of the family's holdings into contiguous estates, the adoption of fixed surnames for the first time and the recording and interest in genealogy lineage and place. Through patronage of new bardic fashions and the generation of pedigrees and family histories, these elements were strengthened and formed the basis of a stable Tivyside into the early 20th century.

History has been invariably written by middle aged scholars and Wales is particular in this respect. Perhaps this has influenced the scant attention to female histories in Wales that have been introduced here but not expanded on and must form the basis of a project beyond the scope of this thesis at present. Of obvious importance is the inferred female cult in place in the Aeron valley, one perpetuated by Rhys's foundation of a female Cistercian house and one that replaced an earlier women's house with links to St Non and St Ffraid. This is echoed in the unidentified holding of Dau Marchty (the two women's houses) granted to Strata Florida in the 13th century and located somewhere in the vicinity of the Aeron valley. Women held obviously powerful positions in medieval Wales. Gwenllian, Rhys's mother, had led an assault on Kidwelly castle and Owain Gwynedd had provided for his wife Angharad by way of a dower with the cwmwd of Anhuniog (Beverley Smith, 1983).

Another aspect of Rhys's reign that has emerged only partially here is the European context of his lordship and his kingdom. The desire by him to introduce European aspects of the French court in his 'new' Eisteddfod held at Cardigan Castle demonstrated his desire to modernise Wales and the awarding of prizes to participants from both the north and south demonstrated his desire perhaps for a united Wales. This should be read alongside the new landscape information to fully inform us where the better survival of documentary evidence from elsewhere has distracted attention away from his significant reign.

Theme 3: Landscape Management

It has never been one of the primary aims of this project to be able to contribute to the methods familiar to landscape archaeologists in any spectacularly new way. What has emerged, however, is the success of the application of a suite of techniques in a region not previously approached in this way. This approach has demonstrated that excavation and other direct techniques such as survey and geophysical prospection must be at the forefront of research in rural areas. The support of research departments can be harnessed and was successfully employed at Llanfair where simple, relatively non-destructive, techniques were able to re-date an 'Iron Age' site to the early 13th century. We must move on from the production of endless resource audits and thematic reviews and concentrate on more specific themes and areas. We must challenge the premise of preservation in situ in these rural areas and the generalised historical narratives generated by the current Historic Landscape Characterisation process favoured by landscape management institutions leaves an appalling lacuna in our understanding. Ceredigion as one of the least commercially developed parts of Wales has lagged behind the rest of Wales in this respect, but the deficiencies in the record are beginning to be addressed by a more proactive approach by Cambria Archaeology where, for example, a series of unique rectangular Iron Age enclosures have been the target of research survey and excavation centred around the lower Teifi valley and this project is going some way to address the archaeological deficiencies. This is vital in an increasingly developed landscape with wind farms, gas pipelines and by-passes currently under construction in west Wales, and is the overwhelming message from the recent research framework for the archaeology of Wales (http://www.archaeoleg.org.uk/).

A Final Word

People do not use landscapes according to its physical attributes but according to its histories. The approach of much of this research has been essentially an empirical one but one that has considered individual, community and lordship as fundamental to the process of landscape use and history. What was once considered an opaque and inscrutable landscape has turned out to be a rich resource that will have resonance for a number of targeted studies outside the scope of this thesis.

Throughout my analysis I have been constantly amazed at how little people understand the rural landscapes of Wales; People lived in tribes on the tops of hills, ate grass and died after a hard, short life. This attitude is changing but very, very slowly. Common approaches have lagged behind the kind of studies carried out elsewhere and the emphasis has traditionally been on documentary analysis with little thought to the lives of the people who wrote them. Perhaps this is the influence of that fantastic institute of scholarly learning the National Library of Wales at Aberystwyth that attracts documentary historians of repute but distracts one away from the wonderful view out of the long windows of the library on the hill. This must change and I have been heartened by the enormous potential of the archaeological landscape on my doorstep and if this research has adequately reflected that potential then it has successfully fulfilled its aims.

BIBLIOGRAPHY

Unpublished sources:

      Aberystwyth

Ceredigion Record Office, uncatalogued material relating to Newcastle Emlyn and Llandysul parish.

      Carmarthen

Carmarthenshire Record Office, MS I:31 (Golden Grove Books).

Published sources:

Alcock, L. 1963 *Dinas Powys: and Iron Age, Dark Age and Early Medieval settlement in Glamorgan*. Cardiff, University of Wales Press.

Allen, D. 1979 Excavations at Hafod y Nant Criafolen, Brenig Valley, Clwyd, 1973-74. *Post-Medieval Archaeology* 13, pp. 1-59.

Austin, D. 1984 The castle and the landscape: annual lecture to the society for Landscape Studies, May 1984. *Landscape History* 6, pp. 69-81.

Austin, D. 1988 Excavations and Survey at Bryn Cysegrfan, Llanfair Clydogau, Dyfed, 1979. *Medieval Archaeology* XXXII, pp. 130-165.

Baker-Jones, L. 1999 *Princelings, Privilege and Power: The Tivyside Gentry in their Community.* Llandysul, Gomer.

Bale, R.J. 2005 A 223 year (AD 1779-2001) modern oak tree ring chronology from Allt Lanlas, Llanerchaeron, Ceredigion. *Swansea Geographer* 40, pp. 45-55.

Bevan, R.E. 1926 Notes on Llanarth and its Neighbourhood. *Transactions of the Cardiganshire Antiquarian Society* 4, pp. 60-70.

Beverley Smith, J. 1983 Dower in Thirteenth-Century Wales: A Grant of the Commote of Anhuniog, 1273. *Bulletin of the Board of Celtic Studies.* XXX, pp. 348-355.

Bourdieu, P. 1991 *The Logic of Practice*. Stanford, Stanford University Press.

Bowen, D.Q. 1994 The Land of Cardiganshire. In J.L. Davies & D.P. Kirby (eds.) *Cardiganshire County History, Volume 1. From the Earliest Times to the Coming of the Normans.* Cardiff, University of Wales Press, pp. 3-20.

Bradley, R. 1998 *The Significance of Monuments : On the Shaping of Human Experience in Neolithic and Bronze Age Europe.* London: Routledege.

Breeze, A. 1994 The Bret Glascurion and Chaucer's House of Fame. *The Review of English Studies.* 45(177), pp. 63-69.

Brewer, J.S. (ed.) 1873 *Giraldus Cambrensis Opera Vol. IV* London, Longmans.

Butler, L.A.S. 1963 The Excavation of a Long-Hut Near Bwlch-yr-Hendre. *Ceredigion* IV, pp. 450-457.

Butler, L.A.S. 1974 Medieval finds from Castell-y-Bere, Merioneth. *Archaeologia Cambrensis.* 123, pp. 78-112.

Cadw 1998 *Register of Landscapes of Outstanding Historic Interest in Wales.* Cardiff, Cadw Welsh Historic Monuments.

Cadw 2001 *Register of Landscapes of Special Historical Interest in Wales*. Cardiff, Cadw Welsh Historic Monuments.

Cartwright, J. 1997 The Desire to Corrupt. Convent and Community in Medieval Wales. In D. Watt (ed.) *Medieval Women in Their Community*. Cardiff, University of Wales Press, pp. 20-48.

Cathcart King, D.J. 1959 Castles of Cardiganshire. *Ceredigion* III, pp. 50-69.

Charles, B.G. 1973 *George Owen of Henllys*. Aberystwyth, National Library of Wales.

Charles, B.G. 1992 *The Place-Names of Pembrokeshire*. Aberystwyth, National Library of Wales.

Charles-Edwards, T.M. 1971 The Seven Bishop-Houses of Dyfed. *Bulletin of the Board of Celtic Studies* XXIV(III), pp. 247-262.

CISP 2007 *The Celtic Inscribed Stones Project*. Accessed 2.4.7 http://www.ucl.ac.uk/archaeology/cisp/database/

Colt-Hoare, R.C. (ed.) 1976 *Giraldus Cambrensis. The Itinerary Through Wales: Description of Wales.* London, Dent.

Cowley, F.G. 1977 *The Monastic Order in South Wales, 1066 - 1349.* Cardiff, University of Wales Press & Board of Celtic Studies.

Cule, J. 1977 Some Early Hospitals in Wales and the Border. *National Library of Wales Journal* XX(2), pp. 97-130.

Davies, J. 1993 *A History of Wales.* London, Penguin.

Davies, J. & Hogg, A.H.A. 1994 The Iron Age In J.L. Davies & D.P. Kirby (eds.) *Cardiganshire County History, Volume 1. From the Earliest Times to the Coming of the Normans.* Cardiff, University of Wales Press, pp. 219-274.

Davies, M. 1957 Rhosili Open Fields and Related South Wales Field Patterns. *Agricultural History Review* 5, pp. 85-96.

Davies, T.I. 1959 The Vale of the Aeron in the Making. *Ceredigion* III, pp. 194-206.

Davies, W. 1982 *Wales in the Early Middle Ages.* Leicester, Leicester University Press.

Davies, W.J. 1896 *Hanes Plwyf Llandyssul.* Llandysul, Gomerian Press.

Davis, P. 2000 *A Company of Forts.* Llandysul, Gomer.

Dobres, M.A. & Robb, J. (eds.) 2000 *Agency in Archaeology*. London, Routledge.

Dodgshon, R.A. 1994 Early Society and Economy. In J.L. Davies & D.P. Kirby (eds.) *Cardiganshire County History, Volume 1. From the Earliest Times to the Coming of the Normans.* Cardiff, University of Wales Press, pp. 343-364.

Donkin, R.A. 1962 Cattle on the estates of Medieval Cistercian Monasteries in England and Wales. *Economic History Review* 15(1), pp. 31-53.

Driver, T. 2002 Gazetteer of Sites Explored 2002: Early Christian and Medieval: Tir Newydd Grange, Llanwenog (SN 4925 4814). *Archaeology in Wales* 42, pp. 123-124.

Duby, G. 1988 *A History of Private Life, Vol. 2. Revelations of the Medieval World.* London, Belknap.

Dugdale, W. 1817-1830 *Monasticon Anglicanum: a History of the Abbies and other Monasteries, Hospitals, Frieries, and Cathedral and Collegiate Churches, with their Dependencies, in England and Wales (6 Volumes).* Accessed 4.10.5 http://monasticmatrix.usc.edu/bibliographia/index.php?function=detail&id=2659

Edwards, O.M. 1896 *Cartrefi Cymru*. Wrexham, Hughes and Son.

Edwards, O.M. 1901 *Wales*. London, Unwin.

Edwards, O.M. 1906 *Clych Adgof: Penodau yn Hanes Fydd Addysg.* Caernarfon, Cwmni'r Cyhoeddwyr Cymreig.

Ellis, T.P. 1926 *Welsh Tribal Law and Custom in the Middle Ages. Volume 1.* Oxford, Clarendon Press.

Evans, A.C. (ed.) 1878 *The Royal Charters Relating to the Town and County of Carmarthen and the Abbeys of Talley and*

Tygwyn-ar-Daf. by J. R. Daniel-Thyssen, Esq. F.S.A. of Brighton. Carmarthen, William Spurrell.

Evans, G. 1922 The Story of Newcastle Emlyn and Atpar to 1531, with Concluding Survey. *Y Cymmrodor* XXXII, pp. 58-170.

Evans, H.R. 1960 A Village Worthy: Evan Isaac Thomas, Llandysul. *Ceredigion* IV(I), pp. 146-190.

Evans, N. 2003 The Llanerchaeron estate before emparkment. *Archaeology in Wales* 43, pp. 25-32.

Evans, W.R. 2004 St David and St David's and the Coming of the Normans. *Transactions of the Honourable Society of Cymmrodorion* 11, pp. 5-19.

Fleming, A. 1998 *Swaledale. Valley of the Wild River*. Edinburgh, Edinburgh University Press.

Forester, T. (ed.) 1887 *The Historical Works of Giraldus Cambrensis*. London, George Bell & Sons.

Fox, A. 1939 Early Welsh Homesteads on Gelligaer Common, Glamorgan. Excavations in 1938. *Archaeologia Cambrensis* 94, pp. 163-199.

Giddens, A. 1993 *New rules of sociological method: a positive critique of interpretative sociologies*. Cambridge, Polity Press.

Gilchrist, R. 1999 Landscapes of the middle ages: churches, castles and monasteries. In J. Hunter & I. Ralston (eds.) *The Archaeology of Britain*. London, Routledge, pp. 228-246.

Green, F. 1910 Genealogies of Cardiganshire, Carmarthenshire and Pembrokeshire families. *West Wales Historical Records* 1, pp. 1-96.

Gregson, N. 1985 The multiple estate model: some critical questions. *Journal of Historical Geography*. 11(4), pp. 339-351.

Gresham, C. 1987 Medieval Parish and Township Boundaries in Gwynedd. *Bulletin of the Board of Celtic Studies* XXXIV, pp. 137-149.

Gribben, A. 1990 Tain Bo Cuailnge: A Place on the Map, A Place in the Mind. *Western Folklore*. 49(3), pp. 277-291.

Griffiths, E.A. 1978 *Boroughs of Medieval Wales*. Cardiff, University of Wales Press.

Griffiths, G.M. 1974a A Visitation of the Archdeaconry of Carmarthen. *National Library of Wales Journal* XVIII(3), pp. 287-311.

Griffiths, R.A. 1974b *The Principality of Wales in the Later Middle Ages. South Wales, Volume 1, South Wales, 1277-1536*. Cardiff, University of Wales Press. (Board of Celtic Studies, History and Law Series No XVI).

Griffiths, R.A. 1994 *Conquerors and Conquered in Medieval Wales*. Stroud, Sutton.

Grooms, J.C. 1993 *Giants of Wales*. Lewiston, Mellen.

Hadley, D.M. 1996 Multiple Estates and the Origins of the Manorial Structure of the Northern Danelaw. *Journal of Historical Geography* 22(1), pp. 3-15.

Halliday, F.E. (ed.) 1953 *Richard Carew's Survey of Cornwall*. London, Melrose.

Hankinson, R. & Caseldine, A. 2006 Short Dykes in Powys and their Origins. *Archaeological Journal* 163, pp. 264-269.

Harvey, D. 1997 The Evolution of Territoriality and Societal Transitions in West Cornwall. *Landscape History* 19, pp. 13-24.

Harvey, D.C. & Jones, R.A. 1999 Custom and Habit(us): The Meaning of Traditions and Legends in Early Medieval

Western Britain. *Geografisker Annaler* LXXXI B(4), pp. 223-233.

Hext Lewes, J. 1971 Llanllyr. *Ceredigion* VI(IV), pp. 341-349.

Hicks, D. 2005 'Places for thinking' from Annapolis to Bristol: situations and symmetries in world historical archaeologies. *World Archaeology* 37(3), pp. 373-391.

Howells, B.E. 1955 Pembrokeshire Farming circa 1580 - 1620. *National Library of Wales Journal* IX(II), pp. 239-250.

Hughes, I.T. 1957 The Background of Llandysul. *Ceredigion* III(II), pp. 100-113.

Hughes, I.T. & Jenkins, J.R. 1967 The Church of St Tysul, Llandysul. *Ceredigion* V(IV).

Hughes, P.D.M., Morriss, S.H., Schulz, J. & Barber, K.E. 2001 Mire development and human impact in the Teifi Valley: Evidence from Tregaron (Cors Caron) peatlands. In M.J.C. Walker (ed.) *Quaternary Research Association West Wales Field Guide*, pp. 76-92.

Huws, D. 2000 *Medieval Welsh Manuscripts.* Cardiff, University of Wales Press & The National Library of Wales.

Institute of Field Archaeologists. (2008). *Introducing a Research Framework for the Archaeology of Wales.* from http://www.archaeoleg.org.uk/med.html.

Isaacson, R.F. 1917 The Episcopal Registers of the Diocese of St David's 1397-1518. *Cymmrodorion Record Series* 6.

Jack, R.I. 1982 Fulling mills in Wales before 1547. *Archaeologia Cambrensis* 130, pp. 70-130.

James, D.B. 2001 *Ceredigion- Its Natural History.* Aberystwyth, D.B. James.

James, H. 1992 *Early Medieval Cemeteries in Wales. The early church in Wales and the West : recent work in early Christian archaeology, history and place names.* Oxbow Monograph 16, pp. 90-103.

James, H. 2006 *The Cult of St. David - Study of Dedication Patterns in the medieval diocese of St Davids.* Accessed 24.8.6 http://www.terra-demetarum.org.uk

James, T. 1997 *Bledri Latimer, alias Bledri ap Cadifor ap Collwyn, Lord of Blaencuch and Cil-sant. Fabulator of Arthurian Romance?* Accessed 12.12.6 http://www.terra-demetarum.org.uk/Articles/bledri.pdf

James, T.I.J. 1955 *Exchequer Proceedings Concerning Wales In Tempore James I.* Cardiff, University of Wales Press. (Board of Celtic Studies, History and Law Series No. IV).

Jenkins, D. 1986 *The Law of Hywel Dda.* Llandysul, Gomer Press.

Jenkins, D. 2000 Hawk and Hound: Hunting in the Laws of Court. In T.M. Charles-Edwards, M. Owen & P. Russell (eds.) *The Welsh King and His Court.* Cardiff, University of Wales Press, pp. 255-280.

Johnson, M. 1996 *An Archaeology of Capitalism.* Oxford, Blackwell.

Johnson, M. 1999 *Archaeological Theory: An Introduction.* Oxford, Blackwell.

Johnson, M. 2000 Self-Made Men and the Staging of Agency. In M.A. Dobres & J. Robb (eds.) *Agency in Archaeology.* London, Routledge, pp. 213-231.

Johnson, M. 2005 On the particularism of English landscape archaeology. *International Journal of Historical Archaeology* 9(2), pp. 111-122.

Johnstone, N. 1997 *An Investigation into the Locations of the Royal Courts of Thirteenth-Century Gwynedd. In N. Edwards (ed.) Landscape and Settlement in Medieval Wales.* Oxbow Monograph 81, pp. 55-70.

Johnstone, N. 1999 Cae Llys, Rhosyr: A Court of the Princes of Gwynedd. *Studia Celtica* XXXIII, pp. 251-295.

Johnstone, N. 2000 Llys and Maerdref: The Royal courts of the Princes of Gwynedd. *Studia Celtica* XXXIIV, pp. 167-210.

Joliffe, J.E.A. 1954 *The Constitutional History of Medieval England From the English Settlement to 1485*. London, Adam & Charles Black.

Jolliffe, J.E.A. 1926 Northumbrian Institutions. *English Historical Review* XXXXI, pp. 1-42.

Jolliffe, J.E.A. 1962 (1st ed. 1933) *Pre-Feudal England: The Jutes*. Oxford, Oxford University Press.

Jones, E.G. 1939 *Exchequer Proceedings (Equity) Concerning Wales, Henry VIII - Elizabeth I*. Cardiff, University of Wales Press. (Board of Celtic Studies, History and Law Series No. IV).

Jones, F. 1972a Boundaries of the Lordship of Talley, 1668. *Bulletin of the Board of Celtic Studies* XXIV, pp. 518-526.

Jones, F. 1987 Historic Carmarthenshire Homes and Their Families. Dyfed, Carmarthenshire Antiquarian Society & Cultural Services Department, Dyfed County Council.

Jones, F. 1996a *The Historic Houses of Pembrokeshire and Their Families*. Pembrokeshire, Brawdy Books.

Jones, F. 2002 *Treasury of Historic Carmarthenshire (Edited by C. Charles-Jones)*. Pembrokeshire, Brawdy Books.

Jones, F. 2004 (2nd. edition) *Historic Cardiganshire Homes and Their Families*. Pembrokeshire, Brawdy Books.

Jones, G. & Jones, T. 2003 *The Mabinogion*. London, Everyman.

Jones, G.R.J. 1964 The Llanynys Quillets: A Measure of Landscape Transformation in Wales. *Denbighshire Historical Society*. 13, pp. 133-158.

Jones, G.R.J. 1972b Post Roman Wales. In H.P.R. Finberg (ed.) *The Agrarian History of England and Wales, Volume I. II A.D. 43-1042*. Cambridge, Cambridge University Press, pp. 283-384.

Jones, G.R.J. 1976 Multiple Estates and Early Settlement. In P.H. Sawyer (ed.) *English Medieval Settlement: Continuity and Change*. London, Edward Arnold, pp. 15-40.

Jones, G.R.J. 1984 Early Territorial Organisation in Wales. *Bulletin of the Board of Celtic Studies* XXXI, pp. 332-323.

Jones, G.R.J. 1985 Multiple Estates Perceived. *Journal of Historical Geography* 11, pp. 352-363.

Jones, G.R.J. 1989 The Dark Ages. In D.H. Owen (ed.) *Settlement and Society in Wales*. Cardiff, University of Wales Press, pp. 177-198.

Jones, G.R.J. 1992 The Models for Organisation in Llyfr Iorwerth and Llyfr Cyfnerth. *Bulletin of the Board of Celtic Studies* 39, pp. 95-118.

Jones, G.R.J. 1994 "Tir Telych", the Gwestfau of Cynwyl Gaeo and Cwmwd Caeo. *Studia Celtica* XXVIII, pp. 81-95.

Jones, G.R.J. 1996b The Gwely as a Tenurial Institution. *Studia Celtica* XXX, pp. 167-188.

Jones, G.R.J. 2000a Llys and Maerdref. In T.M. Charles-Edwards, M. Owen & P. Russell (eds.) *The Welsh King and His Court*. Cardiff, University of Wales Press, pp. 296-318.

Jones Pierce, T. 1939 Some Tendencies in the Agrarian History of Caernarvonshire During the Later Middle Ages. *Transactions of the Caernarvonshire Historical Society* I, pp. 18-36.

Jones Pierce, T. 1940 Notes on the History of Rural Caernarvonshire in the Reign of Elizabeth. *Transactions of the Caernarvonshire Historical Society* II, pp. 35-57.

Jones Pierce, T. 1941a An Anglesey Crown Rental of the Sixteenth Century. *Bulletin of the Board of Celtic Studies* X, pp.

156-176.

Jones Pierce, T. 1941b The Growth of Commutation in Gwynedd During the Thirteenth Century. *Bulletin of the Board of Celtic Studies X*, pp. 309-332.

Jones Pierce, T. 1942-3 A Caernarvonshire Manorial Borough, Studies in the Medieval History of Pwllheli. *Transactions of the Caernarvonshire Historical Society IV*, pp. 35-50.

Jones Pierce, T. 1947 Clennenau Letters and Papers in the Brogyntyn Collection. *National Library of Wales* (Supplement, Series IV, Pt. I).

Jones Pierce, T. 1951 Medieval Settlement in Anglesey. *Transactions of the Anglesey Antiquarian Society*, pp. 1-33.

Jones Pierce, T. 1959a *Agrarian Aspects of the Tribal System in Medieval Wales.* Geographie et Histoire Agraires, Annales de L'Est Memoire No 21, Actes du Colloque International Oganise par la Faculte des Lettres de L'Universite de Nancy 1957

Jones Pierce, T. 1959b Medieval Cardiganshire, a Study in Social Origins. *Ceredigion III*, pp. 265-283.

Jones Pierce, T. 1967 Landlords in Wales, the Nobility and Gentry. In H.P.R. Finberg (ed.) *The Agrarian History of England and Wales, Vol. 4.* Cambridge, Cambridge University Press, pp. 357-381.

Jones, R.A. 1998a Early State Formation in Native Medieval Wales. *Political Geography* 17(6), pp. 667-682.

Jones, R.A. 1998b The formation of the Cantref and the Commote in Medieval Gwynedd. *Studia Celtica XXXII*, pp. 169-177.

Jones, R.A. 1998c Problems with medieval Welsh local administration - the case of the maenor and the maenol. *Journal of Historical Geography* 24(2), pp. 135-146.

Jones, R.A. 1999 The Mechanics of Medieval State Formation: Observations From Wales. *Space and Polity* 3(1), pp. 85-99.

Jones, R.A. 2000b Changing Ideologies of Medieval State Formation: The Growing Exploitation of Land in Gwynedd c.1100-c.1400. *Journal of Historical Geography* 26(4), pp. 505-516.

Jones, T. 1955a *Brut y Tywysogion.* Cardiff, University of Wales Press. (Board of Celtic Studies History and Law Series No. XVI).

Jones, T.I.J. 1955b *Exchequer Proceedings Concerning Wales In Tempore James I.* Cardiff, University of Wales Press. (Board of Celtic Studies, History and Law Series No. XV.

Kain, J.P. & Oliver, R.R. 2001 *Historic Parishes of England & Wales.* An Electronic Map of Boundaries before 1850 (CD-ROM). Colchester, History Data Service.

Kelly, R.S. 1982 The Excavation of a Medieval Farmstead at Cefn Graeanog, Clynnog, Gwynedd. *Bulletin of the Board of Celtic Studies* XXIX(IV), pp. 859-908.

Kirby, D.P. 1994a The Coming of Christianity. In J.L. Davies & D.P. Kirby (eds.) *Cardiganshire County History, Volume 1. From the Earliest Times to the Coming of the Normans.* Cardiff, University of Wales Press, pp. 365-378.

Kirby, D.P. 1994b The Political Development of Ceredigion, c.400-1081. In J.L. Davies & D.P. Kirby (eds.) *Cardiganshire County History, Volume 1. From the Earliest Times to the Coming of the Normans.* Cardiff, University of Wales Press, pp. 318-342.

Langton, J. & Jones, G. 2005 *The Forests and Chases of England and Wales c.1500-c.1800.* Accessed http://info.sjc.ox.ac.uk/forests/

Lewis, E.A. 1923 The Account Roll of the Chamberlain of West Wales From Michaelmass 1301 to Michaelmass 1302.

Bulletin of the Board of Celtic Studies II, pp. 49-86.

Lewis, T. 1927 Archaeological Investigations in the Vicinity of Llanddewibrefi and Llanfair Clydogau. *Transactions of the Cardiganshire Antiquarian Society.* 5, pp. 83-99.

Lhuyd, E. 1909-11 *Parochialia*. Supplement to Archaeologia Cambrensis.

Linnard, W. 2000 *Welsh Woods and Forests*. Llandysul, Gomer.

Lloyd, J.E. 1911 *A History of Wales Vol I*. London, Longmans, Green and Co.

Lloyd, J.E. 1935 *A History of Carmarthenshire, Volume I*. Cardiff, London Carmarthenshire Society.

Lloyd, J.E. 1937 *The Story of Ceredigion (400-1277)*. Cardiff, University of Wales Press.

Lloyd, J.E. 1939 *A History of Carmarthenshire, Volume II*. Cardiff, London Carmarthenshire Society.

Lloyd, T. 1989 *The Lost Houses of Wales: A Survey of Country Houses in Wales Demolished Since c. 1900.* London, SAVE Britain's Heritage.

Lloyd, T., Orbach, J. & Scourfield, R. 2006 *Carmarthenshire and Ceredigion.* Pevsner Buildings of Wales. London, Yale University Press.

Longley, D. 1997 The Royal Courts of the Welsh Princes of Gwynedd AD 400-1283. In N. Edwards (ed.) *Landscape and Settlement Change in Medieval Wales.* Oxbow Monograph 81, pp. 41-54.

Longley, D. 2001 Medieval Settlement and Landscape Change on Anglesey. *Landscape History* 23, pp. 39-60.

Longley, D. (2004) Status and Lordship in the Early Middle Ages. In R.A. Griffiths (ed.) *Gwent County History: Age of the Marcher Lords.* Cardiff, University of Wales Press. pp 287-316.

Macalister, R.A.S. 1945 *Corpus Inscriptionum Insularum Celticarum Vol. 1.* Dublin, Stationery Office.

Maund, K. 2000 *The Welsh Kings.* Stroud, Tempus.

McCaroll, D. 2001 The Glacial Geomorphology of West Wales. In M.J.C. Walker & D. McCarroll (eds.) *The Quaternary of West Wales: Field Guide.* London, Quaternary Research Association, pp. 9-16.

McNeill, T.E. & Pringle, M. 1997 A Map of Mottes in the British Isles. *Medieval Archaeology* XLI, pp. 220-222.

Meyrick, S.R. 1810 *History and Antiquities of the County of Cardigan.* London, Longman, Hurst, Rees and Orme.

Morgan, G. 2001 *Nanteos. A Welsh House and its Families.* Llandysul, Gomer.

Morgan, G. 2005 *Ceredigion. A Wealth of History.* Llandysul, Gomer.

Murphy, K. 2007a *Historic Landscape Characterisation: Llangeler.* Accessed 1.4.7 http://www.acadat.com/HLC/drefachfelindre/llangeler.htm

Murphy, K. 2007b *Historic Landscape Characterisation: Lower Teifi Valley.* Accessed 4.4.7 http://www.acadat.com/HLC/lowerteifivalley/plasyberllan.htm

Murphy, K., Ramsey, R. & Page, M. 2006 *A Survey of Defended enclosures in Ceredigion, Gazetteer of OS grid SN44. Cambria Archaeology, Report no. 2006/20. Project Record No. 54269.* Accessed 12.4.6 http://www.acadat.com/

Nash-Williams, V.E. 1950 *The Early Christian Monuments of Wales.* Cardiff, University of Wales Press.

Nash-Williams, V.E. 1969 *The Roman Frontier in Wales.* Cardiff, University of Wales Press.

O' Sullivan, A. & O' Sullivan, W. (eds.) 1971 *Archaeologia Britannica : giving some account...of the languages, histories and customs of the original inhabitants of Great Britain by Edward Lhuyd.* Shannon, Irish Universities Press.

Orser, C.E. 1999 Negotiating our 'familiar pasts'. In S. Tarlow & S. West (eds.) *The Familiar Past? Archaeologies of Later Historical Britain.* London, Routledge, pp. 273-286.

Owen, A. 1841 *Ancient Laws and Institutions of Wales. Volume II.* London, Record Commissioners, Public Record Office

Owen, D. 1979 Chapelries and rural settlement: an examination of some of the Kesteven evidence. In P.H. Sawyer (ed.) *English Medieval Settlement: Continuity and Change.* London, Edward Arnold, pp. 35-40.

Owen, E. 1894 A Contribution to the History of the Premonstratensian Abbey of Talley. *Archaeologia Cambrensis* 11 (5th Series), pp. 35-50, 92-107 & 196-213.

Owen, H. 1892 Owen's Description of Pembrokeshire, Part I. *Cymmrodorion Record Series* 1.

Owen, H. 1897 Owen's Description of Pembrokeshire, Part II. *Cymmrodorion Record Series* 1.

Owen, H. 1906 Owen's Description of Pembrokeshire, Part III. *Cymmrodorion Record Series* 1.

Owen, H. 1936 Owen's Description of Pembrokeshire, Part IV. *Cymmrodorion Record Series* 1.

Peate, I.C. 1940 The Welsh House - A Study in Folk Culture. *Y Cymmrodor* XXXXVII.

Peate, I.C. 1944 *The Welsh House - A Study in Folk Culture.* Liverpool, Brython.

Peate, I.C. 2004 *The Welsh House. (reprinted with a foreword by Dr Greg Stevenson).* Cribyn, Llanerch Publishers.

Porter, E.T. 1993 *The Olivers of Cardiganshire 1778-1993, Their Descendants in Wales, England and North America and Some of their Related Welsh Families.* Accessed 12.4.6 http://www.genuki.org.uk/big/wal/CGN/Olivers.html

Powel, D. (ed.) 1811 *The Historie of Cambria, now called Wales.* London, Reprinted for John Harding.

Preston-Jones, A. 1992 Decoding Cornish Churchyards In N. Edwards & A. Lane (eds.) *The early church in Wales and the West : recent work in early Christian archaeology, history and place names.* Oxbow Monograph 16, pp. 135-185.

Pryce, H. 2000 Lawbooks and Literacy in Medieval Wales. *Speculum* 75(1), pp. 29-67.

Pryce, H. 2001 British or Welsh? National Identity in Twelfth-Century Wales. *English Historical Review* CXVI, pp. 775-801.

Pryce, H. 2005 *The Acts of the Welsh Rulers, 1120-1283.* Cardiff, University of Wales & Board of Celtic Studies.

Pryce, H. 2007 Patrons and Patronage among the Cistercians in Wales. *Archaeologia Cambrensis* 154, pp. 81-96.

Record Commission 1802 *Taxatio Ecclesiastica Angliae et Walliae Auctoritate Papae Nicholai IV.* London, Record Commission.

Redknap, M. 2004 *French pottery in medieval Wales.* Accessed 22.5.4 http://www.nmgw.ac.uk/

Rees, W. 1924 *South Wales and the March 1284-1415. A Social and Agrarian Study.* Oxford, Oxford University Press.

Rees, W. 1932 *South Wales and the Border in the Fourteenth Century.* Ordnance Survey.

Rees, W. 1951 *An Historical Atlas of Wales.* Cardiff, William Lewis.

Rhys, J. 1907 The Capel Mair Stone. *Archaeologia Cambrensis* 62, pp. 293-310.

Rhys, M. 1936 Minister's Accounts for West Wales 1277 to 1306. Part I, Text and Translation. *Cymmrodorion Record*

Series 13.

Richards, M. 1960a Gwinionydd Is Cerdin in 1651. *Ceredigion* IV(I), pp. 388-399.

Richards, M. 1960b Is Coed Uwch Hirwern in 1651. *Ceredigion* IV(I), pp. 374-387.

Richards, M. 1961 Local Government in Cardiganshire, Medieval and Modern. *Ceredigion* IV(II), pp. 272-282.

Richards, M. 1964a Gwinionydd Is Cerdin in 1564. *Ceredigion* V(I), pp. 229-238.

Richards, M. 1964b The Significance of Is and Uwch in Welsh Commote and Cantref Names. *Welsh History Review* 2, pp. 9-18.

Richards, M. 1969 *Welsh Administrative and Territorial Units: Medieval and Modern*. Cardiff, University of Wales Press.

Richards, M. 1974 The Carmarthenshire Possessions of Talyllychau. In T. Barnes & N. Yates (eds.) *Carmarthenshire Studies*. Carmarthenshire, Carmarthenshire County Council, pp. 110-121.

Richards, M. 2007 *Melville Richards Place Name Archive*.
Accessed 2.3.7 http://www.e-gymraeg.co.uk/enwaulleodd/amr/cronfa_en.aspx

Rippon, S. 1996 *Gwent Levels. The Evolution of a Wetland Landscape*. CBA Research Report 105.

Rippon, S. 2004 *Historic Landscape Analysis: Deciphering the Countryside*. CBA Practical Handbook 16.

Roberts, K. (ed.) 2006 *Lost Farmsteads: Deserted Rural Settlements in Wales*. CBA Research Report 148.

Roberts, T. 1992 Welsh Ecclesiastical Place Names and Archaeology. In N. Edwards & A. Lane (eds.) *The early church in Wales and the West : recent work in early Christian archaeology, history and place names*. Oxbow Monograph 16, pp. 41-44.

Rowley, T. 1983 *The Norman Heritage 1066-1200*. London, Paladin.

Rudeforth, C.C. 1994 Soils and Their Use. In J.L. Davies & D.P. Kirby (eds.) *Cardiganshire County History, Volume 1. From the Earliest Times to the Coming of the Normans*. Cardiff, University of Wales Press, pp. 21-25.

Sahlins, M. 1968 *Tribesmen*. New Jersey, Prentice-Hall.

Sayce, R.Y. 1956 The Old Summer Pastures. A Comparative Study. *Montgomeryshire Collections* 54, pp. 117-145.

Sayce, R.Y. 1957 The Old Summer Pastures. Life at the Hafod. *Montgomeryshire Collections* 55, pp. 37-86.

Seebohm, F. 1904 *The Tribal System in Wales*. London, Longmans, Green and Co.

Seebohm, F. 1933 Tribal System. *Bulletin of the Board of Celtic Studies* VI, pp. 255-265.

Smith, P. 1988 *Houses of the Welsh Countryside (2nd edition)*. London, HMSO.

Smith, P. 1998 The Domestic Architecture of the County: The Rural Domestic Architecture: Fermdy, Plas a Bwythyn. In G.H. Jenkins & I.G. Jones (eds.) *Cardiganshire County History Volume 3. Cardiganshire in Modern Times*. Cardiff, Cardiff University Press, pp. 233-288.

St. Joseph, J.K. 1956 Air Reconnaissance in Britain, 1951-5. *Journal of Roman Studies*. XLV, pp. 88.

St. Joseph, J.K. 1961 Air Reconnaissance in Britain, 1958-1960. *Journal of Roman Studies*. LI, pp. 126.

St. Joseph, J.K. 1977 Air Reconnaissance in Britain, 1973-76 *Journal of Roman Studies*. LXVII, pp. 152-153.

Taylor, C. 2000 Medieval Ornamental Landscapes. *Landscapes*. 1(1), pp. 24-39.

Thirsk, J. 1966 The Origins of the Common Fields, *Past and Present* 33, pp. 142-147.

Thomas, C. 1962 Thirteenth-century farm economies in North Wales. *Agricultural History Review* 16(1), pp. 1-14.

Thomas, C. 1971 *The Early Christian Archaeology of Northern Britain.* London, Oxford University Press.

Thomas, C. 1994a *And Shall These Mute Stones Speak?* Cardiff, University of Wales Press.

Thomas, C. & Howlett, D. 2003 'Vita Sancti Paterni' The Life of Saint Padarn and The Original 'Miniu'. *Trivium* 33.

Thomas, J. 1999 *Understanding the Neolithic.* London: Routledge.

Thomas, S. 1959 Land occupation, ownership and utilisation in the parish of Llansantffraid. *Ceredigion* III, pp. 124-155.

Thomas, W.G. 1994b The Early Christian Monuments In J.L. Davies & D.P. Kirby (eds.) *Cardiganshire County History, Volume 1. From the Earliest Times to the Coming of the Normans.* Cardiff, University of Wales Press, pp. 407-420.

Thorburn, J. 1987 Castell Abereinon, Llandysul. *Archaeology in Wales* 27, pp. 55.

Tilley, C. 1994 *A Phenomenology of Landscape, Places, Paths, Monuments.* Oxford: Berg.

Toulmin Smith, L. (ed.) 1906 *Leland's Itinerary in England and Wales.* London, George Bell & Sons.

Turvey, R. 1988 *The Lord Rhys: Prince of Deheubarth.* Llandysul, Gomer Press.

Vinogradoff, P. 1905 *The Growth of the Manor.* London.

Vinogradoff, P. & Morgan, F. (eds.) 1914 *Survey of the Honour of Denbigh.* Oxford, Oxford University Press.

Walker, M.J.C., Buckley, S.L. & Caseldine, A. 2001 Landscape change and human impact in west Wales during the Lateglacial and Flandrian. *Quaternary Research Association West Wales Field Guide*, pp. 17-31.

Ward, A. 1997 Transhumance and Settlement on the Welsh Uplands: A View from the Black Mountain. In N. Edwards (ed.) *Landscape and Settlement in Medieval Wales.* Oxbow Monograph 81, pp. 97-112.

Weeks, R. 2004 Making sense of the censarii: Licensed Traders in Medieval Sources. *The Local Historian* 34(2), pp. 113-117.

Williams, D.H. 1975 Cistercian Nunneries in Medieval Wales. *Citeaux* 26, pp. 155-174.

Williams, D.H. 1990 *Atlas of Cistercian Lands in Wales.* Cardiff, University of Wales Press.

Williams, D.H. 2001 *The Welsh Cistercians.* Leominster, Gracewing.

Williams, G.A. 1985 *When Was Wales?* London, Penguin.

Williams, S.W. 1889 *The Cistercian Abbey of Strata Florida: It History, and an Account of the Recent Excavations Made on the Site.* London, Whiting and Co.

Williams, S.W. 1899 An Ancient Welsh Farmhouse. *Archaeologia Cambrensis* 16 (5th Series), pp. 320-325.

Williamson, T. 2000 Understanding Enclosure. *Landscapes.* 1(1), pp. 24-39.

Willis-Bund, J. 1902 The Black Book of St David's. *Cymmrodorion Record Series* 5.

Wilson, D.R. 1970 Sites Explored: Cardiganshire. *Britannia* I, page 269.

Wmffre, I. 2003 *Language and Place Names in Wales: The Evidence of Toponomy in Cardiganshire.* Cardiff, University of Wales Press.

Wmffre, I. 2004 *The Place-Names of Cardiganshire, Vols. 1-3*. BAR British Series 379.

www.ingramcontent.com/pod-product-compliance
Lightning Source LLC
Chambersburg PA
CBHW061001030426

42334CB00033B/3320